HOW WELL DO YOU KNOW THE BRADYS?

1. How did Desi Arnaz, Jr., find out about Marcia?
a. Alice knew his mother's housekeeper; **b.** Mike designed his mother's house; **c.** Greg jammed with Dino, Desi, and Billy; **d.** Carol belonged to the same women's club as his mother.

2. How did Marcia's nose get broken, jeopardizing her date with the football star?
a. Bobby threw a baseball at her; **b.** Peter threw a football at her; **c.** Greg threw a basketball at her; **d.** Alice threw a brownie at her.

3. What job did Greg *not* have?
a. Office boy for Mike; **b.** Delivery boy for Sam; **c.** Local chairman of Youth for Nixon; **d.** Football team photographer.

4. What was Peter's journalistic nickname when he became a columnist for the school newspaper?
a. Deep Throat; **b.** Flash; **c.** Scoop; **d.** Mr. Broadway.

5. What did the girls end up buying with the ninety-four books of trading stamps?
a. Sewing machine; **b.** Color TV; **c.** Barbie Doll; **d.** Mystery Date Game.

How many did you get correct?
0 You have recently arrived from another planet.
1 Don't bother applying to "The Brady Bunch" Fan Club.
2 You probably have trouble distinguishing the Bradys from the Partridge family.
3 There's hope for you.
4 You've written at least one fan letter to a member of the cast.
5 Fantastic! Mr. and Mrs. Brady would be proud of you.

ANSWERS: 1. a 2. b 3. c 4. c 5. b

THE BRADY BUNCH BOOK

THE BRADY BUNCH BOOK

Andrew J. Edelstein
& Frank Lovece

WARNER BOOKS

A Time Warner Company

Warner Books, Inc., 666 Fifth Avenue, New York, NY 10103
W A Warner Communications Company

Printed in the United States of America
First printing: September 1990
10 9 8 7 6 5 4 3 2 1

Library of Congress Cataloging-in-Publication Data

Edelstein, Andrew J.
    The Brady Bunch book / by Andy Edelstein and Frank Lovece.

        p.   cm.
    ISBN 0-446-39137-9
    1. Brady Bunch (Television show)   I. Lovece, Frank.
    II. Title.
PN1991.77.B7E34   1990
791.45'72—dc20   90-12046
                                                        CIP

Cover design by Ann Twomey

Book design by Giorgetta Bell McRee

To Vincent Thomas Lovece, who I hope
never wants to become a child actor
—FL

To my family, for their very Brady
qualities
—AE

—————————— • • • • • • • • • ——————————

Acknowledgments

The authors wish to gratefully thank Florence Henderson, Ann B. Davis, Sherwood and Lloyd Schwartz, and all the other *Brady* cast and crew members who gave so generously of their time. We thank Bob Hope, Cathy Podewell, Arleen Sorkin and other *Brady* friends and viewers who shared their reminiscences.

Helping out enormously were Pat Mullins, Patty Montiel, Mickey Freeman, Celeste Gomes, Lorena Alexander, Diane Albert of *The TV Collector* (an invaluable TV-buff magazine, at P.O. Box 188, Needham, Mass. 02192), Debbie Gangwer, Dana Friedman and Ira Robbins; Michael Gould and the rest of the folks at CHB3 (who provided many of the photos, originally taken by and for teen magazines); the ever-helpful staff of the New York Public Library's Rose Theatre Collection; *Brady* fans John Abramson and John P. Daley; and Michael Isbell, whose patient modification of our computer wordware saved us more man-hours than it took to build the Sphinx.

Special thanks go to our editor, Rick Horgan, who shares our sensibilities (such as they are), and to our agent, Lori Perkins, whose great foresight, vision and sense of humor led to this book.

Contents

Foreword

by Florence Henderson

I was very pleased to have been asked to write this foreword because this book deals with a subject that has not only touched millions of lives all over the world, but it has especially touched mine in a most profound way.

Little did I know when I was asked in 1969 to play the mother, Carol Brady, on *The Brady Bunch* that I would be asked to play the grandmother, Carol Brady, in 1990!

People always want to know how it feels to be everybody's favorite Mom on TV. I accept it as a great compliment.

It is a privilege to be a part of something that has had such longevity, to be able to have grown along with the audience.

I hope we will continue to share a long and loving relationship.

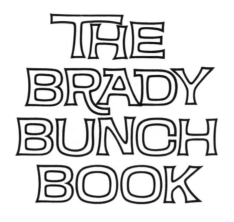

The Bradys in TV-Sitcom History

For most of the '50s and '60s, TV sitcoms were enveloped in the long night of white bread, when white, middle-class families lived in suburban homes where Dad knew best, Mom stayed home and never worked, and the kids ranged from cute to adorable.

Even the '60s shows that focused on monster families, like *The Addams Family* or *The Munsters,* adhered to this middle-class ethos. Herman Munster was Ward Cleaver with green skin.

By the late '60s, however, TV was slowly getting hip to the fact that the world was changing, although early efforts like *The Mod Squad* were patronizing and laughable.

TV began toying with the concept of the nuclear family by creating a spate of widows and widower sitcoms that flourished in the late '60s and early '70s. The idea of a divorced character, even as the real-life divorce rate was climbing, was still a TV no-no as late as 1969. But widows or widowers were perfectly acceptable and there were plenty of them: Diahann Carroll in *Julia;* Doris Day and Lucille Ball in their eponymous shows; Brian Keith in *Family Affair* (bachelor adopts three kids); Fred MacMurray in *My Three Sons;* Bill Bixby in *The Courtship of Eddie's Father;* Hope Lange in *The Ghost and Mrs. Muir* . . . you get the picture.

The Brady Bunch took the w-and-w concept to its next step: Why not bring a TV widow and TV widower together? But instead of marrying off Doris Day with Eddie's Father, say, Sherwood Schwartz created a new TV family, the result of the marriage of two presumably widowed people. (For more on this presumption, see the chapter "A Brady Bunch of Background.")

The term "blended family" was not yet in the national lexicon in 1969, so ABC's flacks liked to call the Bradys a "conglomerate."

This blended family had a nice, demographically appealing symmetry: The boys and girls were each approximately the same age, the boys all had brown hair, and the girls had hair of gold like their mother (the youngest one in curls). And they got the widower's daffy housekeeper to boot.

But even with such a daring (for TV) concept, when the Bradys debuted on September 26, 1969, they were an instant anachronism. The show was a return to the days of *Father Knows Best, Leave It to Beaver,* and *The Donna Reed Show.* Here's how *TV Guide* described the program in its fall preview issue:

> This season's widow-and-widower epidemic reaches an inevitable climax in *The Brady Bunch.* A widow (Florence Henderson) marries a widower (Robert Reed, late of *The Defenders*) and they live happily—if frenetically—after.
>
> "Frenetically" because the man has three sons and a dog and the woman has three daughters and a cat, all of whom have to coexist under one roof without any help from U Thant. There is

also (surprise) a beleaguered housekeeper (Ann B. "Schultzy" Davis). The youngest of the kids, Cindy, gets most of the punchlines. Mom: "I've got a few butterflies in my stomach." Cindy: "Were you sleeping with your mouth open, Mommy?"

The Brady Bunch is produced by Sherwood Schwartz, who brought you Gilligan's Island, which explains why (in the opening episode), the dog and cat make a shambles of the wedding and the bride-groom ends up with cake all over his face.

The Brady ethos was summed up in one of the series' early episodes when Mike tells someone, "We have a wonderful bunch of kids. I mean really marvelous. They don't play hooky. They don't lie. They're not fresh. But boy ... they just won't stay off that phone!"

The problem he was referring to was that the kids kept using the phone and running up the bill. So Mike, in his Ward Cleaveresque wisdom, decided to install a pay phone to teach them the value of money. And that was one of the most complex of the problems the Bradys faced, along with arguing over what to do with ninety-four books of trading stamps and debating how Marcia could get Davy Jones of the Monkees to play at her prom.

The critics were not kind to The Brady Bunch. Writing in TV Guide, Cleveland Amory said:

> There's nothing really wrong with The Brady Bunch. But nothing is really right, either. Everything is so contrived that you don't believe what goes on any more than you believe sketches in a variety show. If the show has a point—except to be a show—it escapes us.
>
> There are millions of stepchildren nowadays and surely their problems and those of their parents deserve, even in a comedy series, something more than this mish-mash.

Meanwhile, of course, America was being convulsed by the greatest generational upheaval ever. And TV was attempting to become relevant by adding ethnic sitcoms and other shows that ostensibly dealt with real-life issues. But the only thing that changed on The Brady Bunch was the hairstyles.

But the '70s was actually a bad time for nuclear families on TV (and in real life as well). Most shows dealt with broken families or singles or the workplace as surrogate family. Not until the 1980s did the nuclear family make a comeback with Family Ties and The Cosby Show.

By that time, all the viewers who had grown up watching The Brady Bunch had come of age, and grown nostalgic over the fantasies—or at least the extremely rarefied environment—that The Brady Bunch depicted. And maybe it's that lack of everyday reality that has given the show its charm and lasting appeal. Sure, the Bradys were corny, pat, out-of-touch, and outlandishly

dressed. So were a lot of us—not to that extreme, of course, but anybody who grew up in that time wore his or her share of plaid bell-bottoms. That's a big reason why we laugh at the Bradys—to an extent, it's laughter of embarrassment about ourselves.

It's easy to understand, then, why this new obsession with the Bradys is so bittersweet. Beneath our laughter is a slight yearning for the kind of family life many of us wish we'd had. We may have worn the plaid bell-bottoms, same as Greg and Marcia, but most of us didn't have a live-in housekeeper, financial luxury, or—most important of all—those open and sympathetic lines of communication.

Still, they really acted like white-bread dorks a lot of the time, didn't they?

A Brady Bunch
of Background

It is 1971, and Sherwood Schwartz is severely ticked off. *Gilligan's Island*, which he had created and produced, had run for three years on CBS and then sailed smoothly into syndication heaven. And since reruns are where the real money is in television, Schwartz—a veteran comedy writer who knows the ropes every bit as well as the jokes—figures he should be reaping a few bucks by now. That's the way it works: You create a series, hook up with a studio that pays the overhead in exchange for ownership, and then split the profits—hence the term "profit participation."

But there's another term bandied about just as frequently in Hollywood: "creative accounting." By 1971, Schwartz was convinced that the accountants at United Artists—the studio that produced *Gilligan's Island*—were being as creative as Salvador Dali. He sued the studio and demanded an audit. The case dragged on for three budget-busting years that might have vacuumed through a lesser man's bank account, before finally ending with a satisfying out-of-court settlement.

To a large extent, Schwartz triumphed because by the time of the lawsuit, he had another successful show already two years old keeping his cash flow steady. It was a classic example of what every producer knows, what Schwartz now likes to call Schwartz's Rule. Which is, you need two hit TV shows: the second one pays for the lawsuit you'll get into over the first.

In Schwartz's case, that second hit show was *The Brady Bunch.*

That wasn't the original name. Not long after *Gilligan's Island* began its network run in 1964, Schwartz had begun concocting a TV script called

Yours and Mine. As is still the general custom, he shopped it around the networks and the studios, trying to arrange a financing deal for a "pilot," or sample show. The networks look at perhaps a hundred pilots a year; only a small percentage make it to series. And for four years, *Yours and Mine* looked like it wasn't going to be anybody's.

"All three networks were interested," the still-active Schwartz recalls today, "but not interested enough to make a pilot. Everyone had a different reason."

It wasn't that the concept wasn't right. Everybody liked the idea of two previously married parents starting a new household with a bevy of stepchildren. They could see the pragmatic possibilities: Scripts could be built around anybody from toddlers to teens, or the parents themselves, or the husband's profession, or the presumably wacky wife. (Wacky wives à la Lucy were still big back then, and the networks knew that Schwartz had been a staff writer on the WASPy *I Love Lucy* clone, *I Married Joan.*) But in time-honored network tradition, a host of cooks decided to try remixing the broth.

"In my script," remembers Schwartz, whose decades in California have only marginally dimmed his Jersey accent, "the parents go off on their honeymoon, and they don't feel right being without their children. And so they go back and get the kids, and all nine of them, including the house-keeper, all go on the honeymoon together." It's believable enough; a less-crowded version actually happened with one of this book's authors as a child. And astute Bradymaniacs know that this is exactly how the pilot eventually aired on ABC. But, "NBC said that's ridiculous, that no two married people would go back and get their kids and bring them back on the honeymoon. And NBC said if I changed the ending, they would do the pilot. And I said, 'No, I won't make the change.' The whole point of the show," Schwartz says passionately, "was that these two people loved their children and felt un-comfortable without them." What an alien concept. NBC passed.

The next stop was the network that eventually adopted the show—but not at this time. With the typically *Alice in Wonderland* logic of entertainment executives, ABC's people felt that if a half hour of this was good, an hour and a half would be three times better. "They *liked* the idea of the couple bringing their kids on their honeymoon," says Schwartz, "and they asked me to make it [TV-movie length]," which at the time was ninety minutes. "I said okay, that then I would show how they meet, and the problems of courtship. I said I could make [the original script] the last half hour of a show in which they meet, get to know each other and the kids, and how that leads up to the marriage. And they said, 'No no no! We like the show just the way it is. Just make it longer!' And I told them, 'I can't make it longer without making it duller!' "

Schwartz and the network parted ways; despite their guarantees, he was sure that if the TV movie turned out dull, the show wouldn't get picked up anyway.

Schwartz zipped the script over to CBS, where *Gilligan's Island* was getting ready to finish its run. But there, he was told, a similar show was in the works: two widowed parents living next door to each other were going to date and, by the eighth or tenth show, get married. But it never went to series.

By now it was 1968. Four years had passed. And in one of those serendipitous circumstances even Shakespeare couldn't have cooked up, a motion picture came out called *Yours, Mine and Ours* that starred Lucille Ball and Henry Fonda as, respectively, a widowed mother of eight marrying a widowed father of ten. It was based on a real-life couple in the news.

Yours, Mine and Ours was a moderate success for the time, earning nearly $11.7 million in domestic rentals (the portion of the U.S. and Canada box-office gross that gets paid to the studio by theaters). It did a little better than the same era's *Goodbye, Columbus* (1969, $10.5 million) and *In the Heat of the Night* (1967, $11 million). Not surprisingly, someone at ABC remembered Schwartz's *Yours and Mine* and shouted something to the effect of "Get me that show!"

With ABC's interest, Schwartz secured a production deal with Paramount Pictures Television. And after a name change to *The Brady Bunch*, the series premiered on September 26, 1969—the start of a five-year, Friday-night network institution, and eternal life in reruns, spinoffs, and whole categories on *Remote Control*. Bradymania had begun.

Like most births, it wasn't easy. The first bit of burping gas was correspondence from a lawyer representing *Yours, Mine and Ours*. "They had immediately sent a letter to Paramount threatening to sue," Schwartz recalls. "So Paramount showed me the letter and I said, 'Why don't you let me answer it and suggest to this gentleman that he look in the Writers Guild files for the date on which I'd registered *The Brady Bunch*, and that mine was called *Yours and Mine*, and that *he* should be happy *I* don't sue *him*!"

Even so, Schwartz changed his new TV project's title. That was never an easy process for him; the name "Gilligan" took ages to arrive at, combining as it does an almost magical combination of silliness and euphony. Yeah, okay, we're only talking about *Gilligan's Island*, but consider that without any other information, these two words tell you (a) it's a comedy (imagine if the title were, say, *Stark's Island*), and (b) who the lead character is.

After much winnowing, the choices came down to *The Brady Bunch* and *The Brady Brood*. "There was a serious question at the time," recalls Lloyd Schwartz, Sherwood's son and eventually the show's risen-from-the-ranks producer, "about whether we should use 'The Brady *Bunch*,' because at that time 'bunch' meant kinda like a street gang or a Western gang [e.g., Sam Peckinpah's *The Wild Bunch*]. So we were afraid it would have that kind of connotation. But 'brood' seemed a little like from a horror movie or something. I think finally we just ran out of other suggestions. Now, today, of course," he believes, "because of *The Brady Bunch,* the word 'bunch' has *good* connotations!" Bring *that* up in your next literature class.

Paramount gave Schwartz an office on their studio lot and assigned him Stage 5, near the historic Bronson Gate—no relation to Charles. Then as now, Paramount was bustling. *Mission: Impossible* was shooting at the studio, gearing up to welcome Leonard Nimoy as Paris. *Star Trek* had been canceled just a couple of months earlier, but the bridge of the *Enterprise* was still intact. All around was a swirl of everything from the ostensibly adult *Love American Style* to the whimsical kiddie show *H. R. Pufnstuf.* Now all Schwartz had to do was find a cast, hire a director, arrange for the sets to be designed and built, scout locations for exterior shots of the Brady house, and assemble the production crew—the sound people, lighting technicians, camera operators, and all the other worker ants who make TV happen. Piece of cake. He'd already done it once, right? But like any parent knows, the second child is always different.

Schwartz tried to minimize the differences by hiring director John Rich, who'd been instrumental in creating *Gilligan's Island* and who, with his distinguished stint on *The Dick Van Dyke Show,* had become something of an industry legend. (If nothing else, these two shows sure demonstrated his versatility.) As a director and sometime producer, Rich would go on to help launch *All in the Family, Barney Miller,* and many other series. And at this point in his career, he would devote himself to the first half-dozen episodes of *The Brady Bunch.*

"The first year of a show is by all odds the most difficult," says Schwartz. "The interrelationships of the characters, which is what the audience tunes in to see, has to be determined. They can be determined to a certain extent by the script and by the producer, but on the set, the director has to make sure that the chemistry continues in the same direction from week to week. This is why John directed the first several episodes of both my shows."

While Rich was doing his work breaking down the script and putting together his crew, Schwartz turned to the physical production of the show. His set designer, Jack De Shields, worked up a plan, and with Schwartz's approval started ordering furniture and other set decorations. And somehow or other, in the last series you'd expect to find it, *The Brady Bunch* wound up with one of the first double beds on a TV comedy.

Up to then, it was always twin beds—just look at Lucy and Ricky, Rob and Laura, Fred and Wilma. But now, new ground was broken. Mike and Carol Brady, the show's parents, would sleep together! And they'd even both been married before! "We just assumed they would sleep together in a double bed," Schwartz asserts, perhaps a little disingenuously considering that a set decorator at the time would have automatically ordered twin beds unless there was a discussion otherwise. But perhaps it was simply the zeitgeist.

"I think at that time, the TV industry was just allowing a little more," speculates Florence Henderson. "It was time to move forward a little bit." Did she feel like a pioneer? "It's strange, but no. It's like, when you're caught up in something, you're working so hard on it—learning, memorizing, constantly putting energy into it—I don't think you're aware actually of how much impact you're having."

Yet perhaps more significantly, not only did Schwartz push the envelope by showing his married couple together in bed, but he slipped in another TV first that has heretofore gone uncommemorated: *Carol Brady may have been the first divorced woman to be a lead character in a TV sitcom!*

"We never said for sure that Carol Brady's spouse died," Schwartz reveals with a devilish grin. "We *did* say that Mike's wife died. But not Carol's. Nope. I didn't want to say there was or wasn't a divorce or that he was killed or he wasn't killed. That was never established." So in a TV era where all single parents were widows and widowers, was Carol Brady the first divorcée? Before Lee Grant in *Fay,* which caused all the commotion? Before Bonnie Franklin on the ground-breaking and much-hyped Norman Lear's *One Day at a Time?* "Maybe," Schwartz says, chuckling. (Now whether he may have told the network or studio people differently is something else. But the only story that matters is the one on the screen.)

Yet while no one raised objections to the double bed or to Carol's ambiguous status, the network, says Schwartz, "did question the fact there was a toilet in the bathroom—and so we had to remove it!" This was, you'll recall, a year and a half before *All in the Family* made flushing fashionable. "The standing joke around the set was that the Bradys had to go to the corner gas station to relieve themselves! Because you could see they had a bathtub, and they had a sink, but no toilet!" In the annals of television censorship, this ranks right up there with Barbara Eden's navel on *I Dream of Jeannie.*

With the interior sets under way, it was time to scout for the Brady house, that famous two-story contemporary ranch on Clinton Avenue* in the unnamed, presumably southern California suburb in which the Bradys lived. The location scouts found the perfect place with amenable owners in Studio City, in the San Fernando Valley—you know, the Vallllley, duuude. Unfortunately, the perfect house was only one story tall. But on the plus side, it *did* have very high ceilings and a huge, high front. So, to create the famous two-story Brady home we saw week after week in the establishing shot, the production crew simply hung a window on wires down the front of the house, high enough to make it seem like it was from a second-story room. Another illusion shattered. (The house is still there, by the way, though we're sure the owners discourage pilgrimages.)

While all this was going on, Schwartz and his casting people were feverishly

*It was also referred to, at least once, as Clinton Way. In any case, it was within walking/bicycle distance of Clinton Elementary School.

The obviously Frank Lloyd Wright–inspired Brady living room.

hunting for the performers who would play the family members. *The Brady Bunch* child-actor casting call quickly became as legendary as the search for Munchkins thirty years earlier.

Schwartz interviewed 464 kids for the roles of the mother's three girls and the father's three boys. "And that's just the number *I* saw," he says, still incredulous. "The casting department saw a lot of others." And it wasn't just six kids they had to find, but twelve—two sets each of three boys and three girls, one set blond and the other brunette.

"I didn't know when I was casting the kids who the [actors playing the] parents were going to be," Schwartz explains, "and I wanted the kids' hair color to match their parents'. That doesn't always happen in real life, but as far as comedy is concerned, I believe in labeling things. You'll remember the uniform structure—blond girls and blond mother. Otherwise, it's another thing to have to ask the audience to remember."

Schwartz's shows, as we all know, don't ask for major intellectual engagement on the part of the viewer. But his notion of uniform structure does have a theatrical history, going back to what the vaudevillians called "funny hats"—a distinctive hat or piece of clothing or some other bit of visual shorthand that an audience could quickly grasp, to differentiate one comic character from another: The Three Stooges' haircuts, for examples. The concept goes back at least as far as the four stock characters of Italian *commedia dell'arte*, which, if not placing *The Brady Bunch* in the realm of Serious Art, does pitch it squarely into traditions of comedy. Which probably says more about audiences than we should care to think about.

For the role of the father, fabulously successful architect Mike Brady, Schwartz found Robert Reed. The lanky, serious-looking Method actor—sort of a cut-rate Steve McQueen—had made his mark opposite E. G. Marshall on the respected dramatic series *The Defenders*. Though he had taken over the male lead in Neil Simon's hit Broadway comedy *Barefoot in the Park* a couple of years earlier, Reed was best known as a dramatic actor who thought himself better suited to Shakespeare than sitcom. Yet if just the right sitcom came up, he would do it. You gotta eat, after all.

"He was an unlikely choice," Schwartz admits. "And he was not particularly thrilled about coming to do the show. He was under contract to Paramount, and he wanted to do the series *Barefoot in the Park*." But that wound up running on ABC from 1970–71 in a black version starring Tracy Reed and the quirkily named Scoey Mitchlll, so obviously that was out. "He was not thrilled about becoming, at his age, the father of six kids," Schwartz recalls. "But he was terrific precisely *because* he hadn't done much comedy. He brought sincerity to the father role that was absent in a lot of other situation comedies. There is something very real there, because he's a classically trained actor, and there's something so honest about him that he gives strength to what could have been a very ordinary role."

The two key roles of Carol Brady and housekeeper Alice Nelson, however, originally went to other than Florence Henderson and Ann B. Davis. Wife Carol was initially Joyce Bulifant, the tiny, blond-bobbed actress who went on to a recurring role as Murray's wife Marie on *The Mary Tyler Moore Show*. Alice was essayed by the late Monty Margetts, who had played housekeeper Una Fields in an earlier ABC sitcom, *The Tycoon* (1964–65), opposite Walter Brennan as an old-coot CEO. (Kathleen Freeman, who'd played house-keepers on the mid-'50s TV series *Topper* and *Mayor of the Town,* had also been considered.)

But Bulifant left the show, either because the chemistry wasn't right, or because Henderson and Reed shared the same agent, or because of a cast offer from *The Bill Cosby Show:* the same season *The Brady Bunch* de-buted, Bulifant played school guidance counselor Marsha Patterson on Cos-by's 1969–71 sitcom. (A few years later, Bulifant joined the Schwartzes on their 1976–77 Saturday-morning kids' show, *Big John, Little John.*)

Florence Henderson—best known up to then as a Broadway and nightclub singer and a New York socialite—had been filling in on the *Today* show in New York and was unavailable the week they were testing for the Carol Brady role. After Schwartz had already decided on Bulifant, "Florence's agent prevailed upon us to give her a test after the fact," Schwartz recalls. "I had known her work [as a singer] for a long time, but she had done no acting on television—she'd done variety shows and talk shows."

"I was living in New York," Florence remembers, "and I had flown out here to do *The Dean Martin Show,* and my agent convinced me to meet all these people about this new series. I was supposed to fly out the next day for Houston, where I was opening at the Shamrock Hotel with my night-club act. But I went down to Paramount and I met them all. It was [Paramount TV executive] Doug Cramer, and [director] John Rich and Sherwood. And I guess they were impressed with me, since they asked if I'd mind coming back later that day and putting a scene on film for them. And I said, 'No, but I do have to catch a flight to Houston tonight.' And they said, 'We'll get you out of here on time, if you could just come and do the film.'"

She went to Paramount again and got ready for the screen test. For some strange reason, they made her up on the nearby *Star Trek* set. "And I *looked* like I was from outer space!" Florence jokes. "This guy did a lousy job on the makeup and he gave me these awful false eyelashes! And I was practically in tears when I went over to the set. I said to John Rich, 'I apologize for this makeup and please don't take it seriously.'" They apparently didn't, but took Florence seriously enough. Schwartz remembers that in the screen test, "She came *alive* for the TV camera. She just is so at home in front of a camera, just like she's in her living room." And so the next day, in Houston, just as she was getting ready to open at the nightclub, Florence got a call from her agent telling her she was wanted for the *Brady Bunch* pilot.

Now what? She had a commitment at the Shamrock, and yet a possibly lucrative series beckoned. "I had to go to Dwight Harris, who booked me in the Shamrock, and say to him, 'Mr. Harris, will you please let me out of my contract, because I have to fly out of here tomorrow, and if we can get someone else to come in, I promise you if this series is a hit, I will be even more valuable to you and I will come back on my first opportunity.' And he said yes. So I got on a plane the *next* day and flew back to L.A. And the show was a success and I did come back my first opportunity and made up the date."

As it happened, Florence's arrival set off the other big change. As Schwartz explains, "Joyce Bulifant is a funny lady. She's just funny. And Monty Margetts was a pleasant, housekeeperly-type lady who could bounce off Joyce Bulifant. Now, Florence Henderson could do comedy, but she herself, her persona, was not comic. Now, if you have a funny person, there should be a straight person, to give you balance. Joyce speaks funny and she moves funny, and I didn't feel she needed support in the kitchen. When it went to Florence, that changed the balance and so we decided to go with a more comic housekeeper and brought in Ann B. Davis."

• • •

Davis by this time was already a well-established character actress who'd won two Emmy Awards for her Schultzy, the comic sidekick on *The Bob Cummings Show.* "I was kind of known as one of the 'funny ladies,' " Davis recalls. "There are probably twenty, thirty of us that are about the same age, size, shape, work for the same money, have the same visibility. And I think we were probably all of us up for the part!" she half jokes. As Schwartz remembers, "She came with a superb background in comedy. She was great as Schultzy—she *is* great."

When Davis got the call to audition for *Brady,* she was in Seattle doing a nightclub comedy act. "My agent called me and said they were seriously interested, but Sherwood wanted to meet me. So," she says in one long breath, "they put me on a plane, flew me down, drove me out to the Valley [to Schwartz's home] where I had about ten or fifteen minutes with Sherwood, drove me back to the plane, and I flew back up and did my show that night. Then I think it was as fast as the next week, I got the word to do the pilot. So I left my car in Seattle, flew down to L.A.—my agent arranged to buy out of the balance of my nightclub act, which was fiiine with me, since I hated it!—and then I flew back up to get my car and drove back down the coast." Good thing the pilot sold, after all that.

Once the adults were in place, Schwartz made his final decisions about the kids. For the boys he chose fifteen-year-old Barry Williams and eleven-year-old Chris Knight, child actors who'd both done several series guest shots, and eight-year-old Mike Lookinland, a TV-commercial veteran. The girls were Maureen McCormick, just turning thirteen, who'd had a recurring role on the sitcom *Camp Runamuck* and had done dozens of commercials and voice-overs; eleven-year-old Eve Plumb, a prolific child actress who'd reportedly already shot four other pilots before this one; and the nearly eight-year-old Susan Olsen, who'd been in commercials since the age of six months, but had only made her TV-series debut, on *Ironside,* a few months earlier.

Now it was time to finalize the opening credits—one of the most important parts of any show since it plays the largest role in establishing genre and mood. It also helps to draw in undecided viewers who might want to indulge their curiosity. And a good theme song, as we all know, can become as evocative a piece of Americana as any piece of folk music.

For the visual part of it, Schwartz chose a checkerboard design that would showcase all the stars equally and evoke an ensemble feel. "I crudely drew what I wanted," he recalls, "and in playing around with the boxes, I noticed that you very neatly fit nine on the screen, which was good because that was how many stars I had on the show." Was there any thought to having instead a montage of family life, or a dad-walks-in-the-door sort of thing as on *The Dick Van Dyke Show* or *Make Room for Daddy*? "No," says Schwartz. "I

The actress rests backstage.

felt [the checkerboard design] was different and unusual, and since TV is a close-up medium, I wanted to use that fact to get people to remember those nine faces."

As with *Gilligan's Island,* Schwartz wrote the lyrics to this show's ridiculously enduring theme song (music by Frank De Vol, a former orchestra leader and the composer of TV themes for *Family Affair* and other shows). It was sung the first season as an upbeat pop chorus by the Peppermint Trolley Company, whose name alone assures the group's placement in the annals of bubblegum-music history. (Remember bubblegum music? When that huge population chunk known as baby-boomers were just reaching pubescence? Makes you appreciate punk and heavy metal, doesn't it?)

From the second season on, the theme—simply titled "The Brady Bunch"—was sung by the Brady kids themselves, with the lyrics slightly modified from third-person to first-person. "The kids would sing for fun around the stage," Schwartz recalls, "and that gave me the idea, Hey, why not use *them?*" Barry Williams recalls that having the kids sing the theme was done "just to make it more homey, not to pilot a career change. I mean, that song was so easy! They just turned down the microphones on the people who couldn't stay in tune. Or Michael Lookinland and I would sing a little louder!"

The Brady Bunch was what is known as a "one-camera show," meaning it was shot in bits and pieces throughout the week, feature-movie style. This is in contrast to *Cheers* and other filmed sitcoms today, which often use three or four cameras, and shoot straight through like a play, in front of an audience. (*I Love Lucy* had actually pioneered that technique many years earlier.) Sometimes on the *Brady* set, a second camera would be set up for a difficult or hard-to-reproduce scene, for backup, or else to have a second angle covered for some special reason.

The adults often reported to makeup as early as 6:00 A.M., Florence remembers, since child-labor laws preclude children working on a film or a TV show past 6:30 P.M. With twelve-hour days typical in the business, that meant having an early start. Complicating logistics further was that then as now, child actors could only work four hours a day and had to be tutored four hours a day, as well as given recreation periods. Schwartz had to stagger the kids' arrival times so that when some were in the studio classroom, others could be available on the set.

The classroom itself *was* a classroom, albeit a small one in a converted dressing room. Presiding was Frances Whitfield, a combination teacher and welfare worker of the type required by child-actor labor laws. Later on, a woman named Beth Compton would teach the older kids. When not on the set, some of the Brady bunch went to professional children's schools, which are geared for this sort of thing (time off for location shooting, etc.). Others transferred their tutorial credits to regular schools.

"The classroom was basically where they hung out," remembers Lloyd Schwartz, a UCLA grad who started out as the kids' dialogue coach on the show and, while completing his master's in television scriptwriting, rose to associate producer and eventually a full producer. "When they weren't on the set doing a scene, they were going to school or on their recreation. Everything is very, very regulated. The teacher/welfare worker had to be there as long as a child was there. The mothers were there practically all the time as well."

At the end of the week, there'd be a wrap party. "We didn't go on till five in the morning [like the famous *Taxi* parties on the Paramount lot a few years later]," remembers Florence, "but they went on pretty late because there were a lot of grown-ups there, too, y'know! And we had a wonderful old property guy who set up, and he was so sweet but he'd bitch and moan as he would start setting up the party as we neared the end, and he was so tough, he didn't want to put the food out too early and having people touching it. And we're like, 'Oh c'mon, Irving, just get me a tortilla chip! Anything!'"

For lunch, they'd order in or eat in the Paramount commissary or cafeteria, or else go out the Bronson Gate to a place called Oblath's. It was one of those workaday eateries of the kind that used to cluster around studios during the golden age of Hollywood—"Nothing fancy," remembers Schwartz, "just a nice restaurant where you could get in and out quickly."

"I remember the gals at Oblath's had been there *forever*," Davis says fondly. "People that had worked at Paramount for years would say, 'My God, is she still here?' They didn't go in for the youngsters there; they went for the tried-and-true veterans who knew how to serve you in time to get back."

Throughout its five-year run, *The Brady Bunch* garnered only moderate ratings—which is strangely true of a lot of syndication hits, including Paramount's *Taxi* (which did have one hit season) and *The Odd Couple*. After the network's first thirteen-week commitment had been fulfilled, the cast and crew could only draw their breath and wait. They did get renewed at mid-season, but, as Ann B. Davis recalls, "I think there was only one year the whole time that we got renewed for a whole season. Every other time, it was thirteen-week orders. That part of it was nerve-racking. But it's something actors get used to."

Still, the show survived, year after year—and with a good share of notable talent passing through. There were veteran movie directors such as Jack Arnold (*The Creature from the Black Lagoon*) and Leslie H. Martinson (*Lad: A Dog*); relative newcomers like Russ Mayberry and Jerry London, who'd go on to distinguished careers in TV movies and mini-series; directing neophytes like Lloyd Schwartz and co-star Robert Reed; and old-hand TV directors like John Rich and Bruce Bilson.

One of the assistant directors was Alan Rudolph, son of the prolific *Brady* director Oscar Rudolph and soon to be a major filmmaker in his own right (*The Moderns, Love at Large, Welcome to L.A.*). "We used to *fight!*" says Lloyd Schwartz, laughing. "Jeez, we fought! We almost came to blows a couple of times. His father, Oscar, was an old-timer who started with Cecil B. De Mille, and he believed that television was a director's medium, which it isn't. It's a producer's medium. And Alan was a very, very talented guy, and it was always for the betterment of the show, but we had very different interpretations. He actually made his first film [*Premonition*, 1972] while working with us."

But among all the changes and personnel throughout the five years, the most tragic undoubtedly was the case of Tiger, the dog. Or actually, Tiger, the dogs.

The Brady Kids in concert. Nice shirts.

"One day we were shooting this episode," Lloyd Schwartz recalls, "I believe the one where Jan thought she was allergic to the dog. And there's a scene where the boys are supposed to say good-bye to the dog. And every time they'd start the scene, the dog would run out of the set. Finally, I went to the trainer and said, 'What's with the dog? We gotta film this scene here.' And he said, 'It's a different dog.' I said, 'What are you talkin' about?' He said, 'The dog got run over.' 'What!'

"The original Tiger had gotten killed the night before," Lloyd goes on. "And the trainer found this one in the pound and hoped we wouldn't notice. Well, it wasn't working. All the dog had to do was just *be* in that scene. And so—and we didn't do anything to hurt the dog—but we nailed his collar to the ground! And if you look at that scene, that's why when they come over to the dog, he's got his head on the ground. It didn't hurt him at all, obviously. But that's what happened. After that, we kind of phased Tiger out."

Around this time, the kids, as kids do, started singing. This being the time (yuck!) of such "family groups" as the Cowsills, the Osmonds, and the Partridge Family, the Brady kids figured (not so coarsely, perhaps, but figured it nonetheless) why not cash in? In 1972, calling themselves the Brady Kids, the six child actors made their debut as a vocal group at the San Bernardino Orange Show, reportedly to a crowd of eight thousand. The group would go on to multicity tours during the show's annual hiatus and appeared a few times on *American Bandstand.* And after Paramount's music division released a 1971 Brady holiday album with Florence Henderson's professional vocals as the centerpiece, the Brady kids followed up with their own three albums of pop tunes. Individually, the kids also unleashed a batch of singles. (See the section, "Musical Bradys.")

"We weren't hired to be singers," says Williams. "We were hired to be exactly what we were—kids. The singing was introduced to Paramount and ABC and Sherwood Schwartz later on because that was what we were interested in as kids, and Paramount saw it as a way to assist our popularity."

The records weren't the only other avenues Paramount and the producers took. There were *Brady* comic books, a *Brady* board game, and an animated Saturday-morning series, *The Brady Kids,* that ran for two seasons and used the actual kids' voices.

The kids themselves became teen and kiddie idols, doing the rounds of shopping-malls holiday parades, the "Teena Awards" sponsored by a teen magazine, and other ventures that, if not making them rich, at least kept their visibility high. Maureen McCormick wrote an advice column for *16,* "Dear Maureen." (Actual letter: "Dear Maureen, I am 14 years old and my boyfriend of three months just broke up with me. I'm so heartbroken that I can't eat or sleep, and I can't even concentrate on my school work. Please help me!") The gang posed for a picture with Keith Moon—yes, Keith Moon—at a party for the L.A. premiere of the Who's rock opera, *Tommy.* Heady times indeed.

Being a teen idol, recalls Barry Williams, "was very exciting. It's maybe one of the most exciting aspects of being in the public eye as a teenager. The fans are very expressive, and when you're singing on stage, there is a kind of electricity where you can understand why rock bands do what they do. And there's a kind of fervor unleashed, especially by younger girls—it's pretty hard to find something to compare it to. But it's very exciting to be the object of that excitement."

Ah, our little boys and girls were growing up. And plot-wise that presented a conundrum for the writers. "When the show began," explains Lloyd Schwartz, "we had kids of very different ages. But as they started getting older, all the [characters' types of] problems got pretty much the same—you get to be a teenager, you start worrying about high school, college, and like that. And when everybody's that age, it limits your stories. So it was felt that bringing in a younger character would add something new to the show. And it was fun for a few episodes."

"I'll tell ya," Sherwood Schwartz reveals, "bringing in Oliver was not my decision. That was a Paramount decision—that since the kids were growing

Posing amid all that endless fan mail.

up we needed a smaller child around. I didn't think we needed one. But I will never fight something which doesn't seem to hurt. On the other hand," he says, "I'll argue to the death if it's something vital to the show that they want to change. CBS originally wanted a kid on *Gilligan's Island*; they wanted the professor to have a twelve-year-old nephew. I couldn't make them understand that to put a twelve-year-old kid on that show would eliminate Gilligan—because Gilligan *is* a twelve-year-old child! They didn't understand that," he says with a sigh. "Their thinking was, 'We're trying to attract children, therefore we need a child.' Now, *that* was a vital battle. But whether they want to add another kid as a cousin who comes to stay with them on *The Brady Bunch*, that's not a vital battle."

Yet, at the same time, another vital battle was being lost—the battle of the Nielsen ratings. *The Brady Bunch* was never a ratings powerhouse, and in most cases was only renewed for thirteen weeks (a half season) at a time. It hung on in the middle ground, never improving, never declining, until the fifth year. Then, against the stiff competition of *Sanford and Son* in particular, the ratings reached a point of diminishing returns.

Schwartz had, nevertheless, amassed five years' worth of shows, considered the minimum at the time for syndication "stripping" (daily Monday-to-Friday reruns). And since most TV contracts run for five years and renegotiating for more is only practical if the show is a blockbuster and not merely respectable, Schwartz and the network reached the same conclusion. It was time to call it quits.

Even if ABC had thought otherwise, says Schwartz, "Re-negotiating [contracts] would have been a mess. And we were no longer comfortably perched at number twenty-two or eighteen, anyway. You know, we spent most of our lives between twentieth and thirtieth [place] in the ratings. We are," he says wryly, savoring the best revenge, "much bigger in syndication than in our original run."

Indeed, *The Brady Bunch* has become a veritable franchise, having been spun off in some form or other on all three commercial networks. Aside from the Saturday-morning cartoon that ran for two years concurrently with the show, the characters later surfaced in an ABC variety show (*The Brady Bunch Hour,* 1977); an NBC sequel series (*The Brady Brides,* 1981), and a further CBS sequel (*The Bradys,* 1990) and two TV movies: NBC's *The Brady Girls Get Married* (a 1981 compression of three *Brides* episodes); and CBS's *A Very Brady Christmas* (1988) which spawned *The Bradys,* a short-run series version that aired in the winter of 1990. The characters have become pop icons, showing up in a dream sequence in a kitschy episode of NBC's *Day by Day.* (See "The Brady Legacy" for details.) And of course, the original show is in syndication all over the world.

What is it? *What* is the appeal? "The stories," believes Schwartz. "Human, family stories. I don't care what the generation is, it's the same: the problems of communicating, of honesty, of being the middle child, of little things like wearing braces or wearing glasses. And," he supposes, "we did a lot of innovative stuff," like one of the first double beds in an American sitcom.

"Several of the plots were things that really *had* happened in our house," says Lloyd Schwartz. "We had four kids in the family, and there were always lots of kids around, and we had a housekeeper. The criticism I hear all the time with *The Brady Bunch* is that no family is like that. And my family was exactly like that!"

Too, the timing and other coincidental factors seem to have been right for a *Brady* revival. As Ann B. Davis observes, "Just about the time we went into syndication, there were a whole bunch of sitcoms on the air that were getting pretty racy. They may not look racy now, but fifteen years ago they did. And when these shows [later] started to move into after-school-hours syndication, the country rose in its wrath and said, 'Don't put *Three's Company* on the air for our children to see.' So they had to go back to *The Brady Bunch* and *Gilligan's Island* and some of those. Also, at about that same time, eighty-five channels opened up [because of cable], and there

Producer Lloyd Schwartz with Maureen McCormick. *Courtesy of Lloyd Schwartz.*

wasn't enough software to go around. And finally, it was in color. Some of the earlier series began to fade out because they hadn't made the transition. So it was the combination of people wanting wholesome shows for their kids and the industry having all that new cable time to fill gave us the impetus.

"Now, of course, fans breed fans. And it's kinda funny in a way, because it's been long enough now that I'll meet somebody thirty-five or thereabouts, and he'll have a three-piece suit and an attache casé, and he'll see me and suddenly his face will light up like he was twelve: 'Heyyyyy! *Alice!*' And I love it! It's great," she says, "to have your fans grow up before your eyes."

For fans in their twenties and thirties, there is nostalgia, true. But just as big as that is the fact that *The Brady Bunch*—like *The Jetsons* and those hygiene films we saw in high school—display unself-conscious kitsch like nobody's business . . . just *look* at those clothes and Carol Brady's famous bubble-do (which Florence Henderson hated even at the time). "Some people might like that [kitsch value]," Lloyd Schwartz concedes, "but I don't think they come back episode after episode to see how Bob's hair looked."

Maybe not—or maybe so, as any fan of MTV's *Remote Control* can testify. But Lloyd is unquestionably right about something else: "We have quite a sense of humor about our show and its place in TV history. None of us are saying it's great. We like what we did, but we've heard all the kidding and the jokes and everything. Same with *Gilligan's Island*. We're not blind to people saying, 'Oh, it's a *Brady Bunch* kind of thing.' Certainly Bob and Florence feel that way—and you know if you saw their performance on the [1989] Emmy Awards [where the Brady parents met the Bundy parents from *Married . . . With Children*]. They were the best thing about the award show," Lloyd happily maintains, "because all of us connected with the show have that sense of humor about it."

The expression, of course, is "laughing all the way to the bank." But there *is* a genuine, heartfelt core to *The Brady Bunch*. Say what you will, it was never cynical or calculated, never took itself too seriously. It wasn't great TV in the sense of Keatonesque slapstick (*I Love Lucy*), poignant tragicomedy (*The Honeymooners, Taxi*), allegory and fancy wordplay (*M*A*S*H*), or hip topicality (*Murphy Brown, The Mary Tyler Moore Show*). But it had heart —it really believed in the things it said. So what if *The Brady Bunch* is like that nerdy kid you made fun of in high school. A lot of times, twenty years later in this barracuda world, you realize that while they might not have been cool, you could always count on them to be genuine.

•••••••••

The Brady Legacy

As pop icons, the Bradys naturally can be manifested in many ways. And they have been, they have been. . . .

BRADY COLLECTIBLES

Paperback Books include:

The Brady Bunch
The New York Mystery
The Treasure of Mystery Island
Showdown at the PTA Corral
Count Up to Blast–Down
The Quarterback Who Came to Dinner
Adventure on the High Seas

Comic Books:

The Brady Bunch
   Dell Publishing Co.
   Two issues: February 1970, and May 1970
The Brady Bunch Kite Fun Book
   PG&E, 1976

Board Games

The Brady Bunch
  Whitman, 1973

Bubblegum Cards

Set of 88.
  T.C.G. Productions, 1969

THE SERIES

The Brady Bunch

ABC: September 26, 1969–August 30, 1974; 117 episodes (including the pilot).

The Brady Kids

ABC animated series: September 9, 1972–August 31, 1974; 22 episodes.

The Brady Bunch Hour

ABC: January 23–May 25, 1977 (sporadically).

The Brady Girls Get Married / The Brady Brides

NBC: February 6, 1981–April 17, 1981; 9 episodes; name change after third episode.

The Bradys

CBS: February 9–March 9, 1990; two-hour premiere, plus 4 additional episodes.

THE TV MOVIES

The Brady Girls Get Married

NBC: October 27, 1981. Reedited, 90-minute version of the three-episode series that ran February 6–20, 1981. Originally scheduled as a two-hour TV-movie for February 6, 1981.

A Very Brady Christmas

CBS: December 18, 1988; rerun December 22, 1989.

THE DETAILS

The Brady Kids

Executive producer: Sherwood Schwartz. Producers: Lou Scheimer, Norm Prescott. Director: Hal Sutherland. Music: Yvette Blais, Jeff Michael

In this animated, Saturday-morning series, all the Brady kids (supplying their own voices) had their adventures and misadventures without the interference of grown-ups, but with the help of their talking dog, Moptop; Marlon the magical mynah bird; and pandas Ping and Pong. Twenty-two episodes were stretched out over two seasons. The episode of September 8, 1973, "Teacher's Pet," was the pilot for the 1973–74 ABC animated series *Mission: Magic*.

Sherwood Schwartz says he's now speaking to a company about producing a *new* animated *Brady Bunch* series. Why not? He did two of them for *Gilligan's Island*!

The Brady Bunch Hour

Executive producers: Sid and Marty Krofft. Producer: Lee Miller. Co-producer: Tom Swale. Music: George Wyle. Music arrangements: Sid Feller, Van Alexander. Writers: Carl Kleinschmitt, Ronny Graham, Bruce Vilanch, Steve Bluestein, Michael Kagan. Director: Jack Regas

The final episode of *The Brady Bunch* had aired less than three years earlier when the geniuses at ABC decided the time was right to bring back our favorite clan. So on Sunday, January 23, 1977, came the debut of *The Brady Bunch Hour*, a comedy-variety program that was to air once every fifth week in the *Nancy Drew/Hardy Boys Mysteries* time slot. (It eventually aired all over the place; see the episode mini-guide, page 243.) The biggest changes were that Geri Reischl played Jan, and that Mike had put aside his architecture career to help the family star in their own TV variety show and move from their famous house into a new beachfront home.

"I had nothing to do with it," says Sherwood Schwartz today, obviously pleased. The show was produced by Sid and Marty Krofft, the puppeteer producers of *D.C. Follies* and many children's series. The Kroffts had been doing the Osmond variety show *Donny & Marie*, "and Florence and Bob and a couple of the kids were on as guests one week. [ABC then-president]

It's Saturday morning fun with *The Brady Kids*!

The Brady Bunch Hour, featuring Geri Reischl (left) as Jan.

Fred Silverman saw them and called the Krofft brothers and said he wanted to do a variety show with the Brady bunch. He loves *The Brady Bunch*," says Schwartz. "And he also loves *Gilligan's Island*. His dream show was for me to do *The Brady Bunch on Gilligan's Island*." Enticing as that and the variety-show prospect must have seemed, Schwartz foresaw the problems that eventually doomed the latter—mainly, that the kids really weren't singers. But, Schwartz says fondly, "Fred Silverman's the kind of guy who runs with an idea without stopping for reality."

The Brady Girls Get Married

Written by Sherwood and Lloyd J. Schwartz. Directed by Peter Baldwin. Producers: Lloyd J. Schwartz, John Thomas Lenox. Executive Producer: Sherwood Schwartz.

The Brady Brides

Executive Producer: Sherwood Schwartz. Producers: Lloyd J. Schwartz, John Thomas Lenox. Music: Frank De Vol. Art Director: Jack De Shields. Photography: Lester Shorr.

The family that refused to die surfaced again four years later, this time on NBC. Originally this was going to be a TV movie called *The Brady Girls Get Married*. But at the last minute, NBC execs decided to break up the telefilm into the first three episodes of a new series, which would air on Friday nights for familiarity's sake. Beginning with the fourth episode, the series' title became *The Brady Brides*.

The plot involved the double wedding of Marcia and Wally Logan (played by Jerry Houser), a toy designer/salesperson for the Tyler Toy Company, and of Jan and Phillip Covington III (played by Ron Kuhlman), a college chemistry instructor. Marcia now was a designer for Casual Clothes, and Jan—following in her father's footsteps—was an architect. Yet when they started looking for houses (with the help of Carol, who's now a real-estate agent—who says the Bradys didn't acknowledge the real world?), both couples realized they each couldn't afford one. So they came up with a typical Brady togetherness solution: Buy a house together! This meant, however, that the laid-back Wally and the stiffer Phillip had to learn to live with each other.

Lending a hand was their old housekeeper and new neighbor Alice—who had married Sam the butcher and was now Alice Franklin. Of course, stopping by for the wedding were Greg, now a doctor; Peter, now in the air force; and Bobby, a college student. All the original Brady performers were in the TV-movie episodes. The guest cast included Barbara Cason as neighbor Elvira Fritzinger; Richard Brestoff as Carol's boss, Ben Richards; Jean Byron as Claudia Covington, Phillip's mother; Ryan McDonald as his namesake father; and James Gallery and Carol Arthur as the Logans. Florence, Ann,

The Brady Girls Get Married—to Wally Logan (Jerry Houser) and Phillip Covington III (Ron Kuhlman).

---

and Barbara Cason turned up regularly on *The Brady Brides,* along with young Keland Love as Harry, Wally's toy-tester.

The cutesy-sexy repartee between Mike and Carol carried over onto *The Brady Brides.* Take this exchange, as Phillip installs a new lock on the front door:

> JAN:
> This lock is a deterrent.
> PHILLIP:
> That's right. Like some people think leaving the
> light on is a deterrent.
> MARCIA:
> Wally doesn't feel that's a deterrent at all. In fact,
> he kinda likes it.
> JAN:
> We're not talking about the bedroom.
> MARCIA:
> You weren't, but I was.
> (Giggles all around.)

Variety actually gave the first episode an upbeat review. "Introduction of Kulhman was nicely set up and subsequent intro of Houser was nicely handled as well. . . . Peter Baldwin's direction gave the pleasant plot variations a nice sense of pace, provided parents Robert Reed and Florence Henderson with enough to do to make their presence felt (while sliding them gradually into the background)—and it was easy to see why NBC quickly snapped up *Brides* for its primetime sked." But *TV Guide* critic Robert MacKenzie ruminated that "It's pointless to dwell on the negligibility of the acting and writing in this series. Doters don't care. They will be right there, snuggling in their rockers, when *Sis and Cindy at the Old Folks Home* makes its debut in 2040." Damn right!

As Sherwood Schwartz remembers, *The Brady Girls Get Married* "was written and produced originally as a two-hour film, but it never ran that way. It ran as half-hour shows leading into another series [titled *The Brady Brides* starting with the fourth episode] because that's what Paramount and NBC decided to do. I'll never forget it: We had to, on a weekend, take apart a two-hour show and put in logical endings at different places to turn it into half-hour shows!" Indeed, *TV Guide* had already gone to press with the two-hour movie in its listing for February 6, 1981—there was even a full-page ad for it. "Boy, we ate and slept and worked at it all weekend," Schwartz remembers. Nor was there any time for reshooting. "No, it was too late for that," he says, "because this had to happen like right now. That was a tough thing to do."

The first three episodes were later *re*-reedited into a ninety-minute TV movie that aired on NBC on October 27, 1981, under the original title, *The Brady Girls Get Married.* It still pops up in syndication.

It would be the last of the Bradys (except for reruns, of course) until . . .

A Very Brady Christmas

Written by Sherwood and Lloyd J. Schwartz. Directed by Peter Baldwin. Producer: Lloyd J. Schwartz. Executive Producer: Sherwood Schwartz.

This drama ended up as the third highest-rated TV movie of 1988. And since it aired on CBS, it means the Bradys have appeared on all three commercial networks—a rare feat.

The story: The clan is reunited at Christmas, amid flashbacks from the first-season Christmas episode. There is, unfortunately, plenty of Brady trouble this yuletide. Marcia has two kids and an out-of-work husband, Jan's marriage is falling apart, electronics salesperson Peter is angry because his girlfriend makes more money than he, Bobby's dropping out of grad school to race cars, and, worst of all, some actress named Jennifer Runyon is playing Cindy.

Just as Christmas dinner is about to be served, there's an accident at a construction site for which Mike is the architect. He's called away, and then,

Jennifer Runyon as Cindy in *A Very Brady Christmas*.

as he's investigating the accident, the site collapses! Does Mike survive? What do you think?

Lloyd Schwartz has a particularly fond memory of working on that TV movie. "When the boys came back for this last movie, I took them all to a Dodgers game," he says. "And on the way back, they said they wanted to see the house. And I felt really like—when I drove 'em by the house—that they *are* like brothers, they are that close. And they viewed the episodes kind of as home movies, because that was their formative time growing up. So we went to see the house, and it was like they were going to see *their* old house, even though they obviously never lived in it. Then they wanted to see the house where they filmed the pilot—Carol's parents' house, where they had the wedding. That was a pretty moving day."

The Bradys

Executive Producers: Sherwood Schwartz and Lloyd J. Schwartz. Producer: Barry Berg. Music: Laurence Juber. Photography: King Baggot.

In the fall of 1989, while the Schwartzes were in the planning stages for two new Brady TV movies—*The Brady 500* (with Bobby racing in the Indianapolis 500) and *The Bradys on the Move*—CBS astonished the world by asking them instead for a new Brady series! The TV movies were scrapped, and on Wednesday, December 13, 1989, production began on six new one-hour episodes—shot on the same Paramount soundstage, Number 5, as the original series. All the original cast returned with the exception of Maureen McCormick; she was replaced by Leah Ayres, a former regular on the HBO series *1st and Ten* and a guest on such shows as *St. Elsewhere, 9 to 5*, and the soap opera *The Edge of Night*. And in the Brady version of a psychedelic flashback, virtually *all* the regulars of *every* Brady permutation were also back: Jerry Houser as Marcia's husband Wally Logan, Ron Kuhlman as Jan's spouse Phillip Covington III, and Caryn Richman as Greg's wife Nora (from *A Very Brady Christmas*). Added were three members of yet a third Brady generation: Marcia and Wally's kids Jessica (Jacklyn Bernstein) and Mickey (Michael Melby); Greg and Nora's son Kevin (Jonathan Weiss); and Jan and Phillip's adopted daughter Patty (Valerie Ick). Former MTV veejay Martha Quinn came aboard as Bobby Brady's wife, Tracy. Ken Michelman played Cindy's radio-station boss, Gary Greenberg.

"A one-hour drama based on a half-hour sitcom from twenty years ago," marvels Lloyd Schwartz, co-creator of the new series with his father, Sherwood. "I have never," he says, laughing, "heard of that happening before." Once again, as always, the Bradys rule.

AND ALSO ...

The MTV and syndicated game show *Remote Control,* hosted by Ken Ober, is positively obsessed with the Bradys. Among the popular categories on this game-show parody are the Brady Network, Brady Physics, and Brady Metaphysics.

Three grown-up Brady kids, Barry Williams, Eve Plumb, and Susan Olsen (looking very hippie-ish in her floppy hat and T-shirt), played for charity when a syndicated version of *Remote Control* debuted on September 23, 1989.

The question to decide who goes first was, "How many times did Mike get Carol pregnant?" In another category, the grown-up Brady kids had to guess which 1976 headline from a Louisville newspaper was accurate. The choices: "Barry Williams: I'm the Next Elvis," "Ann B. Davis Says 'Aliens Ate My Shrubs,'" or "Success as Hooker? Wait and See, Says Eve [Plumb]." The correct answer, of course, is number three.

In the Brady Physics category ("Physics the fun way ... the Brady way!"):

"Bobby enlists in the British navy and commits an indiscretion with the admiral's favorite cabin boy. If he's drawn and quartered, how many parts is he in?" Eve got this one.

Later, in the "Casey's Big Poll" category, a poll of college students supplied the answer to "Which two Bradys were most likely to do it?"

The answer: Greg and Marcia (but you knew that, anyway). The other four finishers in the poll were: Cindy and Bobby, Marcia and Bobby, Jan and Bobby, and Carol and Tiger.

In the Brady Network category, the question was which performer did not appear on *A Very Brady Christmas*. Barry Williams knew it was Susan Olsen even before Susan could hit her buzzer.

In the two-person challenge round between Barry and Eve, the quick-response category was "Which Brady did it?" Let's see how *you* do, in your comfy chair without a screaming audience, flashing lights, and a sexy co-hostess with a drop-dead dress:

—Got caught smoking
—Loved a boy who only loved bugs
—Owned Kitty Karry-All
—Stole Kitty Karry-All
—Had sex with Mike
—Hung dead cows in his freezer
—Was scared of heights

Barry eventually beat Eve 115–90, and even took the grand prize during the "Wheel of Jeopardy" segment.

AND . . .

One of the most memorable homages to *The Brady Bunch* aired on the February 5, 1989, episode of the NBC sitcom *Day by Day*. Teenager Ross Harper (C. B. Barnes) fantasizes becoming a member of the Brady family because his parents (Linda Kelsey and Doug Sheehan) yelled at him when he got a bad grade on a test. "Mike and Carol Brady wouldn't do that," he says.

Falling asleep in front of yet another Brady rerun, Ross materializes in the Brady household. Still clad in his bathrobe, he runs into Carol, and when he sees Florence Henderson, he wipes the sleep from his eyes and exclaims, "Mrs. Brady? Carol Brady?" Carol doesn't understand why he's being so formal, especially since he's *the Bradys' long-lost son Chuck*!

Taking off his bathrobe, Ross discovers to his shock that he's dressed in the height of Brady fashion: bell-bottoms, a polyester print shirt, and platform shoes.

Mike tells Ross/Chuck that he has to do something about his hair. Chuck replies that his hair is sacred and that he's not cutting it. Mike says, "I don't want you to cut it. You have to get it permed. All the Brady men have perms." Sure enough, the next time Ross comes down the stairs, his hair has been permed.

Ross really digs being part of the Brady household. But he changes his mind when Mike and Carol start repeating dialogue they recited when he first arrived. When Ross tells them they just said that, he is told that of course the dialogue repeats—it's a rerun! Everything we do is a rerun, Mike informs him. Ross/Chuck suddenly wakes up and, much to his relief, finds himself back at the Harper residence.

The episode contains many neat-o Brady references, including bully Buddy Hinton, two Brady siblings running against each other for class president, Marcia's cheerleading cheer, and the Bradys' Roaring '20s party.

The Bradys making this groovy scene were Florence Henderson, Robert Reed, Ann B. Davis, Chris Knight, Mike Lookinland, and a very pregnant Maureen McCormick.

AND . . .

Eve Plumb had an unusual bit part in Keenen Ivory Wayans's 1988 blaxploitation spoof, *I'm Gonna Git You Sucka*. She plays the wife of a leftover '60s black militant, who watches over their two blond, blue-eyed kids and rewards them by letting them watch *The Brady Bunch*. (The theme plays in the background.)

In Jazzy Jeff and the Fresh Prince's rap video "Parents Just Don't Understand," the hero gets angry at his parents because his mother chooses clothing for him—including a pair of ugly pants described as *"Brady Bunch bell-bottoms."*

Looking back, it's clear that *The Brady Bunch* did try to promote positive values: togetherness, sharing, getting along with strangers, respect for parents, telling the truth. The crises the episodes explored are the universal anxieties of adolescence—first dates, first day in a new school, self-consciousness, self-esteem—although each was wrought to Wagnerian proportions. It's also interesting to note that *The Brady Bunch* often featured black actors in nonracial supporting roles, usually as friends of the kids.

There's a comforting (or numbing) sameness to *The Brady Bunch*. Virtually every episode begins with an establishing shot of the Brady's residence. The plots are variations on a very few themes: a minor crisis hits a family member, a prank doesn't succeed, a Brady's ego goes out of control. And each episode is usually resolved with a lesson in which we learn about the wrongs of selfishness, teasing, pigheadedness, fibbing, bragging, and other antisocial behavior.

But like we said before, didn't they really act like a bunch of white-bread dorks sometimes?

———————— • • • • • • • • • • ————————

Brady Sightings

"As a kid, [black-activist film director Spike Lee] was more of a sports fan, organizing games on the block, sending baseball cards away for autographs, fighting to watch Knicks games on TV when his sister wanted to watch *The Brady Bunch*."
—*Rolling Stone*, July 13–27, 1989

Question: "What are some of your all-time fave TV shows?"
Pop star Belinda Carlisle: "*Green Acres, I Love Lucy*, and *The Brady Bunch*."
—*Movieline*, September 1989

"Every morning before going to work, [blond bombshell Christina Applegate of *Married ... With Children*] has breakfast with her mom, and then the two of them watch back-to-back episodes of *The Brady Bunch*. Maybe an hour of watching the squeaky clean Brady clan prepares Christina for what *not* to do when she transforms herself into Kelly Bundy, daughter from hell."
—*Us*, June 12, 1989

"Like the Brady Bunch possessed by tacky, bad-ass demons ..."
—Lead of a review of Brooklyn band the Lunachicks, whose debut EP, *Sugar Luv*, contains the ditty "Jan Brady"; *New York Press*, July 7, 1989

Buddy Hinton's Revenge
—Salt Lake City rock band named for the famous Brady bully

"I loved *The Brady Bunch*! I was totally in love with Bobby and wanted to have long blond hair like Jan."
—*Dallas* actress Cathy Podewell, to the authors; she eventually fulfilled her dream of meeting Bobby when Chris Knight showed up at a frat party at the University of California, Santa Barbara, where she was a freshman.

"[H]ere now I sit with my hands shaking, barely able to write, and my eyeballs pulsing, longing for a cathode ray tube on which to affix their gaze. TV theme songs and episodes are racing through my head. No, not *The Brady Bunch* theme again! It's the one where Cindy reads Marcia's diary."
— Editorial, *New York Daily News,* October 24, 1989

"That whole week, it was terrible! I couldn't get [*The Brady Bunch* theme] out of my head! That same week, I saw Florence Henderson shopping for shoes. No offense to Florence, but I was with my mother, shopping for her."
—*Days of Our Lives* star Arleen Sorkin, who also played the recurring role of Geneva the maid on *Duet,* to the authors; speaking about the week she had to seduce guest star Robert Reed on that sitcom.

"This one-hour *CBS Summer Playhouse* drama, a failed pilot about a New York columnist and his family, dredges up the hackneyed format of the 1970s family sitcom, without the laughs. However, it doesn't have any of the redeeming elements that made similarly themed family shows like *The Brady Bunch* a hit."
—Lead of a review of *American Nuclear,* starring James Farentino; *Variety,* August 2–8, 1989

"Where *is* Murphy? . . . [W]e have to come up with five minutes of cultural advancements, and all we've got is *A Very Brady Christmas.* . . ."
—Joe Regalbuto as Frank Fontana, bemoaning the difficulty of compiling a 1980s decade-in-review news segment; *Murphy Brown,* CBS, October 2, 1989

"A prisoner in Massachusetts' Deer Island House of Correction refused to climb down from the jail roof unless prison officials could name all six Brady kids."
—*Entertainment Weekly*, February 16, 1990

Meet the Brady Bunch

MIKE BRADY

The type of dad most kids would be proud to have: a loving husband and a concerned, caring father involved in all aspects of his kids' lives. He spends Saturday mornings teaching the boys how to play baseball and football, and serves as council master for Greg's "Frontier Scouts." Athletically inclined himself, he is known to play golf. He went to Norton College. No male midlife crisis or wimpy self-confessionals for him.

"We have a wonderful bunch of kids," he tells a friend. "I mean really marvelous. They don't play hooky. They don't lie. They're not fresh. But boy . . . they just won't stay off that phone."

MIKE AT WORK

Unlike Ward Cleaver and Ozzie Nelson, we knew what Mike did for a living. He was an architect, and must have been a pretty darn successful one to be able to support a non-salary-earning wife, six kids, and a housekeeper/cook. He had a drafting table in his den at home and we even saw him at "the office," one of those late '60s ultramodern L.A. buildings.

Here are some of the things that went on with Mike Brady and his work:

- He called Mr. Crawford on the pay phone to make a "multimillion-dollar deal."
- He built a new house for Don Drysdale.
- He designed the Penelope Fletcher Cultural Center for Penelope Fletcher, a wealthy, grouchy doyenne played by Natalie Schafer.
- His firm was going to build the courthouse in Woodland Park.
- His boss sent him to Hawaii with his family to work on a project.
- His boss sent him to Cincinnati, where his firm was submitting plans to build an addition to an amusement park.
- The president of his company, Mr. Matthews, gave him a pool table as a gift for having landed "the Whitley project."
- An FBI agent checked up on Mike because his firm was designing a building for a "classified government agency."

LESSONS FROM MIKE

An integral part of nearly every *Brady Bunch* episode were the lecture/homilies delivered by Mike and Carol, which taught the kids the meaning of life and helped them, we hope, grow up to be responsible adults. Of course, Mike's were delivered in a firm but loving voice. Someday, some marketing whiz might want to edit all the Bradys' lectures down, put them on a videotape, and release it as a primer for parents. Here's a selection of some of Mike's best lessons.

To Marcia: "Honey, you should never really promise anything unless you're sure you can deliver." ("Getting Davy Jones")

To Jan: "A Brady never goes back on her promise. . . ." ("Miss Popularity")

To Carol about Bobby (when Bobby tells his friends he knows Joe Namath): "He's got to learn that when you bluff, someone's gonna call you on it." ("Mail Order Hero")

To Marcia when she gets anxious about entering high school: "Marcia, there's an old saying: You can't take a step forward with two feet still on the ground." ("Today I Am a Freshman")

To Bobby in "Law and Disorder," on the importance of rules: "We always have to have rules and laws, but we have to use them with reason and justice."

Still, Mike could be a stern disciplinarian when he needed to be. In "Out of This World," in which Greg fakes creating a UFO to pull a prank on Bobby, Mike grounds Greg by taking away his car privileges for the weekend when Greg needs the car to go on a fishing trip.

"How am I supposed to get there without a car?" asks Greg.

"I suppose you'll have to hitch a ride on a UFO," responds a sarcastic Mike.

Sometimes, Mike disciplined with a wry sense of humor. Like when he found out that Cindy and Bobby schemed to get Joe Namath to come to their house: "I think you two are going to be penalized for illegal procedure."

Other times, he could really be harsh. When the kids conspired to scare Alice in "Fright Night," he responded by taking away their allowances for two weeks. And in "Greg Gets Grounded," he forbade Greg from driving for a week because Greg tried to cover up a near accident. And the kids, because they were Bradys, never disobeyed him.

CAROL BRADY

Carol Brady was a true domestic goddess, a "homemaker" who had stay-at-home help even though she herself stayed at home. Unlike June Cleaver, she didn't wear pearls while vacuuming or cooking. But she didn't do much of those latter activities, anyway, since Alice was always available. Still, sometimes Carol did the shopping and would help Alice chop and slice and dice.

She graduated from State University. A concerned woman, she belonged to the PTA and a "women's club" (obviously the kind that didn't have consciousness-raising sessions). In her one foray into community activism, she was the chairman of the drive to save Woodland Park. She helps Jan become a pom-pom girl because she once won a twist contest. She did dabble in a few hobbies: she attempted to become a free-lance writer, trying to sell the story of her family to *Tomorrow's Woman* magazine. At other times, she showed an interest in photography and sculpture.

Carol was kind and selfless, always ready with a smile and fresh-from-the-oven advice. She was a loving mom who would line up at the head of the stairs and hand individual brown-bag lunches to each of the six kids as they went off to school.

ADVICE FROM CAROL

To Jan: "Find out what you do best and then do your best with it." ("My Sister's Shadow")

Later in the same episode: "Sometimes when we lose . . . we win."

To Greg when he decides he'd rather be a rock singer than go to college: "Fame is a fleeting thing, but a college education lasts a lifetime." ("Adios, Johnny Bravo")

To the kids en masse, when they are thinking of voting Peter out of the family singing group, "The Brady 6," just because Peter's voice is starting to change: "Money and fame are very important things, but sometimes there are other things that are more important—like people!" ("Dough Re Mi")

To Cindy, when she finds out she can't rent a theater for her production of *Snow White:* "I never thought you were a quitter . . . you knew you accepted a big responsibility and now you're dropping it. . . . No person has ever solved a problem by crawling into a hole." ("Snow White and the Seven Bradys")

To the kids after they've scared Alice with a practical joke: "If you carry a joke too far, somebody could get hurt." ("Fright Night")

To Marcia when she complains about people not liking her because she wears braces: "Braces can never change the feelings of a real friend . . . and they can never change the feelings of someone who loves you." ("Brace Yourself")

On the other hand, she didn't want her daughters growing up too fast. In "Going . . . Going Steady," she spies Marcia trying on her false eyelashes in an attempt to look older.

CAROL:
False eyelashes are out!
MARCIA:
A lot of girls my age wear makeup.
CAROL:
I'm sorry, that's their mothers' problems, not mine.
Now off they come!
MARCIA
(taking them off):
Ouch! Like Harvey said, "Parents just don't un-
derstand our generation. . . ."

(Note how rap stars Jazzy Jeff and the Fresh Prince reiterated this theme—see "The Brady Legacy.")

To Bobby when he gets down on himself for not selling any bottles of hair tonic door to door ("The Hair-Brained Scheme"):

> CAROL:
> There's an old saying, quitters never win and winners never quit.
> BOBBY:
> That's corny, Mom.
> CAROL:
> It may be corny, but it's also true. Listen, honey, the great ones never quit no matter how rough things get.

To Cindy: "You shouldn't put down a loser, Cindy, because you might be one yourself someday. Just remember that." ("You Can't Win Them All")

DOUBLE-BARRELED PARENT LECTURE

Sometimes the problems were so overwhelming that both Mike and Carol had to talk to the kids at the same time:

> MIKE (to Bobby):
> You should have thought of all the problems you could have caused by hiding the fact you've been exposed to mumps.
> CAROL:
> Honey, don't ever be afraid to come and tell us something. ("Never Too Young")

When Greg and Marcia argue about who should move into the attic:

> MIKE:
> You're not gonna solve anything by arguing.
> CAROL:
> Right. ("Room at the Top")

Mike is yelling at the boys, who want to keep the $1,100 Bobby found and not share it with the girls:

> MIKE:
> This is quickly becoming a house divided and you should be ashamed of yourselves.

CAROL:

And all because of something you don't even have.

MIKE:

Your mother and I always share our good fortune with all of you.

CAROL:

Every day.

MIKE:

It's about time you pull yourself together and call a truce to this civil war. AND THAT'S AN ORDER! ("The Treasure of Sierra Avenue")

ROMANTIC INTERLUDES OF MIKE AND CAROL

The Brady Brunch at least acknowledged that couples slept in the same bed and could even be romantic there (although a couple of closemouthed kisses and murmured *mmmmmms* was all we saw). Still in the early '70s, Mike and Carol were the smoochingest couple in prime time.

CAROL:

There are some things that men and women do equally well. . . .

MIKE:

Yeah, I agree with that. Especially one thing. Pucker up and I'll show you.

Carol and Mike (kissing): Mmmmmmm ("The Liberation of Marcia Brady")

Anticipating a second honeymoon at a dude ranch, Carol greets Mike dressed like a cowgirl. Responds Mike: "Wow! You can ride my range anytime!" ("Miss Popularity")

Mike and Carol are in bed talking about the kids' report cards, when Mike leans over and kisses Carol:

MIKE:

Good night, honey.

CAROL:

I'd give it a C.

MIKE:

A C?

CAROL:
That kiss—I'd give it a *C.*
MIKE:
How about a chance to improve my grade?
CAROL:
That seems fair.
(Mike gives Carol another kiss.)
CAROL:
Mmmmmmm, yes that's definitely a *B.*
MIKE:
A *B?*
CAROL:
I'm sorry, I call them as I feel them.
MIKE:
How about another chance for a willing pupil?
CAROL:
Fire when ready, Gridley. . . .
(Mike turns out the light and gives Carol a big
smack and a big embrace.)
CAROL:
Now, that's an *A!* ("Power of the Press")

In "The Subject Was Noses," Mike and Carol have to sleep on separate couches in the guest room because their room is being wallpapered and painted.

CAROL:
Do you realize that this is the first time since we
were married that we haven't slept in the same
bed?
MIKE:
Breaks up the monotony, doesn't it?
CAROL:
Now, Mike, don't start that. . . .
MIKE:
Can't you take a joke?
CAROL:
Sure, I married you, didn't I?
(They laugh. They kiss. Mmmmmm.)

THE BRADY KIDS

You just knew the Bradys were Republicans, members of the so-called Silent Majority. The squarest family on the block, they were relentlessly middle-class during a decade when to be middle-class was considered by some to be totally uncool.

The family carried the concept of "togetherness" to the nth degree; rarely did they pursue separate activites. They were the kind of kids you hated because they were so involved in so many extracurricular activities. They were milk-drinking goody-goodies who listened to their parents. What kind of world did they live in?

The kids did tease each other. But when they did, they would be chastised by their parents or would resolve the problems before the episode was over. They didn't often scream, usually reserving their emotional expressions to pouting as they dealt with the normal problems of adolescence—sibling rivalry, first dates, braces, new schools, etc.

THE BRADY GIRLS

The Brady girls were not the type you would call bad girls. Like their parents and brothers, they were even-tempered and lovable—and had beautiful hair.

MARCIA

Marcia is an overachiever. At various junctures, she is editor of her junior-high newspaper (the *Fillmore Flyer*), senior-class president, and winner of various awards. When she became a freshman at Westdale, she worried about her popularity and joined a half-dozen clubs. She would run for head cheerleader and school-banquet hostess. She was chairman of the enter-tainment committee and the Fillmore Junior High chapter of the Davy Jones fan club, and her shining moment came when she persuaded Davy Jones to appear at her prom.

The other girls may have been jealous of Marcia, but Marcia was jealous of Greg, especially when she felt he was being given preferential treatment.

"Why should I be penalized for being born a year too late? I'm sick and tired of being second around here." ("A Room at the Top") They ran against each other for student-body president, and competed with each other to see who got the higher score on their driving test. But generally, she liked Greg (what lusty thoughts ran through both stepsiblings' minds, one can only speculate) and once even told him, "You're the greatest brother a girl ever had."

Maureen McCormick primps.

LOVE LESSONS FROM MARCIA BRADY

Poor Marcia, always falling in love. And you *knew* when she was in love, because her eyes glazed and she pranced around the Brady residence as if in a trance. But did she ever really kiss a boy? Don't count on it.

MARCIA:

I'm in love. . . .

JAN:

Who is it this time?

MARCIA:

What do you mean this time? The others were just schoolgirl crushes.

JAN:

Is there a difference?

MARCIA:

Is there a difference? Is there a difference be-tween a shooting star and a firecracker?

JAN:

Is he gorgeous?

MARCIA:

He will be when his complexion clears up.
("The Private Ear")

Marcia to Cindy, who has a crush on a boy: "Cindy, you don't ask a boy to call you. You get him to call you by being mature and playing cool. . . ." ("Cindy Brady, Lady")

THE MANY LOVES OF MARCIA BRADY

Marcia's first crush was on Desi Arnaz, Jr. She writes about him in her diary: "Every time I see him on TV, I think Wow! Desi Arnaz, Jr. . . . He's so cute. In my dream of dreams, I dream of being Mrs. Desi Arnaz, Jr." And at the end of the episode, when Desi has showed up at the Brady house, he tells Marcia, "As far as you're concerned, I think you're the tops yourself," and he kisses her on the cheek. And Marcia screeches, "I'll never wash this cheek again as long as I live!"

Marcia's first steady was a nerdy guy named Harvey Klinger, whose hobby was collecting bugs. Marcia was so bug-eyed over Harvey that she spent hours studying insects so she would have something to talk to him about.

Alas, it was a relationship, like all of Marcia's, that did not last beyond one episode.

Marcia's first date with a "high-school boy" was a trip to the pizza parlor with Warren Mulaney, the guy who just so happened to be the same "crumb" who beat out Greg for first-string basketball team and student-council president.

Marcia's biggest crush was on twenty-eight-year-old dentist Dr. Stanley Vogel. After she comes back from a dental appointment dreamy-eyed, she raves: "You should see him! He is far out . . . mmm . . . he has dark, gorgeous hair, dreamy eyes, groovy bell-bottom pants, neat shoes, and he plays the best rock-and-roll music in his office."

Later in the episode, she fantasizes about being "Mrs. Marcia Dentist." Ironically, Marcia had been traumatized earlier in the series when she had to wear braces: "I'm Ugly! Ugly! Ugly! Every time I smile, I look like an electric can opener."

MARCIA BRADY, PROTO-YUPPIE

Like many of today's dressed-for-success women, Marcia put career ahead of romance—at least temporarily. In a final-season episode, she gets a job as a server at Haskell's Ice Cream Hut. A guy she's been dating wants to ask her out, but she turns him down because she wants to work: "You know what they say: Business before pleasure."

Later, she spots the same guy in the ice-cream store with a new girl, and gets angry. "Boys! From now on, I'm dedicating myself to my own career!"

MARCIA MINUTIAE

Marcia's Sunflower Girl pledge (as recited by Peter): "I am a little sunflower/sunny, brave and true/from tiny bud to blossom/I do good deeds for you."

The text of the letter Davy Jones sent to Marcia: "I want to thank you for the interest in my career. If I'm ever in town, I'd be happy to show you my appreciation anytime. With best wishes, I am your friend, always . . . Davy Jones."

And here is Marcia Brady doing the school cheer when she tried out for Westdale High cheerleaders:

> One! Two! Tell me who are you?
> THE BEARS [said breathlessly each time]
> Three! Four! Tell me who's gonna score?
> THE BEARS
> Five! Six! Tell me who's got the kicks?
> THE BEARS!

JAN

To many, Jan was actually more attractive than Marcia. She always seemed sensible and more approachable. She had wavier and longer blond hair than her sister Marcia, which she often wore pulled back from her forehead. A bit of a tomboy, she also had problems that may be endemic to being the middle child. She thought people were always making fun of her and often put herself down ("What a dumbhead I am"). She felt insecure around big sister Marcia, and she suffered a major trauma in the third season when she had to start wearing glasses:

> JAN:
> Glasses! I'll look positively goofy! When Bernie
> McGuire sees me, he'll go positively bananas.
> CAROL:
> Bananas? That's bad, isn't it?
> JAN:
> It's the worst.

But by the final season (without the glasses), she will be named "The Most Popular Girl in the Class."

CINDY

Cindy specialized in whining, pouting, and being overly cute. Maybe it was the ribbons in her pigtails (always color-coordinated with her pants or skirt) that caused the discomfort. But in actuality, much of her sense of being victimized was due to her being the youngest child, a feeling she often shared with nearly-as-young Bobby.

A teenaged Eve Plumb, as she never appeared on *The Brady Bunch*.

In "The Teeter-Totter Caper," the older kids are going to Aunt Gertrude's wedding, but not the little kids. Cindy whines: "Why can't us little kids do something important, too?" She and Bobby decide to break an endurance record on a teeter-totter.

In "Cindy Brady, Lady," Cindy complains that she's not as old as her sisters: "Why did I have to be born so young?" Carol tries to console her by telling her that in a few short years, "You're gonna be a teenager, too." Cindy responds, "I wanna be a teenager *now*!"

When Jan complains that her opponent in the Most Popular Girl contest has "the three *B*'s: beautiful, brainy, and built," Marcia tries to be sympathetic: "Jan, that's not everything." Leave it to Cindy to add the topper: "At my age, it's nothing. . . ."

When Cindy accidentally loses Marcia's diary, Marcia talks about how important it is to have a diary, a place to write your innermost thoughts. Cindy: "I never had an innermost thought in my life."

CINDY MINUTIAE

She attends Clinton Grammar School. She's a snoop who reads Marcia's diary, and a bit of a tattletale. She must be smart because she got onto the quiz show "Question the Kids." She wore braces during the final season, but unlike Marcia, she never complained about it.

THE BRADY BOYS

Both the Brady boys and girls adhered to very rigid sex roles. Girls didn't play sports and boys didn't cook. That was that. No questions asked.

GREG

Good ol' Greg. Lovable and even-tempered, a red-blooded boy who liked girls, cars, and sports. As the oldest child, he was usually the leader who would call Brady-kid meetings where they would plot negotiation strategy with Mom and Dad.

As he shot past puberty, he developed into quite a ladies' man; in fact, Alice once referred to him as "The Casanova of Clinton Avenue." But far from being a rogue, he was a kind of good-natured ogler who never got too hung up on just one "chick" (as Greg would have called them).

Sports also filled his leisure time. As a youngster, he was pitcher on his Pony League team, the Tigers. And once, encouraged by Don Drysdale, he was going to drop out and become a major-league ballplayer. He likes to surf and was a high-school letter man, although he couldn't make it to the first-string basketball team. At Westdale High, he was involved in everything from sports to student government, and once even combined the two as head of the committee to name the lead cheerleader. How on earth did he find time to do everything?

PICKUP TIPS FROM GREG BRADY

In "Greg's Triangle," Greg is approached by Jennifer, a curvaceous coed whom Greg (or Greggy, as she calls him) has been eyeing, and vice versa. Note the smooth dialogue, dudes:

JENNIFER:
I bet we have a lot in common.
GREG:
I bet we have. What do you like? Movies? Sports? Surfing?
JENNIFER:
You're a surfer? Fantastic! I should have known with a physique like yours.
GREG:
Well, I kind of lift weights to stay in shape.
JENNIFER:
Maybe I should try that.
GREG:
What for? Your shape doesn't need any improving.
JENNIFER:
Thanks. I'd still like to learn how to surf, though.
GREG:
Maybe I can teach you a few things.
JENNIFER:
Great. I'm not doing anything Saturday.

GREG:
You are now. Pick you up at ten.

Greg's all-purpose line to break a date: "Tell someone 'something suddenly came up.' " ("The Subject Was Noses")

PETER

Another even-tempered, lovable, red-blooded boy, who loved tinkering with science projects, his bicycle, etc. Peter, the middle boy, always looked up to Greg, and in fact as the show wore on, he became a kind of cut-rate Greg, whose primary interests were girls and sports. In fact, when Greg graduated high school, he gave Peter his letter sweater, saying Peter would have to get his own letter . . . "probably in chasing girls."

BOBBY

The youngest even-tempered, lovable, red-blooded boy of the clan, Bobby started out being sensitive about his height; Sam the butcher once called him "Shrimpo." Because of his place in the family hierarchy, he was always linked to the youngest girl, Cindy. And he was often forced, like Cindy, to sound overly cute. By the final season, he became interested in girls and started looking like "Butch" of the Little Rascals. Bobby was known for his active fantasy life, often slipping into dreamland where he would rob trains with Jesse James, play football with Joe Namath, and become the world-champion pool player.

He wore braces during the last season, and it was also during the last season that Mike referred to him more often as "Bob" rather than "Bobby."

ALICE

Cheerfully answering the phone, "Brady residence," Alice Nelson was a TV domestic in the tradition of Hazel and Beulah. She was good-natured, somewhat simple, yet practical. She was free with advice and always at the beck and call of her employer. Alice had a severe self-esteem problem and was always putting herself down; when she had a toothache, she half joked, "I'm glad it's not my wisdom tooth. I need all the smarts I can get." None of this kept her, of course, from her appointed rounds—such as taking fresh-baked cookies out of the oven and serving them, with milk, to the famished Brady kids when they came home from school.

Yet even more than cooking, cleaning, and sewing for the Bradys, Alice's true mission in life was to snag a husband—specifically Sam the Butcher (whom she once described as six feet, two hundred pounds of "unbudgeable bachelor"). They'd met at an army dance, and though they did date, we can only speculate about their private love life.

Alice was verbally creative, and was a contender in the Countess of Cornball competition: "Anyone for flapjacks? Hot off the grill and still flapping?" ("Out of This World")

Mike to Alice: "Alice, your talk is like your meat loaf: a little bit of everything and all mixed up."

Alice on her food: "My Mexican dinner comes in three degrees: hot, very hot, pass the fire extinguisher."

Carol (to Alice): "You know, Alice, raising a family gets to be a habit."

Alice: "I know, Mrs. Brady. It's a habit I'd like to talk Sam into."

Alice, telling Carol how she was planning to redecorate Sam's apartment with some frilly curtains: "The idea is to turn that man's apartment into this woman's apartment." ("The Babysitters")

Mike: "How do you feel about helping two people fall in love?"

Alice: "I'm all for it, especially if one of those two people turns out to be me!" ("You're Never Too Old")

OLIVER

Oliver, Carol's nephew, was introduced toward the end of the final season. A tyke whose blond bangs and wire-rim glasses suggested a pint-sized John Denver, he was brought in when Bobby and Cindy outgrew their cutesy-kid phase (at twelve and eleven, respectively). When Greg moved up to the attic, Oliver moved into the top bunk in the boys' room and got to say all the cutesy-poo lines that Bobby and Cindy used to say during the early days of the show.

Biographies of the Cast

ROBERT REED

Peter O'Toole. Albert Finney. Diana Rigg. Robert Reed.

What do they have in common? They are all alumni of London's Royal Academy of Dramatic Arts. Yes, the man who played Mike Brady is a classically trained actor. O. Henry couldn't have written a more ironic tale.

"I hear it on the street from the kids," Reed once recalled, mimicking them: " 'Hi, Mr. Brady!' They think of me from *The Brady Bunch* and as E. G. Marshall's kid" from his years on *The Defenders*. "I guess I'll be remembered for that—unfortunately. I guess it's an actor's ego. He'd rather have *Hamlet* on his tombstone than *The Brady Bunch*."

Robert Reed may not even have "Robert Reed" on that tombstone—he was born John Robert Rietz in Highland Park, Illinois, a suburb of Chicago, on October 19, 1932. He changed his name for the stage—and hated doing so. ("I think of vanilla pudding or tapioca when I think of 'Reed,' " he once said bitterly.) His father, also named John Rietz, moved the family to Texas when Robert was six, then on to Missouri and to Muskogee, Oklahoma. They were solid midwesterners, raising cattle and turkeys.

A self-proclaimed conservative (his idea of marriage in 1963 was "to have a little wife to make that 5:00 A.M. coffee, do the dishes, and wash my laundry"), Reed nonetheless decided early in life to become an actor. His

54

parents, rather liberally, went along. "The fact that I didn't want to become anything but an actor didn't upset my parents at all," he recalled. "I'm an only child and they're well adjusted. As long as I'm happy, they are." He was still attending Central High School in Muskogee when he began writing for local radio stations KMUS and KBX, eventually also producing shows for them and working as an announcer.

The midwesterner went on to Northwestern, studying theater there under Alvina Krause and summering at her theater in Eagles Mare, Pennsylvania. He left Northwestern in 1954—"just shy of graduating," he once admitted, before changing his story in later years—and studied at the Royal Academy for a year. He was accompanied by his new bride, Marilyn Rosenberg, a fellow student at Northwestern. "She was a drama major, too," he recalled, "but primarily a dancer." They had a daughter, Carolyn, in 1957, and were divorced in 1959.

By that time, Reed had helped to further the growing success of off-Broadway theater through the troupe the Shakespearewrights, among whose number was Pernell Roberts. During 1956–57, he worked in Chicago with the Studebaker Theatre. There he met Sir Cedric Hardwicke, Geraldine Page, and E. G. Marshall, who would play his father for four years on *The Defenders*.

"I started out as E. G. Marshall's son in *Desire Under the Elms,*" he recalled. But, "I lost the role during rehearsals. They said we were not a good father–son team."

Reed went on to a town-by-town tour of Shakespeare that in 1957 brought him to Hollywood. He and Hollywood didn't take. For one thing, the town insisted he change his name from Rietz. At least supposedly—Reed has recounted the story in different ways. "When I was at MGM," he told the *New York Post's* Sidney Skolsky in 1964, "I was told 'TZ' is not going to look good on a marquee." A year earlier he'd told Alan Gill of *TV Guide*, "Somebody at 20th Century Fox felt that the 'TZ' wouldn't look good on the marquee."

Is it any wonder he landed at an ad agency? Reed worked himself up to proofreader, copywriter, and finally media buyer, but he couldn't give up acting, and so decided to go on the dole while looking for parts. (This is a self-proclaimed conservative?) "It was wonderful," he later said of the experience. "I used to get up in the morning, get into my new car, drive down to the unemployment center, where I would meet other unemployed actors, who also had new cars. We'd gab, have coffee, talk shop, complain [about] how small the checks were ... Man! It was Socialsville!" he gushed some years ago, sounding disturbingly like a *Brady* script or a Reaganomics nightmare.

Little by little, Reed got acting work. His break came with a 1959 episode of *Father Knows Best,* "The Imposter," where he played a young lawyer. His scene lasted only about a minute, but it was an important minute.

Shortly thereafter, the pilot for the law drama *The Defenders* was in preproduction. (It had grown out of the two-part *Studio One* live drama "The Defender" by Reginald Rose, starring Ralph Bellamy, William Shatner, and Steve McQueen.) Reed's agent sent the producers the clip from *Father Knows Best,* and, reportedly, that show's producer, Gene Rodney, also recommended him. Whatever it took, Reed got an audition for the part of Ken Preston, the son and law partner of crusty attorney Lawrence Preston (E. G. Marshall). Nine months later, he got a phone call telling him the part was his and that *The Defenders* would be shooting back in New York.

The Defenders was a tough, justly acclaimed show that took on subjects that are still controversial today, such as abortion and euthanasia. For his part, Reed became a TV heartthrob, getting fan letters and marriage proposals from as far away as Japan. The show ran four years, amassed a cache of Emmy Awards, and turned Reed into the James Brolin or Chad Everett of his time. He was so much in demand that during the show's last year he shuttled back and forth between the set and Broadway, where he succeeded Robert Redford in the male lead of Neil Simon's *Barefoot in the Park.*

After *The Defenders* ended in 1965, Reed went on to guest-star in episodes of *Dr. Kildare, Family Affair, Ironside*, and many other shows, and was the

Looking very debonair.

Robert Reed and co-star E. G. Marshall in *The Defenders*.

star of an unsold ABC military sitcom, *Somewhere in Italy . . . Company B.* (Maybe it was the name that killed it.) A guest shot in a 1969 episode of *Mannix* led to a recurring role as Lieutenant Adam Tobias from then until 1975—concurrent with *Brady!* "When Bob and I worked in a scene, it was like sign language," *Mannix* star Mike Connors told author Ric Meyers. "It clicked, there was a spark. He was only going to do one episode originally, because he was starring in *The Brady Bunch,* but we had such a good time and there was so much chemistry, he wanted to come back."

It's not surprising he did. Reed—who was very good as Mike Brady, seemingly a natural—was not wild about *The Brady Bunch.* He'd done it largely because he was a Paramount contract player back in the days when the studios still had stables of actors, and Paramount had the show, and Reed wanted to work. He gave virtually no interviews for it, unlike the acres of press he'd done for *The Defenders*. And yet, Sherwood Schwartz reveals, Reed did develop a soft spot for Mike Brady.

"I'll tell you an amazing thing that he did," says Schwartz. "We were doing the two-hour *Brady Girls Get Married* [the original TV movie that got edited at the last minute to become the initial episodes of *The Brady Brides*] and he was on stage in New York [in *Deathtrap*], and we decided that since he was unavailable, we were gonna do it without him. And he was furious! Not at us, just furious with the fates. And he bought himself out of a weekend [of performances] to come out here and be in that show as much as he could. He needed the weekend and two extra days, and he did that on his own at great expense and problems and flying back and forth. But he said, 'Nobody's gonna marry off my two oldest daughters but me!'"

Reed could also be incredibly generous. Florence Henderson, in her book

A Little Cooking, A Little Talking and a Whole Lot of Fun, recalls that one year he took the Brady kids to Europe at his own expense. Another time, he arranged for the cast to all go on a catered fishing trip. "I didn't know it at the time," Reed told her when he appeared on her cooking show in the mid-'80s, "but those years on *The Brady Bunch* were some of the happiest years of my life."

In his career, Reed has continued to do well. He's appeared in an endless string of TV movies and mini-series, and he earned three Emmy nominations from 1975–77—twice for Outstanding Single Performance by an Actor in a Drama or Comedy (losing both times to the same person, Ed Asner) and once for Outstanding Supporting Actor in a Drama Series. He's come back for nearly every permutation of *The Brady Bunch;* it'd be as hard to imagine the sequels without him as it would *Star Trek* without William Shatner.

Hamlet on his tombstone? No, Robert Reed will remain the Brady patriarch forever.

FLORENCE HENDERSON

Florence Henderson grew up in a family something like the Brady bunch. Only not, ah, *quite* as well-to-do. "There were five girls and five boys," Florence recalls. "I'm a country girl from a very large, poor family in Indiana. And yet people always thought I came from a wealthy background. Y'know," she adds, sad and perky at once, "one Christmas, my gift was my school reader—and believe me, I loved getting it!"

A lot has changed. Today, Florence Henderson has without question the most successful career of all the *Brady* cast—her own show on national cable TV, a high-visibility position as a commercial spokesperson, many TV guest appearances, and lots of theater and nightclub gigs. And even if things hadn't worked out so well, it's clear from her personality and the opinions of others that she would still be as sweet and lovely and as much of a joy to be around and to talk to as she is. A cynic would say no one can *really* be as nice as that. But Florence is—while remaining nobody's fool. "Florence is one sharp lady," says an admiring Ann B. Davis. "Raised with all them brothers, she learned to stand up for herself. Nothing gets by her."

It's true. In the middle of a conversation filled with the kinds of fond recollections you'd have with an aunt, Florence, without missing a beat, says of *A Very Brady Christmas,* "No, we never expected it to do a thirty-nine share [in the ratings] and pick up viewers at every half-hour sampling." Wow. Silken strength—the perfect *Brady* mom!

"I loved it," Florence says of her stint as Carol Brady. "I loved every minute of it. I loved the idea of going to work, of seeing my friends on the crew, of seeing Bob and Ann B. and all the kids. I'm having a wonderful life now, but it was just as wonderful then."

If Florence expresses a more refreshing appreciation of life than many others in the cast, it's likely because she started out with much less material support than any of them. Her childhood was beyond humble—it was down-right *Grapes of Wrath*.

Florence Agnes Henderson was born February 14, 1934, in the village of Dale, Indiana, and raised in nearby Rockport and in Owensboro, Kentucky; she was the last child of rent farmers Joseph and Elizabeth Elder Henderson. "My father didn't marry till he was forty-seven," she says, "and *then* he had ten children. I was born when he was sixty-seven. He never did tell us his age—we only knew he was twenty-five years older than my mother. And *she* never knew for sure how old he was; we didn't know until after he died [at age eighty-two]. When we were little, he would say to us, 'Now if anybody asks you how old I am, you just tell them that I'm old enough to take care of myself, and I'm old enough to mind my own business.' "

Florence's mom passed away in 1984, at age eighty-eight. "She was still on a bowling team," Florence says proudly. "She was a great lady—kinda unique. She was one of the last of the pioneer types. She taught me music and she taught me how to sing when I was a baby. I don't ever remember not being able to sing." Florence's press releases always claimed she had a repertoire of fifty songs when she was just two years old. "Well, that's what my mother always said!" she answers, laughing.

Singing was Florence's ticket out of the hills. She was encouraged by the Benedictine nuns at St. Francis Academy elementary school and joined the choir at St. Bernard's Church. To help make ends meet, she sang for the Elks, the Kiwanis, the American Legion, whomever. During her senior year of high school, she got heard by the entertainment duo the Medley Brothers—relatives of a friend—who had become local brewery moguls. They sponsored the poor but talented girl to a year at New York City's prestigious American Academy of Dramatic Arts, the alma mater of Robert Redford, Edward G. Robinson, and many others.

Unfortunately, it was a two-year course, and so Florence quickly found herself auditioning for stage roles. She immediately landed a big break—a one-line part in director Joshua Logan's summer-resort musical *Wish You Were Here*. It opened on Broadway on June 25, 1952. Yet by the time it closed late the following year, Florence had been spotted in it by the legendary Richard Rodgers and cast as Laurey in the national tour of the Rodgers and Hammerstein hit, *Oklahoma!* Thus began Florence's successful, critically acclaimed career in theater and light opera. "She is the real thing," wrote the esteemed *New York Herald Tribune* critic Walter Kerr, "right out of a butter churn somewhere. . . . You not only like this Laurey, you believe in her; and for as long as *Oklahoma!* finally manages to run, I never expect to see a better one." She made her TV debut on *The Ed Sullivan Show* in 1952, as an off-camera singer, and soon became a fixture of New York variety television.

On January 9, 1956, Florence married the theatrical producer and company manager Ira Bernstein, son of the legendary New York press agent Karl Bernstein, who represented the likes of Cole Porter and George Gershwin.

They had four children: Barbara Ellen, Joseph Karl, Robert, and Elizabeth. Barbara made three appearances on *Brady Bunch* under the name Barbara Bernstein; she's now Barbara Chase, a comedienne with the troupe the Groundlings and the administrator for the Daytime Emmy Awards. The two boys live in Boston, where they have a band called Big Train.

Throughout the 1950s, Florence was known as a theater and nightclub chanteuse and New York City socialite—quite a change from the barefoot girl of the Kentucky hills. She was one of the first women to substitute-host *The Tonight Show,* and joined the ranks of what was then known as "The *Today* Girl," doing weather and light news. (Don't laugh *too* hard—Barbara Walters, among others, followed her in that position.) With Bill Hayes, her song-and-dance-act partner, she hosted the *Oldsmobile Music Theatre* (a.k.a. *Hayes and Henderson*) on NBC, and did Oldsmobile industrial shows back when they were musical extravaganzas featuring name talent. In 1966, she even got to sing with fabled New York City Mayor John V. Lindsay, in the annual Inner Circle political writers' revue. When most of the TV industry emigrated to Los Angeles, Florence adapted by making occasional forays to the West Coast and taking her nightclub act on tour.

One day in 1969, she was scheduled to perform at the Shamrock Hotel in Houston, immediately after taping *The Dean Martin Show* in L.A. In the midst of all this, her agent got her an interview with the producers of a promising new sitcom eventually titled *The Brady Bunch.* They liked her, called her back for a screen test the same day, and then rushed her to her plane to Houston—where the very next day they called her to come back and shoot the pilot. An understanding nightclub booker released her from her contract (she eventually made it up to him). Florence made the pilot, and the pilot sold the series. And by then she was in Norway.

Norway? What was she doing in Norway? Singing, as it turned out. She was the star of a movie not surprisingly titled *Song of Norway.* It was one of those big, splashy musicals that came in the wake of *The Sound of Music* (1965). Most of them—including *Hello, Dolly!* (1969), *Paint Your Wagon* (1969), and *Willy Wonka and the Chocolate Factory* (1971)—were embarrassing flops. *Song of Norway,* about the classical composer Edvard Grieg and featuring weak and watered-down versions of his music, was no exception. (At least it had gorgeous scenery shot in Super Panavision widescreen, and supporting performances by no less than Edward G. Robinson and Robert Morley.) Florence starred as Nina Grieg, the composer's wife— at exactly the time *The Brady Bunch* was supposed to begin shooting. Correction: At exactly the time *The Brady Bunch* actually *did* begin shooting.

"It was a really hair-raising year for me!" Florence remembers—meaning it literally, as it turns out. "I was supposed to be through *Song of Norway* in time to get back for *The Brady Bunch,* and I wasn't. The shoot ran late, and I was still in Norway, and they had to start *The Brady Bunch* without me. So I had, like, six episodes to catch up on when I got to L.A.! They shot everything they could that I wasn't in, and saved those scenes for when I got back. It was crazy! Amazing!" she says, laughing. "I met myself coming and going! Plus, for *Song of Norway*, I wore my own hair in front, but [hair]pieces elsewhere, and so they had cut my hair very, very short as well as make it very blond. And that's how I wound up with the bubble-do, as I called it, the first year on *The Brady Bunch*, because that was a wig! Oh gosh, the headaches it gave me—I hate wigs and hairpieces and things like that." So another *Brady* mystery is solved—Carol's famous first-year hair.

Florence went on to spend five productive and highly visible years on *The Brady Bunch*. And who better, here and now, to answer a burning question for all *Brady* fans: Just what the hell *did* Carol do all day?

Florence laughs, but her answer is serious. "Well, I stayed busy—I had six kids, don't forget." You also had Alice. "I had Alice, but I was very much involved in what the kids did, in all their activities. Being a mother myself with four kids, and even though I had help, I was always driving someone somewhere. So was Carol. Kids all have different interests, they've all gotta be in this place or that place, in totally different directions. There's a lot to be said for a woman that just runs her home—I don't think people realize what's involved in running a home smoothly, keeping it clean, doing laundry, organizing. You need the organizational skills of a general."

And so it went for five years in the life of Carol and Florence both. Yet as important as the series was to her—it is, after all, how she's best known, even with her ubiquitous Wesson Oil commercials—*The Brady Bunch* is merely one piece of a sturdy, steady career. She was busy before it and busy after: there was theater, including a 1974 national tour of *Annie Get Your Gun;* game shows, including *Hollywood Squares* and *The Magnificent Marble Machine;* her commercials, of course; and lots of TV guest shots. She's published two books: *One-Minute Bible Stories: New Testament* by herself and Shari Lewis (1986), and *A Little Cooking, A Little Talking and a Whole Lot of Fun* (1988), a recipe-and-anecdote book culled from her TV show—*Country Kitchen* on cable's The Nashville Network (TNN).

Country Kitchen is an odd combination that somehow works for her—a cooking/talk show. She's such an infectiously good-natured type, and such a natural at drawing out the celebrity guests who drop by with their recipes, that in the series' five-year run, Florence has played host to everyone from Willie Nelson to Robin Leach—and, of course, *Brady* compatriots Robert Reed and Barry Williams.

The show came about, indirectly, through her second husband. Florence had gotten divorced after twenty-five years of marriage, and on August 4, 1987, she married Dr. John Kappas, a hypnotherapist, an author (*Success Is Not an Accident: The Mental Bank Concept*), and the founder of the twenty-four-year-old Hypnosis Motivation Institute. They share a seventy-foot

yacht in Marina del Rey, California, once displayed on *Lifestyles of the Rich and Famous*.

Her husband's program, she says, "is just a simple thing that you do before you go to sleep that takes about ten minutes and involves a little writing. And one of the things you do is write down two or three of your goals. And I had been writing for about a week that I wanted a talk show—I've always loved that format. About a week later, I got a call from my manager asking if I'd like to do a talk show and I said yes. He said, 'Don't you want to know anything about it?' I said, 'No, I think it's right.' He said, 'Well it's in Nashville and it involves cooking.' And I said I didn't want to do just a cooking show —that if I could be allowed to make it entertaining and funny and all that, then I was interested." Somewhere, somehow, Wesson Oil got into the act, sponsoring the show and very visibly supplying cooking oil and other products. In any case, "The producer came to see me—I was performing my act in New York—and we talked and we firmed up the deal, and now here we are!"

And here, it seems, she'll stay—on our TV screens forever and ever. "I think it was really that essence of behavior," she muses today about the *The Brady Bunch*'s enduring appeal, "bringing out the best of the family life rather than all the shades that are there in real life. And people sometimes take us to task for that. I think you can laugh about *The Brady Bunch* because it was idealized and all that, but I think that was the strength of it. Parents, kids—we all strive for that ideal of a family that is communicating and working together, that cares about each other. I think that's what came across the most. We cared about each other, supported each other, and protected each other like a family should. *We* might criticize each other, but don't let anyone else. I think that's one of the reasons," she says simply, "that we've lasted so long."

As no less an authority than Bob Hope told us, "Florence? Ah, she's a great gal, a great gal. I took her to Australia with me, y'know [for a TV special]. Yeah, Florence is a dear, sweet lady." Bob, we couldn't agree more.

Florence with guest Sally Struthers on *Country Kitchen*.

MAUREEN McCORMICK

Ah, was there ever a Brady girl so fair as Maureen McCormick? The object of every young male's desire in an era before Samantha Fox, the oldest Brady daughter was unquestionably the most popular Brady daughter among the show's fans. And did you know she once interviewed Richard Nixon for TV?

We'll get to that. But first: Maureen Denise McCormick was born August 5, 1956, in Encino, California, the youngest child and only daughter of Richard and Irene McCormick. Her dad, a public-school teacher in Burbank when *The Brady Bunch* started, had performed with amateur theater groups. A strain of show business runs through her family: her brother Michael, eight years older, has been a nightclub manager, and her seven-years-older brother Kevin was an artist and musician. (She also has a three-years-older brother, Dennis.) When *The Brady Bunch* began, she was attending public junior high in Woodland Hills, California.

Maureen—nicknamed Mo as a child—made her acting debut in 1964, in a little-theater production of *Wind It Up and It Breaks* at the La Jolla Playhouse. She segued into commercials, doing some four dozen by 1970—including one as the voice of "Peanuts" tomboy Peppermint Patty. She also recorded about twenty-five soundtracks for talking toys and dolls, so the next time your kid pulls the string on her Chatty Cathy (or Kitty Karry-All), listen close.

Her first major TV-series exposure came with the NBC sitcom *Camp Runamuck,* in which she made occasional appearances as happy camper

Maureen Sullivan. She had bit parts on other sitcoms, including *Bewitched, I Dream of Jeannie,* and *My Three Sons.* But it was *Brady* that really got her career going.

And go it did. Even in the days before the *People/Us* publicity machine got cranking, Maureen was a teen idol par excellence. She won *16* magazine's Female Star of the Year award (which may have had something to do with her writing an advice column, "Dear Maureen," for sister magazine *16 Spec*). She got to go on *The Dating Game* a couple of times, once choosing a bachelor number-two named Rick Feldman with more than a little dab of Brylcreem in his slickly parted hair. (They got to go on a fabulous, fun-filled trip to Vancouver, British Columbia.) Around the same time, she interviewed President Richard Nixon for the TV special *Art Linkletter's Kid's-Eye View of Washington.* A few years after Brady, she still had enough pull to land an album deal, and recorded a duet LP with Chris Knight.

As a teen, Maureen liked to ski and water-ski and play at guitar; she had a golden Labrador retriever named Sage. Aside from her co-stars, her closest friend at the time was probably Barbara Bernstein, Florence Henderson's daughter.

Unlike many of the other Brady children's, Maureen's career didn't fall apart after *The Brady Bunch.* She developed into a beautiful and voluptuous young adult, and provided cheese cake in such films as *Moonshine County Express* (1977); *Take Down* (1979), a well-regarded drama of high-school wrestlers, also starring Edward Herrmann, Lorenzo Lamas, and Stephen Furst; *Skatetown U.S.A.* (1979); and *Texas Lightning* (1981). She had a more serious role in *The Idolmaker* (1980), actor Ray Sharkey's tour de force about the music business.

But though she continued to work, her career never ignited, and like the other Brady girls, she's extremely ambivalent about *The Brady Bunch;* her agent once barked to a reporter for *Cable Guide,* "Maureen doesn't want to be associated with *The Brady Bunch* anymore." She opted out of the 1990 sequel series, *The Bradys.* Nonetheless, reviewing her options, Maureen did appear in *A Very Brady Christmas.*

Acting, she conceded, "hasn't been the primary focus of my life." And like many stars of old series, she partially blamed the show. "I think it's hard, to a degree, to move beyond the typecasting that happens after a series like *Brady Bunch,*" she said right before the Christmas reunion aired. "I'm just starting to get beyond it now. I've been doing a lot of work in theater, where you really have a chance to take a role and build it. And I'm getting into producing. And I want to start having a family."

The latter, at least, has proven a successful wish—she and actor Michael Cummings had a child not long after she expressed it, making Maureen the first of the Brady girls to do so. The former teen queen now has a little starlet of her own.

EVE PLUMB

"Success as Hooker? Wait and See, Says Eve."

No, Eve Plumb's acting career after *The Brady Bunch* didn't go *that* badly. In fact, the middle Brady daughter has probably had the most consistent (albeit not overwhelming) TV and film career of any of the show's kids. The headline of *The Courier-Journal & Times* of Louisville, Kentucky, merely spotlighted the extent to which she would seek roles as far away as possible from cute tomboy Jan.

This particular project was *Dawn: Portrait of a Teenage Runaway,* a 1976 NBC TV movie. Two years after *The Brady Bunch* was canceled, Eve played a fifteen-year-old small-town girl, Dawn Wetherby, who out of desperation goes to the big, wicked city and finds herself turning tricks. It was a ratings success that inspired a 1977 sequel, *Alexander: The Other Side of Dawn.* Then in *Secrets of Three Hungry Wives,* produced by *Penthouse* magazine's Penthouse Productions, Eve co-starred with Susan Dey and Ann Dusenberry as one of three women who had affairs with a slain billionaire. But just so she wouldn't get typecast *that* way, she also played Beth March in the 1978 TV movie *Little Women.* People apparently liked her so much that even though her character died, Eve came back for the short-lived TV-series version playing Melissa Jane ("Lissa") Driscoll, Beth March's lookalike cousin. (Sounds like a *Brady* episode, doesn't it?)

Still, the post-Jan roles have been few and far between, and after marrying and getting divorced from lighting technician Rick Mansfield, whom she met on the set of the *Little Women* series, Eve seems a little bitter today. She performs in the *Brady* reunions half grudgingly, out of loyalty and friendship but also a lack of other opportunities, and, in the words of one *Brady* producer, "can be a little difficult about the subject."

That's a shame, but not uncommon in a second-generation showbiz family where expectations are inordinately high. Eve was born April 29, 1958, in Burbank, California, the second daughter and third child of Neely and Flora Plumb. Her folks lived in the San Fernando Valley, with weekends and holidays spent at a Malibu beach house. Dad was an independent record producer who had been a manager at RCA Records on the West Coast for nine years; Mom was a journeyman actress and a ballet dancer; Eve's sister, Flora June Plumb, a graduate of the UCLA theater department, also followed her mother into the arts. Brother Ben, a Harvard grad, had gone to Brazil to work in a food program for the poor, before becoming a businessperson in Central America.

Eve's acting career began at age six, when she went on her first interview for a TV commercial. She was successful in that field and had done about forty by the time of *The Brady Bunch.* She also sang as a child and recorded albums with the Jimmy Joyce children's chorus. Years later, aside from her stint as part of the Brady Kids singing group, she recorded at least one single for RCA Records ("How Will It Be").

She made the usual rounds of bit parts in such series as *The Big Valley, It Takes a Thief,* and *Lassie* and played a girl named Pony Alice on the *Lancer* western series. (She later named her pet dog after her character.) By 1969, she had already reportedly appeared in four TV pilots; *The Brady Bunch* was her fifth.

Eve was a sixth-grader in a Van Nuys, California, public school when the series began. When she reached eighth grade, her parents transferred her to private school in the San Fernando Valley. They tried to keep her as normal as possible under the circumstances—adhering, for instance, to her fifty-cents weekly allowance.

Possibly the most artistic of the Brady kids, she has sculpted in copper wire and painted and, in addition to studying ballet, took judo and karate lessons for two and a half years. She has also ridden horses in show competition. A voracious reader as a child, she belonged even then to several book clubs.

"It seemed normal to me," she mused about growing up in a TV series. "But then, I never knew anything else."

She got a quick lesson in normal life after *Brady* folded. At fifteen, she could find no roles since producers preferred casting eighteen-year-olds to play teenagers, since as adults they're not subject to stringent child-labor laws. "I was disappointed," Eve recalled. "But I didn't get too down about it.

I kept busy being a cheerleader and a homecoming queen." Why isn't that surprising?

With Brady nostalgia on the rise, Eve is finding herself a little more in demand than usual—though mostly to appear as herself or in a spin on her image. The best and most hilarious of these bits was her part in the 1988 spoof of '70s "black exploitation" films, *I'm Gonna Git You Sucka,* in which she played the very blond wife of a very black revolutionary (played by *The Mod Squad's* Clarence Williams III). After she greets director-star Keenan Ivory Wayans with a perfectly executed series of black handshakes, she and Clarence send their two adorable blond children to the other room to watch TV—as *The Brady Bunch* theme comes out of the set! Terrific!

Several years ago, Eve formed her own production company to develop projects for herself. She chose *The Sweetheart: The Story of Mary Pickford,* about the legendary silent-movie ingenue. But the movie never got made, and now, amazingly, Eve at thirty-two is too old to play the part. Our little girl has grown up.

Of course, she'll remain forever young as long as there's a Brady bunch. As she's avowed, "I am anxious to go in with an idea of my own and follow it through to the end." She's reportedly trying her hand at stand-up comedy. And with *The Partridge Family's* Susan Dey a hit on *L.A. Law,* who knows just where Eve Plumb will end up?

"I think anytime an actor is out of work, they think, what else can I do?" Eve mused. "But I stay with acting because it's so much fun when you do work. And it's the best potential salary that I can think of."

SUSAN OLSEN

She reportedly once told Milton Berle that she retired from show business at age three and made a comeback at five. She wasn't much exaggerating.

Susan Olsen, the youngest of the Brady clan, was already a grizzled veteran when *Brady* began—and she was only seven at the time! That was the way it was in her family. Her sister Diane, three years older, had retired from show business at eight; her much older brother Christopher had made his debut at age fourteen months in the movie *The Iron Curtain,* a.k.a. *Behind the Iron Curtain* (1948); and her even older brother Larry Jr. began his career at age five and reportedly appeared in fifty films before growing up to become an aircraft engineer.

Into this greasepaint gang, Susan was born on August 14, 1961, in Santa Monica, California; the family later moved to Tarzana. Her dad, Lawrence, worked for Douglas Aircraft; her mom De Loice, nicknamed Dee, stayed at home and raised/managed the kids. The littlest Brady got her start as an infant in commercials, and after a few years took a breather. Then at five or six, she was plucked from kindergarten to sing "I'm a Believer" on Pat Boone's daytime talk/variety show. She made her TV-series debut not long after that, in the 1968–69 season of *Ironside.*

Growing up, she had a Siberian husky named Tanuck; two Persian cats, Princess and Tippy; two desert tortoises, Hildegard and Jumbo; and a puppy

named Angela that somehow or other passed through the Paramount *Brady* set.

Susan wanted to be either an actress or an archaeologist when she grew up. Neither worked out; though she reprised her role of Cindy on *The Brady Bunch Hour* and the TV-movie *The Brady Girls Get Married,* she was not in the casts of either *The Brady Brides* TV series or the recent *A Very Brady Christmas* TV-movie reunion. "The wholesome, Goody Two Shoes image worked against me," she complained. "That is, when I could get any auditions at all."

No, what she became was a sneakers mogul. A graphic artist based in Playa del Ray, California, she began six years ago to paint high-top sneakers for her rock-and-roll friends. (She was encouraged by her artist husband Steve Ventimiglia, whom she married in August 1988.) In 1985, she went to Converse, the Massachusetts-based footwear giant, to see about marketing her night-glow exotic-animal prints and other sneaker designs. Her Glow All-Stars proved a fair hit when they finally arrived in stores in 1988, and since then, Olsen won a license to silkscreen her drawings of Disney characters on T-shirts.

A smart move. "This is really just one of those fads that'll be over when it's over," she's said of her sneakers. But until then, "I'll just sit at home and open the royalty checks." From her first career, Susan Olsen has, it seems, learned a lot about survival.

BARRY WILLIAMS

"I did smoke joints," Barry Williams is quick to admit. He's talking about his teen years, when Greg Brady only got as far as cigarettes. Barry, of course, lived in the real world. "I was a [cigarette] smoker, too—God, all through that period," he goes on. "I just quit smoking a few years ago. I was," he says with a verbal smile, "a lot more experimental than Greg was."

Just another affluent California beach kid, when you come right down to it. Born Barry William Blenkhorn on September 30, 1954, in Santa Monica, California, and raised in the tonier L.A. suburb of Pacific Palisades, Barry grew up privileged. His father Frank owned three credit bureaus—data warehouses like TRW, on a smaller scale. His mom Doris stayed at home and watched the kids—Craig, the oldest; Scott, a year younger; and Barry, born two years after Scott. Barry half jokes that he modeled the oldest Brady kid after "some of my brothers' not-so-desirable qualities—like how to take advantage of little brothers, how to manipulate. . . ." But Barry adapted: at an early age he became a good enough actor to go to convenience stores and buy girlie magazines for his brothers' backyard clubhouse, making up stories about an invalid father who counted them among his few precious luxuries.

Clearly, he was never your typical little brother. He began taking acting classes at eleven and shortly thereafter played the symbolic Johnny in a documentary titled *Why Johnny CAN Read,* about new educational techniques. He landed a toy commercial at eleven and a half, then made his TV-series debut at age twelve, in an episode of *Run for Your Life.* More episodic TV followed, bit parts in *That Girl; The Mod Squad; The Andy Griffith Show; Gomer Pyle, USMC,* and other shows. He even made his movie debut, in the cult classic *Wild in the Streets* (1968), playing the lead character, Max Frost, as a child.

His first regular series role was on the ABC soap opera *General Hospital* in early 1969, playing a young rheumatic heart patient named Jack Larson (which, yes, is the name of the actor who played Jimmy Olsen in *The Adventures of Superman*). Years later, a grown-up Barry would return to *General Hospital* as a sleazy dance teacher named Hannibal.

Back in his pubescent years, Barry also shot an unsold NBC sitcom pilot, *The Shameful Secrets of Hastings Corners,* a soap-opera spoof. He was also up for the role of Tom Sawyer in a Disney TV production—and the day he lost the part was, he recalls, almost the day he lost everything.

"I had a callback [e.g., a second audition] from Disney, which I took. I had a paper route as well, which I'd given to a guy that would deliver the newspapers for me if I had an appointment. But he missed two houses and one of them called and wanted their paper." After Barry returned from the audition, he remembers, "My dispatcher called me and said to get that paper down there. It was dusk, I jumped on my bicycle, and was off to deliver the paper, and while I was crossing the street on my bike, a gal in a Volkswagen ran a red light and hit me broadside. It sent me into the asphalt, stripped a lot of my face and hands and elbows, and I had to go to the hospital, etc. But I didn't have a concussion and I healed up okay."

Sensing that a nice, safe soundstage was better than a busy California street, Barry and his folks put his career in gear. And in mid-'69, he landed the highly visible role of the Bradys' oldest son. Pretty soon, he became a

teen idol, getting a reported five hundred to eight hundred fan letters a week. (Elsewhere it said 6,500 a month—does anybody *really* count these things?) He did photo spreads in teen magazines. He attended openings and awards shows. With the Brady Kids, he went on concert tours and on *American Bandstand*. He bought a horse named Ya-Teh-Ha (reportedly an Indian word for "hello"), a pet monkey named Eddie, and a German shepherd, Tassie. He took up singing and considered pursuing a music career. And then, just as quickly as it happened, it was over.

"After *The Brady Bunch* ended," he recalls, "I had about another year and a half where I was swinging pretty much off the popularity of that show. Then I found myself in a bit of trouble. Some of that was attributable to typecasting, but part of the problem," he admits, "was that I blamed the show. I was used to having things always come my way, and suddenly I had to put myself on the line. Y'know, it had always been one way, so I was surprised when it was any other way."

He had at least planned ahead and taken vocal lessons, and quickly landed a spot on the first touring production of the Broadway hit *Pippin*. But then things began to slow down. He tried enrolling at Pepperdine University, but dropped out because, he admitted, like many child actors, "I didn't have any social skills." He started drinking, and gambling away unemployment checks.

"Around my midtwenties there, things got pretty tough, and I had to do some re-evaluating. That period is what I usually liken to my teenage rebellion—just a little delayed," he says, chuckling ruefully. "Then about seven, eight years ago, I kinda got myself in gear and in a sense started all over again. I made a decision I wouldn't let *The Brady Bunch* be either a negative *or* a positive force in my life, and to just go ahead with my career."

The critical factor was the downfall of his pop-music career—or rather, his attempt at one. As he recalls today, "I knew I wanted to pursue music, but I found it *very* difficult to get a record deal. I did, finally, when the owner of [the independent label] Private Stock Records told me that if I could get [TV-theme king] Mike Post to produce, that he would give me a deal. So I hounded the guy. And finally Mike said to me, 'Look, if you can come to me with material that I think is credible, I'll consider it.'

"So I got set up with a pianist and I went to music publishers and told them I had a deal. And I would go through volumes and volumes of songs, take home tapes, go over 'em with the pianist, and see which ones were suitable. I got it down to about eight and sang them for Mike. And Mike said, 'Ah, Barry, this one's horseshit, this is good, this works, this doesn't. Take these four and woodshed those.' So I spent *another* five weeks with that. We got it down to three songs—Larry Carlton played on all three—and Mike liked these tunes and got excited and said, 'Okay, let's go!' And then Private Stock Records went out of business, so I didn't have the kind of distribution push I needed.

"Now I was faced with a choice: Take these songs that are already done and try to sell them, which is very difficult to do since everybody wants to develop their own material; start over again from scratch, and I had already invested eighteen months; or take up these offers I was getting to do musical comedy. So I made a choice. I wanted to work. And I fell in love with musical theater and since then have not pursued recording."

That was the start of a long, slow climb to respectability. Barry did regional and dinner-theater productions of such evergreens as *Grease, Oklahoma!, I Do! I Do!, West Side Story, They're Playing Our Song,* and *Promises, Promises.* Then in 1988, he got his chance at Broadway. Scott Bakula, the male lead of the acclaimed two-person musical *Romance/Romance,* was leaving the show (ironically, to pursue television). Barry, at his own expense, flew to New York to audition—and won the role. From October 1988 to January 14, 1989, when it closed, Barry Williams was the male lead in a Broadway hit.

Since then, however, it's been back to the old regional and off-off-Broadway grind—except that he's now based in theater-intensive New York City, where he lives on the Upper West Side with his two cats and fiancée Diane Martin, a former Miss Arizona.

"You gotta be realistic," he says with a shrug. "It's important to understand what people's perception is. For me to think that people aren't considering me somewhat of a speculative risk as an artist would be unrealistic.

"People ask me all the time am I bothered with *Brady Bunch* trivia. Well . . . no. That is a part of the perception. I expect that'll be part of the perception forever. It doesn't inhibit my moving ahead. I always thought my ability could take me beyond any stereotyping they were trying to lace me with.

"I'm fortunate that I have another venue in theater," he realizes. "Television certainly hasn't supported me since the *Brady* days. Maybe for a year here or there, but not on a long-term basis." And as for his new visibility, he says optimistically, "I got my head down, I'm runnin', and I'm not lookin' back!"

CHRISTOPHER KNIGHT

The middle *Brady* boy was almost as big a heartthrob as Barry Williams. But unlike Barry, he came from a theatrical background.

His father Edward was an actor who began his career, as many do, performing Shakespeare in New York; he later became co-owner of The Onion

Co., a little-theater group that worked out of Los Angeles' Horseshoe Theater. His mother Wilma, nicknamed Willie, was a housewife and stage mother who helped to preside over the TV-commercial careers of his three-years-younger sister, Lisa, and his seven-years-younger brother, David. Chris also has a brother Mark, one year older.

Born Christopher Anton Knight on November 7, 1957, in the New York City area, and raised first on Long Island and then around Los Angeles, Chris had professional head shots taken by age seven. By the time he got the part of Peter on *The Brady Bunch*, he had already shot about two dozen commercials and had had bit roles on *Bonanza*, *Gunsmoke*, and *Mannix*. Around 1970, he made his film debut playing Don Murray as a child in the apparently unreleased movie *The Narrow Chute*, about a rodeo rider.

When *The Brady Bunch* began, Chris was living with his family in Canoga Park, California, and going to public junior high; they moved to nearby Woodland Hills in 1971, and Chris went on to a professional children's high school. Among the Brady kids, he was probably the most enamored of pets: his family had a boxer named Matt; two cats, Calipson and Dickens; a tortoise, Touche; a rat, a rabbit, tropical fish; and Chris's pride and joy, several dozen pigeons for which he and his older brother were awarded ribbons at a national bird show. His hobbies were the same as most kids', except that he took up golf when he was about fifteen.

Chris was also probably more interested in a singing career than most of the others except Barry Williams; around 1973, he and Maureen McCormick even released a non-Bradys record album.

Still, neither singing nor acting really happened for him after *The Brady Bunch*. He did land a cast role in the short-lived NBC sitcom *Joe's World* and appeared in a couple of TV movies. But later, he made a lateral move to become a casting director for a short while. Today, newly married, he's a salesperson in the computer business. "I figure, as an actor you're a salesman—you're always selling yourself," he said. "Now, I feel like an agent. I'm selling someone else's commodity." But he still takes time off, of course, for an occasional foray back into Bradyville.

"I haven't had the successes I wanted," he said, "nor have I felt I had the successes that I felt my talents could support. A lot of the problem I have in the industry is that my identity is so grounded in *The Brady Bunch*," he complained. "So I might go into an audition trying to prove them wrong. But when I'm trying to prove that I'm no longer Peter Brady, what I'm trying to prove to them is that I'm no longer Chris Knight. Because those two are so close.

"I mean," he went on, "when you're talking about *The Brady Bunch* characters—and Peter versus Chris—it's virtually the same person. Peter was always an outgrowth of me, anyway. As a child, I wasn't trying to do a character study or anything. I wasn't trying to bring anything different than who I was to the character. So of course, he was me."

MIKE LOOKINLAND

It all came down to a photo on his father's desk. A colleague of Paul Lookinland's was host of a Spanish-English TV show on the Los Angeles PBS station KCET. Taking note of Mike's freckles and reddish hair, she suggested to Paul that his youngster should seek work in commercials. He thanked her for the idea, and then promptly did nothing about it.

Several months later, Paul Lookinland finally took his middle child and oldest son to a commercials agent. And whaddya know? Within a week, the seven-year-old Mike was cast in a Johnson's Band-Aid spot. As his mother Karen once recalled, "There were several kids playing football in the commercial and Michael was just a blur in the background." But it was the start of a very successful child-acting career.

It seemed meant to be. Michael, who was born December 19, 1960, in Mount Pleasant, Utah, got transplanted to the movie capital when his teacher father got work there in the public-school system—as registrar at El Camino Real High School in the San Fernando Valley—when Mike began on *The Brady Bunch,* then as vice-principal of Bret Harte Junior High School in San Pedro, where the family lived, and then as vice-principal of Gompers Junior High School in the same town. Mike's mom was an elementary-school teacher before her three kids all eventually went into show business: Terese, two years older than Mike, did magazine-ad modeling and a commercial or two, and Todd, four years younger, had a fairly consistent child-acting career for several years.

After the Band-Aid commercial, Mike followed up with a Cheerios spot. That led almost immediately into *The Brady Bunch*. And young as he was, he went out for and landed other roles even while he was busy as Bobby Brady: a *Wonderful World of Disney* drama, "Bayou Boy"; the TV movie *Dead Men Tell No Tales;* and the voice of the character Oblio in the acclaimed animated special *The Point*. (Interestingly, Dustin Hoffman provided the narration in its initial network showing; apparently for contractual reasons, his voice was replaced by Alan Thicke's for later showings, and by Ringo Starr for the video version. But Mike's always there.)

As a kid, Mike did all the usual things and also developed such an interest in rocketry that he built and launched model rockets in the desert. He was in the Cub Scouts and later made a trip down the Colorado River with the Boy Scouts. His childhood pets included a dog, a cat, a turtle named Myrtle, a rabbit named Bun Bun, and a rat named—how minimalist!—Rat.

The family also had an amateur folksinging group; Mom played autoharp. Mike sang with them, and continued his interest in singing past the teen-idol stage. He even recorded a Capitol Records single, "Love Doesn't Care Who's in It"; the record contract reportedly followed a favorable newspaper review of a Brady Kids concert at Knotts' Berry Farm. Despite this, Mike's childhood ambitions were to become either an orthodontist, an architect, or a football photographer.

None of that came true after his child-acting career was over, though he did come close to the latter: Mike is now an assistant cameraperson/production assistant/assistant director in Salt Lake City, where he lives with his wife, Kerry, whom he married in May 1988. Mike's also helped to produce sports shorts for home video and ESPN.

"I did continue acting when the show first ended," Mike once recalled. "I did commercials, guest spots on other series. And the following summer [1974] I got *Towering Inferno* and worked for three months. But in high school, I sort of faded away from it a little bit. I still went on auditions and stuff, but I just wasn't getting the jobs." Not to worry, Mike—the other side of the camera is a lot more secure.

ANN B. DAVIS

The first two parts of Ann B. Davis's name—Ann Bradford—mean "Graceful Broad Ford by a River." We don't know about the river part, but as Ann herself would be the first to tell you, she's won her Emmys and made her career as the quintessential Graceful Broad.

She was born May 5, 1926, in Schenectady, New York, where her father, Cassius Miles Davis, was an electrical engineer for General Electric. When Ann and her twin sister Harriet were three years old, they moved with their parents to Erie, Pennsylvania, where Dad became head of the town's physical plant, the Erie Works. Their mother, Marguerite Stott Davis, was an actress in amateur theater groups; Ann's older brother Evans was a dancer actor with Broadway credits.

Ann herself sort of started in show business at age six, when she and Harriet put on a puppet show that earned them two dollars. "Boy, I was impossible to live with for weeks after that!" Ann recalls impishly. Yet while her sister went on to study acting at the University of Michigan, Ann took up pre-med there, wanting to become a doctor. But one Christmas vacation when the two sisters went to Chicago to see Evans in *Oklahoma!* and to glimpse backstage life, a reversal occurred—Harriet decided not to pursue acting anymore, and Ann decided she'd found her lifeblood. She switched to drama and speech—where one of her classmates was John Rich, who, coincidentally, would go on to direct the first several episodes of *The Brady Bunch.* "We worked together on some things at the University of Michigan way back when," Ann recalls. "We both were graduated from there the same year, 1948."

After college, Ann apprenticed at the Erie Playhouse (where her mother had performed) and toured in a sixteen-week tent-theater tour to earn twenty dollars a week. When she'd managed to save a hundred dollars, she took off for California. There she worked the rounds of the Barn Theatre in Porterville, the Wharf Theatre in Monterey, the San Francisco Theatre Guild and other places, and helped found a summer theater.

By 1954, she was living at the Studio Club, a women's dorm in Los Angeles. She'd appeared a couple of times on the historic live variety series *The Colgate Comedy Hour,* then hosted by Eddie Cantor, but had had little luck otherwise. She was working as a temp in a department store, and most of her professional appearances had been free showcase gigs at a bistro called the Cabaret Concert. "It was at the unfashionable end of Sunset Boulevard, under a bridge," Ann remembers. "It was later called El Cid. A loooong way from the Strip!" she says with a laugh. "It was kind of a tryout spot in the coffeehouse era. They served beer and wine and what they called mingle-muffins, which were English muffins with pizza topping. And a friend of mine, Jim Layton, who I'd worked with in the Barn Theatre in Porterville, had written some material, so he and I put together this act and performed down there on and off for a couple of years."

A friend of hers from the Studio Club was having a birthday and talked her boyfriend into taking her out to see Ann perform. The boyfriend was a casting director, and though he was unconnected to this new sitcom starting up, *The Bob Cummings Show,* he thought Ann would be perfect for the role of a photographer's plain-but-funny "gal Friday." He suggested she have her agent contact the producers to set up an interview. "So I did and he did and they did!" she says, laughing.

At the audition were Cummings, financial backer George Burns (yes, *that* George Burns), producer Paul Henning, and pilot-episode director Fred DeCordova (now the producer of *The Tonight Show*). "I read a scene with Bob Cummings," Ann recalls. "He was very sweet. He gave me everything he possibly could to make the audition go well. When I was leaving, George Burns said, 'I think we'll be calling you,' and everybody else went, 'Well, of course, you know, we have other people to see and interview' and like that. And George Burns goes, 'Yeah, but I think we'll be calling you!'" The audition had taken place at around 11:00 A.M.; at about two in the afternoon, she got the phone call telling her that the role of Charmaine "Shultzy" Schultz was hers. "You could have heard me scream all the way to the Hollywood Bowl!"

As Schultzy, the nominally sane antidote to the parade of models entertained by rakish photographer Bob Collins, Ann established herself as one of TV's great funny ladies. The show, a midseason replacement, was a popular success for five years. Ann was the only one on it to receive Emmy nominations, earning four in a row: in 1956, '57, and '58 (for the 1955–56, 1956–57, and 1957–58 seasons, respectively), and in 1958–59 (the year the designation changed to reflect TV seasons' overlapping years). She won the award two times.

In 1958, Ann began a long side career headlining in regional theater during hiatuses and between series. She's since performed summer stock in all fifty states, appearing in *Auntie Mame, Blithe Spirit, Funny Girl,* and many, many other productions. In 1960, Broadway's George Abbott even selected her to succeed Carol Burnett in *Once Upon a Mattress.* ("I was not good," she concedes. "I spent the whole time doing a bad imitation of Carol Burnett.") A dedicated supporter of the USO, the performers' organization that tours and provides entertainment for the American armed forces, she spent many years as a member of the USO National Council, its Hollywood Overseas Committee, and its West Coast Auditioning Committee, herself going out on tours to Vietnam, Korea, and Thailand.

She also made her only four movies around this time (see filmography) and shot an unsold series pilot, *Too Many Sergeants.* She starred as WAC Sergeant Ann Gruber in this military female comedy that "offscreen we called 'Knockers Up, Sergeant'! It would have been a very funny show if it had sold." Afterward, she became a regular on the 1963 summer musical-variety series *The Keefe Brasselle Show.*

"That was a short summer," Ann recalls. "A very exciting time—I hated it!" she says with perfect timing. "No, that's not quite true," she amends. "I had a good time, but it was a weird summer. I played opposite Fred Gwynne. We were a kind of a couple on that show. The critics in New York *hated* that show—I mean they tore the show to shreds and Keefe Brasselle into tinier shreds than anybody. But they thought that Fred and I were awfully good together and wondered if they didn't have anything in mind for us. I'm sorry they didn't, 'cause Fred's a sweet man. I remember he was playing the guitar when I met him."

Two years later, Ann co-starred in *The John Forsythe Show,* playing the physical-education teacher, Miss Wilson. Afterward, of course, came *The Brady Bunch* and its spinoffs.

As Alice the housekeeper, Ann was, like Schultzy, a somewhat off-kilter sea of calm in the midst of four hundred cast members. And like many performers, she constructed a "back-story" biography for her character, in order to help her better play and understand her role. "What I decided—and of course, it never came out in the series—was that Alice had a twin sister and that they were both orphaned early in their lives, and the twin needed to go to college. And so Alice went to work at whatever jobs I could find," she continues, adeptly switching into the first person, "so that she could afford to go. And the sister went on and did that, which pleased me very much and I was happy to do it, and I found myself moving very happily into the housekeeper-taking-care-of-children role. That's why I was happy with my work, why I was single and I didn't have a better job. That's interior stuff. I don't think I've ever talked about that before."

As the role of Alice went on, she acquired the neighborhood butcher, Sam Franklin, as a beau. He was played by Allan Melvin, a highly familiar character actor who in some ways is a male version of Ann. Amazingly, given how busy they both were in the same circles, they hadn't worked together before. "He and I got along very well," Ann recalls. "We'd both been in the business for a hundred years. We enjoyed working together. He was good at his work. We were a funny couple."

In January 1976, Ann put show business largely aside and moved to Denver to join an Episcopal community run by Bishop William C. Frey, whom she'd met two years earlier while doing summer stock in that city. "I never heard a large voice from above saying, 'Get out of show business, Ann.' I just found that my priorities had changed and I knew that I needed some space. I called my agents and said, 'Look, guys, I'm not exactly sure what I'm doing, but I think I need at least a year to figure it out, so don't call me for a year for anything.' They were wonderful," she says, grinning. "They all four said, 'Nobody else is going to understand this, Ann, but *I* do and I'm very happy for you.' They all four said that!"

The following year she was asked to pitch in on *The Brady Bunch Hour.* "That was after I moved here," she says. "I went back and did a few bits on that, a couple songs and stuff, had a lot of fun. They had already started it, given out the [cast and crew commemorative] T-shirts and all that, and somebody insisted that my agent call me, just to come in and do a cameo

'cause they didn't feel it was complete without me." Then and now, whenever she does a TV appearance in California, "I take somebody from the household with me, and it gives them a chance to see how I used to make a living. It also gives people a chance to sit with them and ask, 'What's Ann doing in *Denver?*'" Starting early 1990, they can begin asking what she's doing in Pittsburgh, near where the community recently moved.

Today, Ann lectures once a week and does occasional TV roles, including one in Australia for a Christian Broadcasting Network (CBN) series called *Butterfly Island*. "That was a children's adventure show. I played a guest at this resort. The producers asked me a few months later if I would like to be a regular in the series. And it was in the works for the longest time. Finally

I was supposed to go, and three or four weeks beforehand, the company in Australia went under!" Down under, as it were.

A longtime sports-car nut, Ann no longer has the orange Porsche 914 that became her trademark during the *Brady* years. Lloyd Schwartz remembers it well. "I also bought a Porsche 914, and she taught me to drive it," he still marvels. "Ann Davis taught me how to drive a stick!" Ann has since switched to a Mazda RX-7—still pretty snazzy for a religious lady. "Maybe it's a case of arrested development!" she says happily. "I love small cars, I always have, and I like to be able to go up and down hills and in and out of traffic at a good clip. I just love sports cars. They're fun to drive. Besides, it blows people's minds. I went into a car wash one time, and a young man and I were both waiting for our cars, and he got into his old Dodge and I got into my RX-7, and the girl at the counter did a double take!"

Now, she's enjoying the *Brady* resurgence as much as anybody—though it *does* seem a little odd to her sometimes. "Whenever I check into a hotel, one of the things that I do is make sure the TV works. So every once in a while I'll come across an episode, just flipping around the dial, and I'll sit down and watch it 'cause I don't remember how it came out. And that makes it kind of fun. Some I recognize right away, some I literally don't remember having shot. It's amazing to me that it's lasted twenty years."

But it is, she is sure, a good legacy. "I helped raise you, my dear!" she tells us. "And look how well you turned out!"

SHERWOOD SCHWARTZ

He is the creator of *Gilligan's Island* and *The Brady Bunch* and virtually all of their numerous spinoffs, and yes, Sherwood Schwartz is his real name. And after all these years he's as busy as ever with those darn family problems and getting those castaways off and back onto the island.

"I'm gonna disappoint you," he says when asked his reaction to the *Brady* resurgence, "because I just accept it. Apparently the public loves the characters, thanks to a group of terrific, honest performers. I think *The Brady Bunch* is simply one of the most honest family shows—because in a lot of shows today, everyone who walks into a room tries to say something funnier than the last person who spoke. I think it's a dreadful thing that's happened to TV comedy in the last ten, twelve years," he says in curmudgeonly fashion, "and it's due to this business of sitting around the table with five, six writers, all of them pitching lines as the script goes along, and everyone wants to show how clever or funny they are. And the result is that characterization goes out the window, scenes are longer or shorter than they should be, and the determination is not character or plot, but *lines,* this insane desire on the part of the networks for quick, funny lines. And I think that has destroyed a lot more shows than it ever helped."

This is, of course, the man who speaks of *Gilligan's Island* as a "social microcosm," but give him his due: Sherwood Schwartz has made a business of comedy for more years than there's been commercial television. He was born November 14, 1916, in Passaic, New Jersey, where his father had a wholesale grocery outlet—and like virtually everyone else at that time got wiped out in the Depression. But if times were tough, so, of necessity, were the people. The family moved to nearby New York City, where Schwartz was graduated from DeWitt Clinton High School in 1934 (receiving a Lifetime Achievement Award from there fifty-one years later). He went on to earn a bachelor's degree from New York University, then emigrated to Los Angeles to pursue a master's in biological sciences at USC.

Already in L.A. was his older brother, Albert A. Schwartz, who had attended Fordham University and then Brooklyn Law School—only to chuck it all and become a comedy writer and producer. "Al is who got me into this whole business in the first place," Schwartz recalls. "He was a writer, for radio originally. I had finished my master's work, and Al was working on Bob Hope's radio show. I had no money—nobody did, it was still the Depression, 1939—and it didn't seem to me to be very difficult to write some jokes. So I said to my brother Al, 'If I write some jokes, will you give them to Bob?' " Al lent a brotherly hand, Sherwood's jokes got Bob Hope some laughs, and the next thing Sherwood knew, "Bob Hope's agent called me and said 'Bob wants you to come on the show next year as a writer.' So my whole career took a turn." He did get the master's, though. "I was on my way to becoming a doctor. Instead I went right to work for Bob Hope."

He spent four years there, polishing his craft with some of the top writers in the field. "A strange thing happened [in 1988]," Schwartz says sadly. "Of the original group of Bob Hope writers, six of them died in one year—my brother Al, Mel Frank, Lester White, Jack Douglas. . . . Only three of us are left from the old gang."

During World War II, Schwartz entered the U.S. Army and as a corporal began writing for the Armed Forces Radio Service. There he met George "Rosey" Rosenberg—one of his sergeants—who would become his agent from 1946 to 1962 and (after Sherwood's stint writing for radio's *The Adventures of Ozzie and Harriet*) would represent Schwartz in the fledgling medium of television.

Schwartz's first TV-writing job was on the staff of the *I Love Lucy* clone, *I Married Joan* (NBC, 1952–55)—which co-starred future *Gilligan* icon Jim Backus (whom Schwartz knew from radio) and also featured future *Brady* guest Hal Smith. "There was no head writer on *Joan*," Schwartz recalls, "and Joan [Davis, the star] insisted on one writer on the set every week. We hated to do it, but she insisted she would not perform unless there were a writer there to give her a line in case she needed it. We used it call it our turn in the barrel!" he says, laughing, conjuring images of Niagara Falls.

Schwartz segued to *The Red Skelton Show,* spending seven years there and becoming head writer. He shared a 1960–61 Comedy Writing Emmy Award with brother Al and the other Skelton writers, and was similarly nominated the following year. He also co-wrote *The Red Skelton Chevy Special* (CBS, October 9, 1959).

In 1963, Schwartz made the natural progression from writer to producer with his creation of *Gilligan's Island*. He tells the story behind that infamous sitcom's creation in his 1988 book, *Inside Gilligan's Island: From Creation to Syndication*. And *Gilligan,* of course, begat the Bradys.

Among Schwartz's other executive-producer credits are *It's About Time* (CBS, 1966–67), a broadly played time travel sitcom starring Imogene Coca and Joe E. Ross; *Dusty's Trail* (syndicated, 1973), an equally broad western sitcom starring Bob Denver and Forrest Tucker, with music co-written by the Bradys' Frank De Vol; the Saturday-morning cartoon *Big John, Little John* (NBC, 1973–74) starring Herb Edelman and the Bradys' cousin Oliver, Robbie Rist (and giving an early writing credit, Lloyd Schwartz says, to future *Airplane!* and *Police Squad!* co-creators David and Jerry Zucker); the first half season of the Barbara Eden sitcom *Harper Valley PTA*, later just *Harper Valley* (NBC, 1981–82); an unsold Bob Denver sitcom pilot, *Scamps,* about a writer who opens a home day-care center (NBC, June 3, 1982); and another unsold Bob Denver sitcom pilot that ran as the TV movie *The Invisible Woman* (NBC, February 13, 1983).

He also created, with Michael Jacobs, the 1986–87 CBS series *Together We Stand*, about a married couple with a multiracial household of adopted kids. It was the *Brady* episode/pilot, "Kelly's Kids," done over. Or as Schwartz puts it, "It was 'Kelly's Kids' done badly. I was executive producer for the pilot only, because I immediately got into difficulty—'creative differences'— with the producer, with Universal [the studio], and with CBS." Even after Schwartz's success in that type of show, "They not only argued with me, they told me I was wrong and refused to do the kinds of stories I wanted to do, and in my opinion destroyed the show." And it is indeed hard to see what possible improvements they would have had over Schwartz's vision: the series limped through the fall season, got pulled from the schedule, and returned in revamped form with a single parent before being canceled for good.

A family man nearing his golden wedding anniversary, Schwartz has eight grandchildren and four children: Lloyd (who started out as a *Brady* dialogue coach and has since become Sherwood's producing partner), Ross, Hope (who as Hope Sherwood appeared in several episodes of *Brady* and who is now an actress/comedienne), and Don. Schwartz's brother Elroy is also an old-hand comedy writer (*My Favorite Martian, McHale's Navy, My Three Sons,* and other shows) who's written for *Harry O* and other dramas as well. And to continue the dynasty, Elroy's son Douglas is also a writer/producer (*Manimal, Baywatch*).

These days, Schwartz stays busy writing plays (the latest is called *Rockers*) and screenplays—especially for his TV-movie reunions. "I believe that each reunion show should be an event," he says. "Just getting people back together again to see how they look ain't gonna make it. And just to do the same kind of show you used to do won't make it, either."

And Sherwood Schwartz means what he says. His newest project—a theater piece with "some wonderful songs, a good story, some very funny stuff, and we hope to get it on Broadway"—is titled *Gilligan's Island: The Musical.*

• • • • • • • • • •

Filmographies

Included, in this order, are: All *Brady* projects in which the actors were cast members or played recurring roles; TV series and mini-series in which they were cast members or played recurring roles; TV movies and TV-movie pilots; other pilots; specials; TV-series guest appearances; Emmy Awards or nominations; movie appearances; and selected theater appearances. **NOTE:** Most of the Brady kids' early TV appearances were uncredited bit parts.

ROBERT REED

b. October 19, 1932, Highland Park, Illinois; raised Muskogee, Oklahoma
The Brady Bunch; The Brady Bunch Hour; The Brady Girls Get Married/ The Brady Brides; A Very Brady Christmas; The Bradys

TV-SERIES CAST

The Defenders
CBS: September 16, 1961–September 9, 1965
 Kenneth Preston

Mannix
CBS: September 16, 1967–August 27, 1975
 Lt. Adam Tobias (guest role, March 29, 1969; recurring role, 1969–75)

Operation: Runaway, a.k.a. *The Runaways*
NBC: April 27–May 18, 1978; August 10–31, 1978; May 29–September 4, 1979
 Dr. David McKay (1978)

Galactica 1980
ABC: January 27–February 10, March 16–May 4, June 29–August 17, 1980
 Dr. Donald Mortinson

Nurse
CBS: April 2, 1981–May 21, 1982
 Dr. Adam Rose

MINI-SERIES

Rich Man, Poor Man
ABC: February 1, 2, 9, 16, 23, March 1, 8, 15, 1977
 Teddy Boylan

Roots
ABC: Daily, January 23–30, 1977
 Dr. William Reynolds

Scruples
CBS: February 25, 26, 28, 1980
 Josh Hillman

TV MOVIES AND TV-MOVIE PILOTS

The City (pilot for *The Man and the City;* guest cast; ABC: May 17, 1971)
Assignment: Munich (pilot for *Assignment: Vienna;* guest cast; ABC: April 30, 1972)
Haunts of the Very Rich (ABC: September 20, 1972)
Snatched (ABC: January 1973)
The Man Who Could Talk to Kids (ABC: 1973)
Pray for the Wildcats (ABC: January 23, 1974)
The Secret Night Caller (NBC: February 18, 1975)
Lanigan's Rabbi, a.k.a. *Friday the Rabbi Slept Late* (pilot; guest cast; NBC: June 17, 1976)
Law and Order (NBC: 1976)
Nightmare in Badham County (ABC: November 5, 1976)
The Boy in the Plastic Bubble (ABC: November 12, 1976)
Revenge for a Rape (ABC: November 19, 1976)
The Love Boat II (pilot; guest cast; ABC: January 21, 1977)
SST—Death Flight, a.k.a. *Death Flight,* a.k.a. *SST: Disaster in the Sky;* working title: *Flight of the Maiden* (ABC: February 25, 1977)
The Hunted Lady (NBC: November 28, 1977)
Thou Shalt Not Commit Adultery (NBC: November 1, 1978)
Bud and Lou (NBC: November 15, 1978)
Mandrake (NBC: January 24, 1979)
Love's Savage Fury (ABC: May 20, 1979)
The Seekers (HBO: July 1979; two parts)
Nurse (pilot; as Dr. Kenneth Rose in regular cast; CBS: April 9, 1980)
Casino (pilot; guest cast; ABC: August 1, 1980)
Death of a Centerfold: The Dorothy Stratten Story (NBC: November 1, 1981)
International Airport (pilot; guest cast; ABC: May 25, 1985)

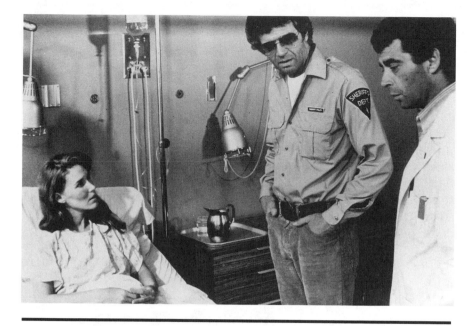

Tough-as-nails Robert Reed as Sheriff Paley in *Revenge for a Rape*.

OTHER PILOTS

Somewhere in Italy . . . Company B (ABC: August 21, 1966; 60 min.)
  Lieutenant John F. Leahy (star of unsold sitcom pilot)
Li'l Abner (NBC: September 5, 1967; 30 min.)
  Senator Cod (in guest cast of unsold sitcom pilot)
Intertect (ABC: March 11, 1973; 60 min.)
  Blake Hollister (in guest cast of unsold drama pilot)

SPECIALS

The Way They Were (Celebrity graduates of Northwestern U.; syndicated,
  February 1981; see Reed's biography (p. 55) for details on his "graduation."
The ABC Afterschool Special "Between Two Loves" (ABC: October
  27, 1982)

SERIES APPEARANCES INCLUDE

The Danny Thomas Show (formerly *Make Room for Daddy*) "Terry
  Comes Home" (October 5, 1959)

Father Knows Best "The Imposter" (October 26, 1959)

Men into Space (January 27, 1960)

Bronco "Volunteers from Aberdeen" (February 9, 1960)

The Lawman "The Left Hand of the Law" (March 27, 1960)

Dr. Kildare Three-part episode: "The Life Machine" (October 26, 1965); "Toast the Golden Couple" (November 1, 1965); "Wives and Losers" (November 2, 1965)

Bob Hope Chrysler Theatre "The Admiral" (December 29, 1965)

Family Affair (December 26, 1966)

Hondo (September 29, 1967)

Ironside "Light at the End of the Journey" (November 9, 1967)

Journey to the Unknown "The New People" (October 3, 1968)

Love American Style "Love and the Wild Party" (November 17, 1969); "Love and the Vampire" (January 29, 1971); (also episode of October 29, 1971)

With Jennifer Hilary in *Journey to the Unknown*.

The Mod Squad "The Connection" (September 14, 1972)
Mission Impossible "Hit" (November 11, 1972)
Owen Marshall "They've Got to Blame Somebody" (February 14, 1973)
Chase "Remote Control" (February 27, 1974)
Harry O "Accounts Balanced" (November 21, 1974)
Medical Center Two-part episode: "The Fourth Sex" (September 8 & 15, 1975)
McCloud (November 16, 1975)
Streets of San Francisco (January 15, 1976)
Jigsaw John (February 2, 1976)
The New, Original Wonder Woman (December 25, 1976)
Hawaii Five-O "The Moroville Convent" (October 18, 1979); "Good Help Is Hard to Find" (November 8, 1979)
Fantasy Island "Room and Bard" (January 29, 1983)
Hotel "Secrets" (October 26, 1983); "Transitions" (November 14, 1984)
The Mississippi (February 7, 1984)
The Love Boat "Seems Like Old Times" (October 27, 1984); "Joint Custody" (October 5, 1985)
Matt Houston "Stolen" (December 21, 1984)
Cover Up "A Subtle Seduction" (December 21, 1984)
Finder of Lost Loves "From the Hearts" (February 9, 1985)
Murder, She Wrote "Footnote to Murder" (March 10, 1985)
Half Nelson "The Deadly Vase" (March 29, 1985)
Glitter "Suddenly Innocent" (December 27, 1985)
Duet
Day by Day (February 5, 1989)
Free Spirit (December 10, 1989)

EMMY NOMINATIONS

Actor, Single Performance, Drama or Comedy Series: For *Medical Center* —Nomination, 1975–76
Supporting Actor, Drama Series: For *Rich Man, Poor Man*—Nomination, 1975–76
Actor, Single Performance, Drama or Comedy Series: For *Roots*, Part 5— Nomination, 1976–77

MOVIES

Hurry Sundown (1967); *The Maltese Bippy* (1969); *Star!* (1968)

THEATER INCLUDES

A Midsummer Night's Dream; Romeo and Juliet (as Romeo)
   Off-Broadway productions by "The Shakespearewrights"

Barefoot in the Park
   Broadway: October 23, 1963, to June 25, 1967; took over male lead from
   September 1964 to mid-1965.

Avanti!
   Broadway: January 31 to February 17, 1968

Deathtrap
   Broadway: September 26, 1978, to June 13, 1982; took over lead for a
   time beginning September 5, 1980

FLORENCE HENDERSON

b. February 14, 1934, Dale, Indiana; raised Rockport, Indiana, and Owens-
boro, Kentucky
*The Brady Bunch; The Brady Bunch Hour; The Brady Girls Get Married/
The Brady Brides* (recurring); *A Very Brady Christmas; The Bradys*

TV-SERIES CAST

Sing Along
CBS: June 4–July 9, 1958
   regular

The Jack Paar Show ("The Tonight Show")
NBC: July 29, 1957–March 30, 1962 (weeknights)
   semiregular

Oldsmobile Music Theatre, a. k. a. *Hayes and Henderson*
NBC: March 26–May 7, 1959
   co-host

The Today Show
(1959–60)
   Women's editor (the "Today Girl")

The Tonight Show
   occasional guest host in 1960s

The Bell Telephone Hour
NBC: October 9, 1959–April 26, 1968
  summer hostess (1964)

Country Kitchen
The Nashville Network: October 1985–present
  host

Nashville Now
The Nashville Network
  guest performer and occasional host

TV MOVIES AND TV-MOVIE PILOTS

The Love Boat (pilot; guest cast; ABC: September 17, 1976)

SERIES APPEARANCES INCLUDE

The Ed Sullivan Show (1952: off-camera voice)
Coke Time with Eddie Fisher (November 5, 1954)
The Dean Martin Show several appearances
The Jackie Gleason Show
The Jonathan Winters Show
The Hollywood Palace
U.S. Steel Hour "Huck Finn" (November 20, 1957); "A Family Alliance"
  (June 4, 1958)
I Spy "The Abbe and the Nymph" (April 13, 1966)
Kraft Music Hall
Operation: Entertainment
The Don Knotts Show (November 10, 1970)
This Is Tom Jones (November 27, 1970)
Medical Center (September 22, 1975; December 12, 1976)
Good Heavens (March 29, 1976)
Hart to Hart "Hartland Express" (November 3, 1981)
Fantasy Island "The Sailor" (January 2, 1982); "My Mommy, the
  Swinger" (December 3, 1983)
Police Squad!
Alice (October 30, 1983)
The Love Boat "The Return of Annabelle" (April 30, 1984); "The Runaway"
  (February 23, 1985)
Finder of Lost Loves "Forgotten Melodies" (December 22, 1984)
Cover Up "Healthy, Wealthy and Dead" (February 2, 1985)
The New Love American Style "Love and the Piano Teacher"
  (December 26, 1985)

Murder, She Wrote
It's Garry Shandling's Show
Day by Day (February 5, 1989)
Free Spirit (December 10, 1989)

SPECIALS

The Rodgers and Hammerstein Anniversary Show (1954)
The General Foods 25th Anniversary Show (CBS: March 28, 1954)
Little Women (CBS: October 16, 1958)
The Gershwin Years (CBS: January 15, 1961)
Highlights of the Ice Capades: Bell System Family Theater
    (NBC, November 4, 1970)
A World of Love (CBS: December 22, 1970)
City vs. Country (ABC: December 21, 1971)
A Salute to Television's 25th Anniversary (ABC: September 10, 1972)
The Paul Lynde Halloween Special (ABC: October 29, 1976)
Bob Hope's All-Star Comedy Special from Australia (NBC: April
    15, 1978)
The ABC Afterschool Special: Just a Regular Kid: An AIDS Story

MOVIES

Song of Norway (1970)

THEATER INCLUDES

Wish You Were Here
    Broadway debut; one line; June 25, 1952, to November 1953; in first month
    only

Oklahoma!
    First national tour; as Laurey; began Hartford, Connecticut, August 29,
    1952, and lasted nine months. Florence also appeared in the New York
    City Center revival for five weeks beginning August 31, 1953, and then a
    tour that closed May 8, 1954 in Philadelphia.

The Great Waltz
    Los Angeles Civic Light Opera; summer 1953

Fanny
    Broadway; November 4, 1954; 19 months

The Sound of Music
    National tour; as Maria; began Detroit, March 7, 1961, and lasted fifteen
    months; Florence received Sarah Siddons Award, 1962

As Nina Grieg in *Song of Norway*.

The Girl Who Came to Supper
Broadway; December 8, 1963; 112 performances

The King and I
Los Angeles Music Center

South Pacific
Lincoln Center revival; as Nellie Forbush; spring 1967

Jerome Kern's Theater
Lincoln Center benefit, November 1966

New Faces of 1966
Inner Circle political writers' revue; sang with Mayor John V. Lindsay; March 1966

Annie Get Your Gun
National tour; as Annie Oakley; 1974

Bells Are Ringing
Los Angeles Civic Light Opera and San Francisco Civic Light Opera, 1978–79

OTHER

General Motors' annual Oldsmobile industrial shows (1958–62); TV commercials for Oldsmobile (1958; with Bill Hayes); Wesson Oil spokesperson

BOOKS

One-Minute Bible Stories: New Testament by Florence Henderson and Shari Lewis (1986)
A Little Cooking, A Little Talking and a Whole Lot of Fun with Florence Henderson and Her Friends (1988)

ANN B. DAVIS

b. May 5, 1926, Schenectady, New York; raised Erie, Pennsylvania
The Brady Bunch; The Brady Bunch Hour; The Brady Girls Get Married/ The Brady Brides; The Bradys

TV-SERIES CAST

The Bob Cummings Show, a.k.a. *Love That Bob* in syndication
NBC: January 2–September 25, 1955;
CBS: October 5, 1955–September 19, 1957;
NBC: September 22, 1957–September 15, 1959
Charmaine "Shultzy" Schultz

The Keefe Brasselle Show (CBS: June 25–September 17, 1963)
regular

The John Forsythe Show (NBC: September 13, 1965–August 29, 1966)
Miss Wilson

SERIES APPEARANCES INCLUDE

Eddie Cantor (two appearances)
The Bob Hope Chrysler Theatre "Wake Up, Darling" (rerun on *NBC Comedy Playhouse*)
Wagon Train
The Dating Game
Love American Style
The Love Boat
Butterfly Island (CBN)
Day by Day (February 5, 1989)

Alice getting lei'd.

PILOTS

Too Many Sergeants (NBC: January 6, 1963)
Unsold series pilot airing as an episode of *McKeever and the Colonel;*
starring Davis as WAC Sergeant Ann Gruber

EMMY AWARDS AND NOMINATIONS

Supporting Actress: For *The Bob Cummings Show,* "Schultzy's Dream
World"—Nomination, 1955
Supporting Actress: For *The Bob Cummings Show*—Nomination, 1956
Supporting Actress, Dramatic or Comedy Series: For *The Bob Cummings
Show*—Award, 1957
Supporting Actress, Comedy Series: For *The Bob Cummings Show*—
Award, 1958–59

MOVIES

A Man Called Peter (1955); *Pepe* (1960); *All Hands on Deck* (1961); *Lover
Come Back* (1961)

MAUREEN McCORMICK

b. Maureen Denise McCormick, August 5, 1956, Encino, California
*The Brady Bunch; The Brady Kids; The Brady Bunch Hour; The Brady
Girls Get Married/The Brady Brides; A Very Brady Christmas*

TV-SERIES CAST

Camp Runamuck
NBC: September 2, 1966–September 17, 1966
Maureen Sullivan (recurring role)

Fantasy Island
ABC: January 28, 1978–July 21, 1984
Among the stock company that also included Carol Lynley, Mary Ann
Mobley, Lynda Day George, Toni Tennille, Melinda Naud, Fred Grandy,
Ken Berry, Barbi Benton, Arte Johnson, Judy Landers, and Phyllis Davis

Maureen McCormick as a gymnast in *Take Down*.

Maureen in *Texas Lightning*.

TV MOVIES

A Vacation in Hell
NBC: May 21, 1979

SPECIALS

When, Jenny? When
   Syndicated half-hour dramatic special about a promiscuous high-school
   girl: July 1980

SERIES APPEARANCES INCLUDE

Bewitched
I Dream of Jeannie
My Three Sons
The Farmer's Daughter
Honey West "In the Bag" (November 5, 1965)
American Bandstand (December 19, 1970, and other dates; with the Brady
   Kids)
Day by Day (February 5, 1989)

MOVIES

Pony Express Rider (1976)	Rose
Moonshine County Express (1977)	Sissy
Take Down (1979)	Brooke Cooper
Skatetown U.S.A. (1979)	Susan
The Idolmaker (1980)	Ellen Fields
Texas Lightning (1981)	
Return to Horror High (1987)	Officer Tyler

EVE PLUMB

b. April 29, 1958, Burbank, California
The Brady Bunch; The Brady Kids; The Brady Girls Get Married/The Brady Brides; A Very Brady Christmas; The Bradys

TV-SERIES CAST

Little Women (NBC: February 8–March 8, 1979)
Melissa Jane ("Lissa") Driscoll (lookalike cousin of Beth March [played by Plumb], who died in the TV-movie pilot)

SERIES APPEARANCES INCLUDE

The Big Valley
It Takes a Thief
Lassie
Mannix
Gunsmoke
Adam 12
Family Affair
The Love Boat
Fantasy Island

SPECIALS

The ABC Afterschool Special: "Sara's Summer of the Swans"

MINI-SERIES

Greatest Heroes of the Bible: The Story of Noah
NBC: November 19–22, 1978
Lilla

TV MOVIES AND TV-MOVIE PILOTS

In Name Only (ABC: November 25, 1969; uncredited, possibly cut)
The House on Greenapple Road (pilot for *Dan August*; guest cast; ABC: January 11, 1970)
Dawn: Portrait of a Teenage Runaway (NBC: September 27, 1976)
Alexander: The Other Side of Dawn (NBC: May 16, 1977)

Telethon (ABC: November 6, 1977)
Little Women (pilot; as Beth March; NBC: October 2–3, 1978)
Secrets of Three Hungry Wives (NBC: October 9, 1978)
The Night the Bridge Fell Down (NBC: February 28, 1983)

MOVIES

I'm Gonna Git You Sucka (1988)

SUSAN OLSEN

b. August 14, 1961, Santa Monica, California
The Brady Bunch; The Brady Kids; The Brady Bunch Hour; The Bradys

SERIES APPEARANCES INCLUDE

Ironside
Gunsmoke
Julia
American Bandstand (December 19, 1970, and other dates; with the Brady
   Kids)
The Wonderful World of Disney: "The Boy Who Stole the Elephant"
   (unconfirmed)

BARRY WILLIAMS

b. Barry William Blenkhorn, September 30, 1954, Santa Monica, California;
raised Pacific Palisades, California;
*The Brady Bunch; The Brady Kids; The Brady Bunch Hour; The Brady
Girls Get Married; A Very Brady Christmas; The Bradys*

SERIES

General Hospital (ABC soap opera)
   as hospitalized child Jack Larson for short while starting Thursday, April
   10, 1969

PILOTS

The Shameful Secrets of Hastings Corners (NBC: January 14, 1970)
as Junior Fandango in half-hour soap-opera spoof

SERIES APPEARANCES INCLUDE

Run for Your Life
That Girl
The Mod Squad
Here Come the Brides
Dragnet
The Andy Griffith Show
Lancer
Gomer Pyle, USMC
The Invaders
Mission: Impossible
Marcus Welby, M.D.
American Bandstand (December 19, 1970, and other dates; with the Brady
Kids)
Highway to Heaven
Murder, She Wrote

MOVIES

Wild in the Streets (1968); *Wilderness Family Part 2* (1978; theme song
vocalist)

CHRISTOPHER KNIGHT

b. Christopher Anton Knight, November 7, 1957, in the New York City area;
raised on Long Island and the Los Angeles area
*The Brady Bunch; The Brady Kids; The Brady Bunch Hour; The Brady
Girls Get Married; A Very Brady Christmas; The Bradys*

TV-SERIES CAST

Another World (NBC soap opera)
Leigh Hobson

Joe's World
NBC: December 28, 1979; January 2, 1980; May 10–July 26, 1980
  Steve Wabash

SERIES APPEARANCES INCLUDE

Bonanza
Mannix
Gunsmoke
American Bandstand (December 19, 1970, and other dates; with the Brady
  Kids)

TV MOVIES AND TV-MOVIE PILOTS

Diary of a Hitchhiker (ABC: September 21, 1979)
Valentine Magic on Love Island, a.k.a. *Magic on Love Island*
  (pilot; as "Jimmy" in regular cast; NBC: February 15, 1980)

SPECIALS

The ABC Afterschool Special: "Sara's Summer of the Swans"

MOVIES

The Narrow Chute (1970; possibly unreleased)
Just You and Me, Kid (1979)

SERIES APPEARANCES INCLUDE

The Jonathan Winters Show (two appearances)
Day by Day (February 5, 1989)

MIKE LOOKINLAND

b. December 19, 1960, Mount Pleasant, Utah; raised Los Angeles area
The Brady Bunch; The Brady Kids; The Brady Bunch Hour; The Brady Girls Get Married; A Very Brady Christmas; The Bradys

TV MOVIES AND SPECIALS

Dead Men Tell No Tales (CBS: December 17, 1971)
The Point (ABC: 1971; voice-over for animated children's fantasy)

SERIES APPEARANCES INCLUDE

Funny Face (1971)
American Bandstand (December 19, 1970, and other dates; with the Brady Kids)
The Wonderful World of Disney: "Bayou Boy" (c. 1971)
Day by Day (February 5, 1989)

MOVIES

The Towering Inferno (1974)

THE BRADY WANNABES: SELECTED CREDITS

Jerry Houser

b. July 14, 1952, Los Angeles, California

TV-SERIES CAST

The New Temperatures Rising Show
ABC: September 25, 1972–January 8, 1974; July 28–August 30, 1974
  Orderly Haskell

We'll Get By
CBS: March 14–May 30, 1975
  Michael "Muff" Platt

The Brady Girls Get Married/The Brady Brides
Wally Logan

The Gary Coleman Show
NBC animated series: September 18, 1982–September 10, 1983
  Voice of Bartholomew

It Takes Two
ABC: October 14, 1982–April 28, 1983; June 2–September 1, 1983
  Assistant DA Jeremy Fenton (beginning partway through series)

One Day at a Time
CBS: December 6, 1975–September 2, 1984
  Jeff (college roommate of Barbara Cooper's dental-student husband;
  recurring role, 1982–83)

PILOTS

We'll Get By (CBS: March 7, 1974)
  Michael "Muff" Platt

Three Times Daley (CBS: August 3, 1976)
  Wes Daley

The Fighting Nightingales (CBS: January 16, 1978)
  Capt. Jules Meyer (in guest cast)

Living in Paradise (NBC: February 1, 1981)
  Jason Slattery

The Girl, The Gold Watch and Dynamite (Syndicated: May 1981)
  Ed Appleton (in guest cast)

Ron Kuhlman

The Brady Girls Get Married/The Brady Brides
  Phillip Covington III

Keland Love

The Brady Brides
Harry

Pryor's Place
CBS children's series
Meatrack the bully

Larry Storch

b. January 8, 1923, New York City

The Brady Kids
Voices of Moptop the dog and Marlon the bird

Best known as Corporal Randolph Agarn of the cult-classic sitcom *F Troop* (ABC: September 14, 1965–August 31, 1967), Storch had been a summer host of the early TV show *Cavalcade of Stars* and the star of a summer comedy-variety series *The Larry Storch Show* (1953). He also appeared on the 1975–76 CBS Saturday-morning live-action series *The Ghost Busters,* and provided voices for such animated kids' shows as *The Groovie Goolies* and *The Pink Panther.*

Jane Webb

The Brady Kids
Voices of Ping and Pong, the panda bears

A prolific voice-over actress, Webb provided the voices of Betty and Veronica on *The Archie Comedy Hour* and *Everything's Archie,* and for many other Saturday-morning cartoons.

Jennifer Runyon

TV-SERIES CAST

Another World (NBC soap opera)
  Sally Frame (one of several actresses in the role)

Charles in Charge
CBS: October 3, 1984–July 24, 1985; first-run syndication: 1987–present
  Gwendolyn Pierce (1984–85)

PILOTS

Six Pack (NBC: July 24, 1983; 60 min.)
  Heather "Breezy" Akins

TV MOVIES

A Very Brady Christmas
  Cindy

Geri Reischl

TV-SERIES CAST

The Brady Bunch Hour
  Jan Brady

Leah Ayres

TV-SERIES CAST

1st and Ten (HBO)

The Bradys
  Marcia Brady

Brady Miscellanea

RELEVANCE AND *THE BRADY BUNCH*

The real world avoided the Bradys as if a dome had been placed over their split-level house on Clinton Avenue. Alice's meat loaf, not Watergate, was discussed over dinner. Never did Mike yell upstairs for Greg to turn down the volume on *Dark Side of the Moon* or investigate that strange smoky smell coming from the girls' bedroom. But there *were,* indeed, examples of "relevance" shown during the series' five-year run.

Perhaps the most "relevant" of all *Brady Bunch* episodes is "The Liberation of Marcia Brady," in which the burning issue of the day, "women's lib," is discussed.

The episode begins when a black, sideburned television reporter (how groovy!) corners Marcia and her friends outside her junior high school. He asks them, "Do you think girls are the equals of boys in every respect?"

"Well," she answers, "if we're all supposed to be equal, I guess that means girls as well as boys."

> REPORTER:
> I take it you're for women's liberation.
> MARCIA:
> I guess I am.

REPORTER:
Do you have any brothers?
MARCIA:
Yes. Three.
REPORTER:
Do you think you can do everything they can
do?
MARCIA:
Well, I think I should have the chance to try.
REPORTER:
Do they put you down sometimes because you're
a girl?
MARCIA:
They sure do and it's not fair.
REPORTER:
Do you think girls should do something about
it?
MARCIA:
WE CERTAINLY SHOULD!

Later in the episode, the issue also divides Mike and Carol:

MIKE:
Some of the things women's libbers want are
pretty far out ... don't you think?
CAROL:
Well, I never went out marching ... but I do
believe in some of their causes.

The upshot is that Marcia thinks she can join the Frontier Scouts; Peter, to get back at her, tries to become a Sunflower Girl.

Another "relevant" piece of dialogue, from "Miss Popularity," shows that the Bradys were aware that they lived in the early '70s.

ALICE:
Tonight, I'm gonna cook something really far
out, something really different.
CAROL:
What's that, Alice?
ALICE:
A recipe with meat in it.

Explanation: The Bradys were not vegetarians, but during the early '70s, the rising cost of meat caused shortages and a consumer boycott.

MORE RELEVANCE:

In "54–40 and Fight," the girls are talking about what to get with their trading stamps.

> CINDY:
> How about a hair dryer?
> MARCIA:
> Cindy, boys don't use hair dryers.
> JAN:
> They should. Boys have longer hair than girls
> these days.

In "The Driver's Seat," Marcia tries to encourage Jan to have a positive attitude about her next debating-team meet.

> MARCIA:
> You can [succeed]. Money-back guarantee.
> JAN:
> Can you give me a better guarantee? You know
> what money's worth these days?

AND THE ONE AND ONLY TIME THE WORD "SEX" IS MENTIONED IN A *BRADY BUNCH* EPISODE:

In the final show, "The Hair-Brained Scheme," little Oliver is wondering why Cindy's two pet rabbits, Romeo and Juliet, can't reproduce.

> OLIVER:
> Maybe they both can have babies.
> CAROL:
> Well, Romeos don't have babies.
> OLIVER:
> Why not?
> CAROL (embarrassed):
> I'll explain it to you after dinner, Oliver.
> OLIVER:
> You know something, Cindy, I think your mom
> has a problem about discussing sex.

THE BRADY BATTLE OF THE SEXES

With the notable exception of Mike's championing Marcia's right to join the Frontier Scouts, there's virtually no equality of the sexes in this family. Guys were guys and gals were gals and don't mess with "Ms." in between.

> GREG:
> Give me one logical, intelligent reason why you should have all those [trading] stamps?
> MARCIA:
> Because they come from groceries and taking care of groceries is a woman's job.
> GREG:
> Well, eatin' them is a man's job. ("54—40 And Fight")

In "The Grass Is Always Greener," we learned that men's and women's places were immutable. Mike and Carol attempted to switch places: Mike tried cooking with the girls, and Carol tried teaching the boys baseball. Neither made out particularly well, but they learned their lessons. As Carol put it, "Sometimes a man has to be taught how tough it is to be a woman."

> GREG (to Marcia):
> You outscored everyone in driver's ed? Even the guys?
> MARCIA:
> That's a typical male chauvinist reaction. You're prejudiced against women drivers.
> GREG:
> No, I'm not. Not as long as they stay off the roads.
> MARCIA:
> You're prejudiced!
> GREG:
> It's not prejudice. It's just that men are naturally superior drivers. ("The Driver's Seat")

(This was a change from a first-season episode in which Marcia and Greg were running against each other for student-body president. Marcia graciously withdrew, saying, "My opponent has more experience in school government ... and besides he's very groovy.")

Mike: "Boys ought to learn at an early age that girls are gonna cost them money." ("The Treasure of Sierra Avenue")

> MIKE:
> Carol, there are certain places where women are
> just not permitted!
> CAROL:
> Name just one.
> MIKE:
> Boys' clubhouses and men's locker rooms.
> CAROL:
> That's two.

Later in this episode, Carol suggests she wouldn't have a problem if one of the boys wanted to play with a girls' dollhouse. Mike has a different opinion: "If my boys wanted to play in anybody's dollhouse, I'd take them to a psychiatrist!" ("A Clubhouse Is Not a Home")

The last word goes to Marcia: "Men are egotistical, arrogant, smug, and conceited!" ("The Driver's Seat")

TALK HIP WITH *THE BRADY BUNCH*

Whoever said the Bradys weren't a happening crew? *Au contraire.* They were a swinging family who employed up-to-the-minute lingo—up to the minute for 1967, of course.

Dig this Brady banter:

> MIKE (to Carol and kids):
> Your "own thing" is stopping that courthouse
> from being built in Woodland Park. My own thing
> is business as usual.
> ALICE:
> Well, my own thing is getting everyone to the
> dinner table. We're having chicken and its own
> thing is getting fricasseed. ("Double Parked")

And here's Alice commenting on Desi Arnaz, Jr: "Oh, he's with it . . . way out . . . but not too far." ("The Possible Dream")

CAROL:
Maybe ballet isn't your thing.
JAN:
Then, what is my thing? ("Try Try Again")

GREG:
Marcia's a very groovy girl.
ALICE:
I know she's groovy. You know she's groovy. But she doesn't know she's groovy. ("Juliet Is the Sun")

When Greg tells Randy Peterson, a girl he wants to date, about his career goal, she says: "I think architects are outasite!"
Later on:

GREG:
I think [Mike's boss] Mr. Phillips is outasite.
CAROL:
Your dad is pretty far out, too. ("Call Me Irresponsible")

Jan and Marcia are trying to get Great-Grandpa Brady interested in meeting Great-Grandma Hutchins (Carol's grandmother):

JAN:
She's really with it.
MARCIA:
And far out.
GREAT-GRANDPA:
"With it?" "Far out?" Children nowadays seem to have trouble expressing themselves in words from the English language.
JAN:
That's modern English, Grandpa.
GREAT-GRANDPA:
Modern, perhaps. English, no. ("You're Never Too Young")

In "My Sister Benedict Arnold," Alice is explaining to Greg and Marcia how their dates decided to make plans with each other instead of with the two Bradys:
"He said, 'How'd you like to go to the pizza parlor and she said far out.'

And she said, 'How about taking me to the carnival Friday night?' And he said, 'Far out.' They said, 'So long,' and I said, 'Far out' . . . I didn't want them to think I wasn't on it."

Greg: "With it."

Greg is trying to cheer up Marcia by telling her a guy in his class (a high-school boy!) likes her:

> GREG:
> He wants to meet you.
> MARCIA:
> Why?
> GREG:
> Obviously, he thinks you're a really groovy chick.
> MARCIA:
> A high-school boy really thinks I'm groovy?
> GREG:
> A lot of people think you're groovy.
> MARCIA:
> Honest?
> GREG:
> I even think you're groovy—for a sister, that is.
> ("Juliet Is the Sun")

Greg is excited about finally getting his own room ("Our Son, the Man"). Surveying it, he exclaims, "This place is funky!"

> MIKE:
> You mean square?
> GREG:
> No . . . together!

BRADY FASHION

The Brady Bunch are living proof that the early 1970s represented the nadir of popular fashion. In the first couple of seasons, the kids wore kid stuff: striped polo shirts, sneakers, and jeans. Greg preferred kind of nerdy plaid shirts. Mike and Carol were conservatively dressed.

As the series progressed, the outfits became wilder. Epauleted shirt-jacks.

Earth-toned bell-bottoms. Striped bell-bottoms. Plaid bell-bottoms (which served as role models for the "wild and crazy" Czechoslovakian guys on *Saturday Night Live*). There were fringed vests. Crocheted vests. Ponchos. Shirts with ugly geometric patterns and butterfly collars. Miniskirts and wide-body pant suits. Wide-striped shirts and wide-striped ties. You know—the kind of stuff that shows up in thrift shops nowadays, but which back then was kind of MallWorld Hep.

Alice, on the other hand, never changed outfits during the entire five-year run. She always wore an efficient blue work blouse and dress. She kept her hair in curlers when she went to bed. When she'd go out with Sam, she'd wear a solid-colored dress. We don't know, but we're sure she wore sensible shoes.

By the way, the favorite Brady color is burnt orange. It shows up in Mike's cardigan sweater, Mike's turtleneck, Mike's sweatshirt, Jan's turtleneck, Cindy's braids, Jan's dress, Jan's sweater, Marcia's miniskirt. Even the teeter-totter in the backyard.

MUSICAL BRADYS

Noting the success of the Partridge Family, the Brady kids also began singing on their show and eventually released four LPs: *Merry Christmas from the Brady Bunch* (1971); *Meet the Brady Bunch* (1972—it hit number 108 on *Billboard*'s album chart); *The Kids from the Brady Bunch* (1972); and *The Brady Bunch Photographic Album* (1973). Several of the kids also embarked on solo recording careers.

Among their other musical efforts were:

- Barry Williams—"Cheyenne"; words and music by Gary St. Clair and Tim O'Brien (single; Paramount Records; 1972)
- *Barry Williams* (album; Paramount Records)
- Barry Williams—"We've Got to Get It on Again" (single; Private Stock Records; c. 1981; cover of the 1972 Addrisi Brothers top-25 hit)
- Maureen McCormick—"Truckin' Back to You"; words and music by Gary St. Clair and Tim O'Brien; b/w "Teeny Weeny Bit (Too Long)"; words and music by David Sandler (single; Paramount; 1972)
- *Chris Knight and Maureen McCormick* (album, c. 1973)
- Eve Plumb—"The Fortune Cookie Song"
- Eve Plumb—"How Will It Be" (single; RCA Records)
- Mike Lookinland—"Love Doesn't Care Who's in It" (single; Capitol Records)

The singing group the Brady Bunch Kids made their live concert debut in the summer of 1972 at the San Bernardino Orange Show. The group did a multicity tour both that summer and the next. "The group had much more to do with the show and that kind of popularity than with that group's ability or musical prowess," Barry Williams notes today. "But we did the concerts and had screaming girls and wore tight outfits with lots of beads on them and things like that." Sounds rough.

MEET THE BRADY BUNCH—the album:

"Time to Change"
Words and music by R. Bloodworth, C. Welch, B. Mechel

"We Can Make the World a Whole Lot Brighter"
Words and music by Robert John and Michael Gately

"We'll Always Be Friends"
Words and music by Jackie Mills and Danny Janssen

"I Believe in You"
Words and music by Jackie Mills and Danny Janssen

"Love My Life Away"
Words and music by Jackie Mills and Danny Janssen

"Ain't It Crazy"
Words and music by Jackie Mills and Danny Janssen

"I Just Want to Be Your Friend"
Words and music by Curtis Boettcher

"Come Run with Me"
Words and music by Richard Obegi and Jimmy Bryant

"Me and You and a Dog Named Boo"
Words and music by Kent LaVole

"Baby I'm A-Want You"
Words and music by David Gates

A post-*Brady Bunch* LP.

Promotional still for the first
record album.

The Brady songsters. (No tattered jeans for this crew!)

But back in Bradyville:

In "Getting Davy Jones," when Jan tells Marcia that musical superstar Davy is in town, Marcia is disbelieving: "Davy Jones?" she retorts. "How about the Beatles, the Fifth Dimension, and the Carpenters, too?"

In "Dough Re Mi," when the Bradys think they are going to be a recording act, Peter says, "We'll make three times as much as the Carpenters . . . there's only two of them!"

That same episode Greg writes a song called "We Can Make the World a Whole Lot Brighter." It's a simpy thing with ecological overtones. But that's cool even if this was *three years after* Earth Day, because ecology was still a safe "radical" subject. Some of its lyrics: "Come take a stand/and help us save the land/let's go out and try to make it better."

In "Amateur Nite," the kids appear on *The Pete Sterne Amateur Hour* as the Silver Platters, so named because if they win first prize, they'll be able to pay for their parents' anniversary present: an engraved silver platter. For their audition, they sing a sappy Cowsills/Partridge—like song called "It's a Sunshine Day (Everybody's Smiling)," which contains such memorable lines as "I just can't stay inside all day/I got to to get out, get me some of those rays." On the actual show, they sing a groovy rocker, kind of like a watered-down Doobie Brothers thing, called "Keep on Moving." They dance around the stage in elaborately choreographed steps, which they no doubt learned by watching *Soul Train*.

In "Adios Johnny Bravo," Greg is conned by a slick-talking agent to abandon his siblings and embark on a solo career as a manufactured teen idol named Johnny Bravo. (They tell him, "You won't be *in* the top 20, you'll *be* the top 20!")

At the start of that episode, the kids are on *The Hal Barton TV Tonight Review* (where do these TV-show titles come from? Public-access cable?), singing a wimpy number called "You've Got to Be in Love to Love a Love Song." Greg, in all his plaid bell-bottomed glory, sings lead, romantically eyeballing Cindy and Marcia. Later, when Greg realizes he's been manipulated, he makes up with his siblings and they appear on the same TV show and sing "Good Time Music," a happening tune with such lines as: "It's much better to put yourself together/and create a lot of lovin' good vibes for humanity." Far out!

THE PIZZA CONNECTION

The Brady family had a strange obsession with pizza. Not only was the pizza parlor a groovy place to go on a date, but the food often cropped up in conversation, often in the strangest contexts.

Carol: "Judging from the reaction around here, I'd say Davy Jones is the hottest thing since pepperoni pizza." ("Getting Davy Jones")

Mike described Greg as thinking of Don Drysdale as a combination of "George Washington, Neil Armstrong, and the man who invented pizza." ("The Dropout")

The kids are searching through the amusement park, hoping to find Mike's lost blueprints. Bobby decides to look in the pizza parlor.

> CINDY:
> Why are we gonna look in there? Jan didn't say anything about pizza.
> BOBBY:
> Well, somebody could have found our sketches and left them there.
> CINDY:
> That's right, too.
> BOBBY:
> So as long as we're here, LET'S HAVE SOME PIZZA!

And it should also be noted, Peter gets a pizza-delivery job at the Leaning Tower of Pizza Parlor. ("Marcia Gets Creamed")

THE RAQUEL WELCH CONNECTION

Like pizza, *The Brady Bunch* writers seemed to have a strange affinity for Raquel Welch. Note these odd instances.

One of the things Greg wants to trade with Harvey (one of his ubiquitous "phone friends") is an autographed picture of Raquel Welch in *Sorry, Wrong Number.*

In "The Snooperstar," Mike describes a client who has "the face of Elizabeth Taylor, the body of Raquel Welch, and the bank account of Queen Elizabeth."

In "Jan's Aunt Jenny," Jenny (Imogene Coca) admits that while she's come to accept her less-than-flattering exterior, "I'd rather look like Raquel Welch myself."

The goat mascot Greg steals in "Getting His Goat" is named Raquel.

DATING WITH THE BRADYS

GREG'S DATES:

Rachel ("The Big Bet")
Rachel ("Greg Gets Grounded")
Randy Peterson ("Call Me Irresponsible")
Sandra ("Peter and the Wolf"): Her cousin Linda got set up with Peter.
Marge (an amusement park worker he picks up in "The Cincinnati Kids")
Jennifer Nichols ("Greg's Triangle")
Kathy Lawrence ("My Sister Benedict Arnold")
Linette Carter ("Click")

MARCIA'S DATES: REAL AND IMAGINARY

Doug Williams (imaginary; he's taking her to the dance in "Cindy Brady, Lady")
Jeff ("Marcia Gets Creamed")
Allan Anthony (the boy who was taking her to the dance in "Brace Yourself")
Doug Simpson, football star ("The Subject Was Noses")
Charlie ("The Subject Was Noses")
Harvey Klinger ("Going ... Going Steady")
Lester ("Going ... Going Steady")
Danny (just mentioned in "Going ... Going Steady")
Warren Mulaney ("My Sister Benedict Arnold")

Maureen McCormick unwinds.

TEACHERS

They were entrusted with the care and feeding of the Brady kids' growing minds. Some were seen, some weren't:

Mrs. Denhoff (Jan's in "The Not-So-Rose-Colored Glasses")
Mrs. Watson (Jan's in "My Sister's Shadow")
Mrs. Robbins (Marcia's in "Getting Davy Jones")
Mr. Price (Peter's in "The Power of the Press")
Mr. Binkley (Greg's vice-principal in "Getting Greg's Goat")
Mrs. Whitfield (Cindy's in "Snow White and the Seven Bradys")—she was
    played by Frances Whitfield, who was the Brady kids' real-life tutor on the
    set.
Mrs. Pearson (Greg's in "The Dropout")
Mr. Randolph (Marcia's principal in "The Slumber Caper")
Miss O'Hara (Greg's in "The Undergraduate")
Miss Goodwin (Marcia's in "Juliet Is the Sun")
Mr. Hillary (Bobby's principal in "Bobby's Hero")

IMAGINARY PHONE FRIENDS

Since they always had each other, the Brady kids didn't need a Wally or a Lumpy to pal around with. In fact, they never really had any close friends— just casual acquaintances who seemed to change from episode to episode. Sometimes we never even saw their "friends"—they just existed as imaginary telephone-conversation partners.

CAROL'S PHONE FRIENDS:

Gloria ("Double Parked"), a member of Carol's women's club.
Martha ("Sorry, Right Number"), who talks about her hem length.

MIKE'S PHONE FRIENDS:

Harry ("Sorry, Right Number")
Ed ("Sorry, Right Number")
Brad ("Getting Davy Jones")—this guy plays golf with the manager of the hotel where Davy is staying.

GREG'S PHONE FRIENDS:

Harvey ("Sorry, Right Number")—Greg wants to trade him his baseball mitt, his autographed picture of Raquel Welch, and his pet white rabbit for a bike.
Fred and Tom ("Peter and the Wolf")
Eddie Bryan ("Love and the Older Man")—the guy he wants to set Marcia up with
Scott, George ("Greg Gets Grounded")

MARCIA'S PHONE FRIENDS:

Linda ("A Room at the Top")
Katie ("A Room at the Top")
Susie ("A Room at the Top")
Jerry ("Cindy Brady, Lady")

PETER'S PHONE FRIENDS:

Kevin ("Marcia Gets Creamed")
Eddie ("The Power of the Press")

JAN'S PHONE FRIENDS:

Stevie ("Jan's Aunt Jenny")
Cathy ("Love and the Older Man")
Gloria ("The Babysitters")
And a *real* imaginary friend, George Glass (the boyfriend she makes up in "The Not-So-Ugly Duckling").

PHYSICAL FRIENDS

Of course, sometimes we actually did see the Bradys' friends, acquaintances, and classmates—though, curiously, they never seemed to be the ones on the phone . . . or even in subsequent episodes.

GREG'S PHYSICAL FRIENDS:

Hank Carter ("A Room at the Top")—the friend who comes home from college and wants Greg to move in with him
Suzanne ("The Hair-Brained Scheme")
Gretchen ("The Hair-Brained Scheme")
Tom Peterson ("Today I Am a Freshman")
Dick Corsen ("Today I Am a Freshman")
Joey ("Brace Yourself")—yet another guy he tries to set Marcia up with
Rusty ("Vote for Brady")

MARCIA'S PHYSICAL FRIENDS:

Doreen ("Getting Davy Jones")
Laura ("Getting Davy Jones")
Page ("Getting Davy Jones")
Molly Webber (the girl she makes over in "My Fair Opponent")
Vicki ("The Subject Was Noses")
Harold ("Juliet Is the Sun")

PETER'S PHYSICAL FRIENDS:

Iris ("The Power of the Press")
Harvey ("The Power of the Press")
Diane ("The Power of the Press")
Steve ("The Hero")
Jason ("The Hero")
Jennifer ("The Hero")

JAN'S PHYSICAL FRIENDS:

Katy ("My Sister's Shadow")
Clark Tyson (the boy she has a crush on in "The Not-So-Ugly Duckling")
Cathy Williams ("Miss Popularity")
Shirley
Herman
Billy Garst (the most popular boy in the class)

BOBBY'S PHYSICAL FRIENDS:

Eric, Tim, Burt, Eddie ("Mail Order Hero")
Millicent (who kisses him in "Little Big Man")
Tommy Jamison ("Cindy Brady, Lady")

WEIRD RELATIVES

Carol's great-grandmother Connie Hutchins from Owensboro, Kentucky, was a youthful-minded swinger who jogged and played basketball. (She was played by Florence Henderson.) Mike's grandfather was Judge Hank Brady (played by Robert Reed), a pompous windbag.

Jan's Aunt Jenny—actually her great-aunt (played by Imogene Coca)—also was eccentric: an Auntie Mame–like world traveler.

Ann B. Davis played the dual roles of Alice and her cousin Emma—an ex-WAC who tried to bring boot-camp discipline to the Brady household. (The look-alike device was also used by Peter, who played a fellow student named Arthur Owens.)

WEIRD *REAL-LIFE* RELATIVES

Florence Henderson's real-life daughter, Barbara Bernstein, appeared in a handful of episodes. She was Suzanne, a girl in a beauty parlor in "The Hair-Brained Scheme," Marcia's friend Ruthie in "The Slumber Caper," and her friend Peggy in "Everyone Can't Be George Washington." What versatility.

Sherwood Schwartz cast his daughter, Hope Sherwood, in several episodes, usually as Rachel, an occasional girlfriend of Greg's.

Robert Reed's daughter Carolyn played Marcia's friend Karen in "The Slumber Caper."

BRADY IN-JOKES

In "Mail Order Hero"—the Joe Namath episode—Marcia talks about Mike Connors being a "far-out" guy because he went out of his way to visit a sick child. She could have picked the name of any actor in Hollywood. Why Connors? Because Robert Reed had a recurring role on Connors's *Mannix* during the same time as *The Brady Bunch* aired.

In "The Hair-Brained Scheme," Carol is trying to impress Bobby about famous people who never quit, like Thomas Edison. She then mentions "Carl Mahakian." Bobby says he never heard of him. And Carol explains why: "He quit." Carl Mahakian was the show's postproduction coordinator.

In "Miss Popularity," Jan wants to go to the dance with Billy Garst, the most popular boy in school. Bill E. Garst was the show's film editor.

In "You Can't Win Them All," the Bradys are talking about the couples they're inviting for a dinner. Among the couples are the Bernsteins. (In real life, that's Florence Henderson and her then-husband, Ira Bernstein.)

In "The Teeter-Totter Caper," two college boys named Ralph Nelson and Alan Rudolph set the world's record for staying on a teeter-totter. Ralph Nelson was the show's unit production manager, while Alan Rudolph was the assistant director.

In "Juliet Is the Sun," Greg tries to cheer up a depressed Marcia by telling her that a classmate named Lloyd Leeds likes her. That name is a hybrid of two key *Brady Bunch* personnel—production assistant (later producer) Lloyd Schwartz and producer Howard Leeds.

TV AND THE BRADYS

Another hint that the Bradys lived in the real world was the fact that references to real TV shows cropped up occasionally.

Robert Reed enjoying lunch with cast members and others.

Cindy has told her teacher that her family will star in a production of *Snow White*. Carol gets angry and wants to punish her.

CINDY:
Mom, can't we make a deal?
CAROL:
Listen, I'm not Monty Hall. ("Snow White and the
Seven Bradys")

In "Top Secret," Oliver is impressed that Bobby has deduced (erroneously) that Sam the butcher is a double agent.

OLIVER:
Boy, you sure know how to operate.
BOBBY:
Well, thanks. I used to watch *Mission: Impossible* a lot.

In "The Possible Dream," Marcia tells Desi Arnaz, Jr: "When I was younger, I used to think Captain Kangaroo was someone special. But compared to you . . ."

REAL-LIFE ATHLETES AND THE BRADYS

Joe Namath, Deacon Jones, Don Drysdale, and Wes Parker all appeared in *Brady Bunch* episodes. But the names of other real-life jocks are sprinkled throughout several others:

Wilt Chamberlain	Lee Trevino
Jerry West	Roman Gabriel
Hank Aaron	Vida Blue

A typical Brady moment.

Your friends and mine, the Brady boys.

SEVEN THINGS WE NEVER FOUND OUT

1. How did that lady meet that fellow?
2. How did they know it was more than just a hunch?
3. Who lived in the bedroom that became the girls' room?
4. What is Alice's employment history?
5. What were all the Bradys looking at during the opening credits?
6. Why didn't the Bradys ever form a baseball team?
7. When did Alice eat?

THOSE BETTING BRADYS

Great sports all, the Bradys loved nothing more than to engage in a wee bit of wagering. It's amazing that Bobby never grew up to be a racetrack tout.

In "Driver's Seat," Greg and Marcia bet over who will get a higher score on their road test. Loser does the household chores for a month.

Mr. Matthews (in "The Hustler") bets Bobby a pack of chewing gum that he can beat him at pool. Bobby wins.

In "Fright Night," Marcia bets the boys her week's allowance that they aren't brave enough to spend a night in the attic, where there might be a ghost.

In "The Big Bet," the entire episode concerns what happens when Greg bets Bobby that he (Greg) can do twice as many chin-ups. The loser has to do everything the winner says for a week. In a subplot, Mike bets Carol that he won't recognize "Bobo," his high-school girlfriend, when they attend Mike's high-school reunion.

THE *GILLIGAN'S ISLAND* CONNECTION

As we all know, Sherwood Schwartz created both *Gilligan's Island* and *The Brady Bunch*. Two of the Minnow castaways, Thurston and Lovey Howell, showed up on *Bunch*. Or at least the actors who played them: Jim Backus (Thurston B. Howell) played Harry Matthews, the president of Mike's firm, and, in two earlier episodes, a prospector named Zaccariah whom the Bradys meet under unpleasant circumstances during the family trip to the Grand Canyon. Natalie Schafer (Lovey) played Penelope Fletcher, a haughty benefactress (in other words, the Lovey Howell type) for whom Mike was designing a building—and who ended up singing a duet of "On the Good Ship Lollipop" with Cindy.

Jim Backus in the episode "Ghost Town, USA."

BRADY BY THE NUMBERS

The Bradys' phone number is 762-0799 in "The Not-So-Ugly Duckling," but by the time of the Joe Namath episode, it's 555-6161. Did they have it changed because of crank calls?

The California license-plate number on the convertible is TEL 635.

The California license-plate number on the station wagon is Y 18078.

That staircase that the kids and everyone else trundled down contains twelve steps.

ALL ABOUT TIGER

Tiger, that adorable moppet pup, got accidentally iced during the run of the *The Brady Bunch*. (See the chapter "A Brady Bunch of Background.") A replacement Tiger came on the show, but the magic just wasn't there. Tiger *exeunt*.

But fret not. After *The Brady Bunch*, this ersatz Tiger went on to stardom as "Blood," opposite Don Johnson in the science-fiction cult classic, *A Boy and His Dog*. (Tiger played the dog.) The 1975 movie also starred Jason Robards and Alvy (*Green Acres*) Moore, with the late Tim McIntire as the voice of Blood.

There's more! Tiger went on to win the animal kingdom's prestigious Patsy Award for his part in the movie, which is more than either Tiger did on *The Brady Bunch*. For the record, he/they had been beaten out in the "Continuing Series" category by: Scruffy, the dog on *The Ghost and Mrs. Muir*, 1970; Arnold, the pig on *Green Acres*, 1971; Pax, the German shepherd on *Longstreet*, 1972; and Midnight, the multitalented cat on not only *Mannix*, but *Barnaby Jones*, 1974. No award was given in 1973, more's the pity.

PETS OF *THE BRADY BUNCH*

Besides Tiger, there were:

Romeo and Juliet (the rabbits)
Bobby and Peter's frogs Spunker and Old Croaker ("Greg Gets Grounded")
Greg's mouse Myron
Bobby's parakeet ("What Goes Up")
Alice once mentioned her pet goldfish "Herman," although we never saw it.

SOME FAMOUS BRADYS

Matthew Brady: lovable and even-tempered Civil War photographer
Diamond Jim Brady: lovable and even-tempered robber baron
James Brady: lovable and even-tempered former White House press
     secretary
James Brady: lovable and even-tempered *Parade* magazine columnist
Nicholas F. Brady: Secretary of the Treasury, with a lovable, even-tempered
     monetary policy

A MAGICAL BRADY MOMENT

In "My Fair Opponent," the show opens with Cindy drawing a happy face—
that Brady family crest—on a blackboard. Marcia, who's in a foul mood,
comes in and changes the smile to a frown!

A Brady Bunch of Trivia

QUESTIONS

1. How did Desi Arnaz, Jr., find out about Marcia?

A. Alice knew his mother's housekeeper
B. Mike designed his mother's house
C. Greg jammed with Dino, Desi & Billy
D. Carol belonged to the same women's club as his mother

2. How did Marcia's nose get broken, jeopardizing her date with the football star?

A. Bobby threw a baseball at her
B. Peter threw a football at her
C. Greg threw a basketball at her
D. Alice threw a brownie at her

3. What job did Greg not have?

A. Office boy for Mike
B. Delivery boy for Sam
C. Local chairman of Youth for Nixon
D. Football team photographer

4. What was Peter's journalistic nickname when he became a columnist for the school newspaper?

A. Deep Throat
B. Flash
C. Scoop
D. Mr. Broadway

5. What did the girls end up buying with the ninety-four books of trading stamps?

A. Sewing machine
B. Color TV
C. Barbie doll
D. Mystery Date Game

6. In "Katchoo," Jan is allergic to something. Everyone thinks it's Tiger. But of course it isn't. What was causing Jan to sneeze?

A. Alice's meat loaf
B. Carol's polyester housedress
C. Tiger's flea powder
D. The shag carpeting

7. Match the Brady character with the Snow White character

1. Mike	A. Doc
2. Carol	B. Evil Queen
3. Jan	C. Dopey
4. Marcia	D. Grumpy
5. Cindy	E. Happy
6. Greg	F. Prince Charming
7. Peter	G. Sneezy
8. Bobby	H. Snow White
9. Alice	I. Bashful
10. Sam	J. Sleepy

8. In "The Brady Braves" episode, the Indian chief gives each Brady member an Indian name. Match the Brady with their new name.

1. Mike	A. Squaw in Waiting
2. Carol	B. Middle Buffalo
3. Jan	C. Little Bear Who Loses Way
4. Marcia	D. Big Eagle of Large Nest
5. Cindy	E. Willow Dancing in Mind
6. Greg	F. Yellow Flower with Many Petals
7. Peter	G. Stalking Wolf
8. Bobby	H. Dove of Morning Light
9. Alice	I. Wandering Blossom

9. What weird hobby did Marcia's first steady have?

A. Collected stamps
B. Collected bugs
C. Collected baseball cards
D. Collected lingerie

10. Jan or Marcia?

A. Couldn't tap dance
B. Played Juliet
C. Wore glasses
D. Wore a wig
E. Was a cheerleader

11. Bobby or Peter?

A. Scared of heights
B. Was a magician
C. Was a drummer
D. Sang in the glee club

12. What item wasn't found in Tiger's doghouse?

A. Cindy's doll
B. Greg's mouse
C. Marcia's bite plate

13. What present did Aunt Jenny give to Marcia?

A. A shofar from Golda Meir
B. A sari from Indira Gandhi
C. A jewel from Queen Elizabeth
D. A hat from Bella Abzug

14. Four bad things happened when the Brady Bunch went to Hawaii and Bobby found the secret "tabu" tiki. Which didn't?

A. A heavy wall decoration fell down, just missing Bobby
B. Alice hurt her back during a hula lesson
C. Greg wiped out surfing
D. A scorpion crawled on Peter while he was sleeping
E. Marcia's string bikini became unraveled

15. Identify:

A. Kaplutus
B. Harvey Klinger
C. Connie Hutchins
D. Mr. Driscoll
E. The Banana Convention
F. Bobo

ANSWERS

1. A
2. B
3. C
4. C
5. B
6. C
7. 1-F, 2-H 3-E, 4-J 5-D 6-A 7-G 8-I 9-B 10-C
8. 1-D 2-F 3-H 4-E 5-I 6-G 7-B 8-C 9-A
9. B
10. A) Jan B) Marcia C) Jan D) Jan E) Marcia
11. A) Bobby B) Peter C) Bobby D) Peter
12. C
13. A
14. E
15.
A) Kaplutus—the planet where the pint-sized aliens who Bobby dreams about come from in "Out of This World"
B) Harvey Klinger—Marcia's first steady
C) Connie Hutchins—Carol's grandmother
D) Mr. Driscoll—owner of the local toy store
E) Banana Convention—rock band Greg plays with in "Where There's Smoke"
F) Bobo—Mike's girlfriend in high school

A Selective Season-by-Season Mini-Guide to The Brady Bunch

The first season episodes dealt mainly with the adjustment of the new families and their predictable quarrels. Marcia had her hair parted on the side and worn in pigtails. Carol had a bouffant. Mike looked like a Groovy Young Republican with short, razor-cut hair and midrange sideburns. Greg looked like a dork.

The biggest change in the second season was that the Peppermint Trolley no longer sang the theme song. The Brady kids themselves warbled the immortal lines, changing the lyrics from "that's the way they became the Brady Bunch" to "that's the way *we* became the Brady Bunch" (italics ours). Marcia moved her part from the side to the center. Tiger disappeared from the cast. Mike's sideburns got a little longer. Carol grew her hair out in a modified Sassoon.

In the third season, the kids were growing up, gaining inches. Greg's hair grew longer. The younger boys now had hair that made them look like members of a British rock group, circa 1965. Alice was grayer. Jan's hair was long and wavy. Carol grew her hair longer, shag-style in the back, and began dressing in all her earth-toned, paisley-printed glory.

The fourth season began with a three-part episode in which the Bradys went to Hawaii, shot on location. Marcia entered high school. Greg got his driver's license. Mike's hair got really curly, Greg's hair got curly and longer. The family's clothing began getting really weird.

In the fifth and final season, Greg moved into his own room in the attic and prepared to graduate high school. Cindy's pigtails got longer, and eventually she stopped wearing them altogether. Jan began parting her hair in the middle and became cute. Mike's perm got even curlier, as did the boys'. Mike, for all intents and purposes, stopped wearing ties.

THE KIDS BY SEASONS

GREG

1: Runs for student-body president against Marcia
Has a crush on his teacher
2: Gets advice from Don Drysdale
Baby-sits for younger kids
Shoots a family movie
Gets his first job
Gets caught smoking
3: Buys a lemon used car
Carol doesn't want him to join the high-school football team

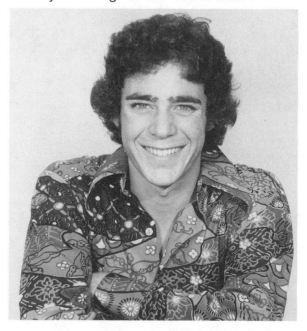

That groovy Greg!

4: Decides he doesn't want to be an architect
Has to choose between Marcia and his girlfriend for head cheerleader
Gets grounded for having an auto accident
Moves into the attic
5: Becomes Johnny Bravo
Steals rival school's team mascot
Double-dates with Peter
Hair turns orange

MARCIA

1: Enters Mike in "Father of Year" contest
Runs for student-body president against Greg
Gets braces
Goes steady with bug collector
2: Baby-sits the younger kids with Greg
Has slumber party
Becomes "liberated"
3: Gets swelled head after getting lead in school play
Meets Davy Jones
Turns plain friend into beauty
4: Starts high school
Has a crush on the dentist
Tries out for head cheerleader
Has a swollen nose
5: Gets first job
Takes driver's test

JAN

1: Seemingly allergic to Tiger
Receives locket from unknown admirer
2: Plays practical jokes
Has her first crush
Becomes a salesperson
3: Gets jealous of Marcia
Needs glasses
Meets Aunt Jenny
4: Wants to be left alone
5: Loses Mike's blueprints
Tries to discover something she's good at
Wins school popularity contest

CINDY

1: Loses Kitty Karry-All
2: Tattles on other kids
   Has nightmares
3: Sets teeter-totter record with Bobby
   Has a secret admirer
4: Appears on a TV quiz show
5: Reads Marcia's diary

PETER

1: Saves a little girl's life
2: Breaks Carol's vase
   Has a fight with Buddy Hinton
3: Is told he has no personality
   Tapes other people's conversations
   Voice changes
   Writes for school newspaper
4: Asks Greg's help for date
   Plays Benedict Arnold in school play
   Gets first job and loses it
5: Double-dates with Greg
   Meets his look-alike

BOBBY

1: Runs away from home
2: Finds $1,100 in wallet
   Is scared of high places
   Feels sorry for himself
3: Sets teeter-totter record with Cindy
   Tries to stretch himself to become taller
   Wins a bet with Greg
4: Becomes power-crazed school safety monitor
   Idolizes Jesse James
5: Meets Joe Namath
   Gets mumps from girl
   Saves Peter's life
   Becomes pool champ

A Brady Bunch of Credits

CREATOR AND EXECUTIVE PRODUCER: Sherwood Schwartz
THEME, "THE BRADY BUNCH": Lyrics by Sherwood Schwartz, Music by Frank De Vol

THE PILOT

PRODUCER: Howard Leeds
MUSIC: Frank De Vol
DIRECTOR OF PHOTOGRAPHY: Lester Shorr
ART DIRECTOR: Bob Smith
FILM EDITOR: Marshall Neilan
MUSIC EDITOR: Dan Carlin
POSTPRODUCTION COORDINATOR: Carl Mahakian
UNIT PRODUCTION MANAGER: Wally Simpson
ASSISTANT EDITOR: James C. Myers
SET DECORATOR: John Burton
CASTING: Joe D'Agosta
SOUND MIXER: Bill Ford

FIRST SEASON

PRODUCER: Howard Leeds
SCRIPT EDITOR: Ruth Brooks Flippen
ASSOCIATE PRODUCER: David M. Whorf
MUSIC: Frank De Vol
MUSIC SUPERVISOR: Leith Stevens

DIRECTOR OF PHOTOGRAPHY: Lester Shorr
ART DIRECTOR: William Campbell
FILM EDITORS: Marshall Neilan, Bernard Matis, Frank Cappacchione
MUSIC EDITOR: Richard Lapham
POSTPRODUCTION COORDINATOR: Carl Mahakian
SUPERVISING SOUND EFFECTS EDITOR: Douglas H. Grindstaff
UNIT PRODUCTION MANAGER: James R. Nicholson
ASSISTANT DIRECTORS: Norman A. August, Robert Birnbaum, Clancy Herne
SET DECORATORS: Pierre Ludlum, Anthony D. Nealis
CASTING: Michael O. Hanks
SOUND MIXER: Carl Daniels

SECOND SEASON

PRODUCER: Howard Leeds
SCRIPT EDITORS: Tam Spiva, Charles Hoffman
ASSOCIATE PRODUCER: Lloyd Schwartz
MUSIC: Frank De Vol
MUSIC SUPERVISOR: Kenyon Hopkins
DIRECTOR OF PHOTOGRAPHY: Robert G. Hager
ART DIRECTOR: John M. Elliott
FILM EDITORS: Marshall Neilan, Bill E. Garst
MUSIC EDITOR: Jack Lowry
POSTPRODUCTION COORDINATOR: Carl Mahakian
SOUND EFFECTS EDITOR: Douglas H. Grindstaff
UNIT PRODUCTION MANAGER: James R. Nicholson
ASSISTANT DIRECTOR: Morrie Abrams
SET DECORATOR: Anthony D. Nealis
CASTING: Michael O. Hanks
SOUND MIXER: James R. Wright

THIRD SEASON

PRODUCER: Howard Leeds
SCRIPT EDITOR: Tam Spiva
ASSOCIATE PRODUCER: Lloyd Schwartz
MUSIC: Frank De Vol
MUSIC SUPERVISOR: Kenyon Hopkins
DIRECTOR OF PHOTOGRAPHY: Robert G. Hager
ART DIRECTOR: Jack DeShields
FILM EDITORS: Bill E. Garst, John F. Schreger, Marshall Neilan
MUSIC EDITOR: Jack Lowry
POSTPRODUCTION COORDINATOR: Carl Mahakian

SUPERVISING SOUND EFFECTS EDITOR: William Andrews
UNIT PRODUCTION MANAGER: Ralph W. Nelson
ASSISTANT DIRECTORS: Ray E. Taylor, Bill Green, Alan Rudolph
SET DECORATOR: Dorcy W. Howard
CASTING: Edward R. Morse
SOUND MIXER: James R. Wright

FOURTH SEASON

PRODUCER: Howard Leeds
SCRIPT EDITOR: Tam Spiva
ASSOCIATE PRODUCER: Lloyd Schwartz
MUSIC: Frank De Vol
MUSIC SUPERVISOR: Kenyon Hopkins
DIRECTOR OF PHOTOGRAPHY: Robert G. Hager
ART DIRECTOR: Jack DeShields
FILM EDITORS: Bill E. Garst, Marshall Neilan
MUSIC EDITOR: Jack Lowry, Al Friede
POSTPRODUCTION COORDINATOR: Carl Mahakian
SUPERVISING SOUND EFFECTS EDITOR: William Andrews
UNIT PRODUCTION MANAGERS: Ralph W. Nelson, Wally Samson
ASSISTANT DIRECTORS: Ray E. Taylor, Bill McGarry
SET DECORATOR: Anthony D. Nealis, Bill F. Calvert
CASTING: Betty Martin
SOUND MIXER: Wallace R. Bearden

FIFTH SEASON

PRODUCERS: Howard Leeds, Lloyd Schwartz
SCRIPT CONSULTANT: Skip Webster
PRODUCTION EXECUTIVE: Jack Sonntag
MUSIC: Frank De Vol
DIRECTOR OF PHOTOGRAPHY: Robert G. Hager
ART DIRECTOR: Monty Elliott
FILM EDITORS: Marshall Neilan, Bill E. Garst
MUSIC EDITOR: Jay Smith
POSTPRODUCTION COORDINATOR: Carl Mahakian
UNIT PRODUCTION MANAGER: Mike Salamunovich
ASSISTANT DIRECTOR: John Morrison
SET DECORATOR: Anthony D. Nealis
CASTING SUPERVISOR: Mildred Gusse
CASTING: Pat Harris
SOUND MIXERS: Wallace R. Bearden, Jim Ford

The Brady Bunch
Episode Guide

PILOT: *"The Honeymoon"*
Written by Sherwood Schwartz. Directed by John Rich.
Original Airdate: September 26, 1969

Most of the key Bradyisms that made the series so lovable were apparent in the debut episode: pseudo-hip talk, sexy repartee between Mike and Carol, pat situations, corny jokes, contrived plot devices and lots o' smiles.

It's Mike and Carol's wedding day and we open at Mike's house as he's eating breakfast with the boys. "It's important to have a good breakfast," Mike tells them. Yet even though his intentions are good, it's obvious his mind is elsewhere. Alice, his housekeeper, notices and says, "I don't blame you for being nervous, Mr. Brady. This is a very important Saturday." Mike responds, "Who said I'm nervous? I'm mature and I'm logical and I know I'm doing the right thing. Why should I be nervous?" Meanwhile, he's pouring twenty-one teaspoons of sugar into his coffee. Greg isn't surprised by his dad's condition. As he tells Mike, "It's a normal male reaction—for your generation."

Alice tries more reassurance: "Mrs. Martin is a lovely woman," she tells him. And the kids—in that hip-speak they would utter so knowingly for the next five years—echo her:

"She's outasite, Dad," says Greg.

"Groovy," chimes in Peter.

"Neat-o," adds Bobby.

"And they knew that it was much more than a hunch. . . ."

Mike spills some coffee, leading Alice to proclaim that "I'm sure the future Mrs. Brady is cool, calm, and collected."

Cut to Carol's house, where an equally nervous Carol Tyler Martin is rushing to get dressed, her hair in curlers, as Jan, Cindy, and Marcia watch. "Brides are supposed to look beautiful and I look awful," she moans. The girls reassure her that she looks fine. "How can you sit there and say I look beautiful?" asks Carol. "Because we love you," whines Cindy. And all four females hug each other.

Carol's phone rings. It's Mike checking on Carol's nervousness. Both admit they're really jumpy.

"Why don't you take a tranquilizer?" Carol suggests.

"I took one," he answers. (So Mike Brady was on drugs on his wedding day—stop the presses!)

Carol suggests that maybe he should pop another one.

"Nothing doing," Mike replies, just saying no. "I wanna be calm for the ceremony, but there's a honeymoon to consider!"

As the boys get dressed, Mike notices that Bobby has removed the picture of his late mother from the bureau. Bobby explains that Carol might not like to see it. Compassionately, Mike tells him to put it back. "I don't want you to forget your mother," he tells him, "and neither does Carol."

And it's off to the wedding—the boys and Mike and Tiger (who comes along, despite Mike's disapproval). The boys reluctantly agree to leave Tiger in the car, an act that will shortly have important ramifications.

The wedding is to be held in the backyard of Carol's house. Mike wears a dark suit and Carol a yellow satin dress. When Mike and Carol see each other, Carol asks him how she looks. Affecting a mock-British accent, Mike replies: "You, my dear, are prettier than the flowers, sweeter than the cake, more appetizing than the hors d'oeuvres, and more sparkling than the champagne."

Carol is overcome by joy. "A few years ago, I thought it was the end of the world."

Mike: "But now it's the beginning for both of us."

Carol: "For all of us!"

Mike: "The whole blooming Brady bunch!"

The actual ceremony goes off without a hitch. But after Mike has kissed Carol, Tiger jumps out of the car window. Spotting Fluffy, Carol's cat, Tiger gives chase and the two animals run amok in the backyard, over the guests, and across the food tables. Mike and Carol yell at the kids. The wedding cake is just about to slip off the table when Mike slides in and, like Ozzie Smith, makes a great save. His heroic act is extremely short-lived, however, as the cake slips from his grip and falls all over him. But this being the Bradys, everybody laughs and Carol plants a big smacker on Mike's cake-covered lips.

"Just what we wanted," Mike muses. "A nice quiet wedding."

Now it's off to the honeymoon. Mike and Carol check into a swank ranch-style hotel, enduring the leers of the prissy hotel clerk, who notes they've booked the honeymoon suite. The clerk looks twice when Mike, from force of habit, signs the register "Mr. and Mrs. Michael Brady and family." "It's obvious this man doesn't understand the modern generation," cracks Mike.

In their room, Mike toasts Carol with some champagne.

"Here's to a great big, bubbly life together."

Carol: "Champagne makes me dizzy."

Mike: "It has a terrible effect on me, too."

Carol: "What?"

Mike: "You'll find out. . . ."

And they kiss.

Back at the Brady house with Alice, the kids are upset. The boys think only they—and not the girls—got yelled at because of their inability to control Tiger. The girls think the boys got preferential treatment.

Cut to the honeymoon suite, where the newlyweds are clearly not enjoying themselves. Mike hears his own angry voice, amplified in his head: "I told you to put that dog back in the car!" And, of course, so does Carol: "Girls! Stop that screaming!"

They both feel guilty and decide to head back to the house, with Mike leaving the hotel in his bathrobe. They go into the girls' room, wake them up, and ask if they'd like to come back with them. "I've never been on a honeymoon!" Cindy squeals. They go grab the boys, and the Bradys head back to the hotel en masse.

"If there's one thing that's better than a honeymoon for two," says a beaming Carol as they walk into the hotel, "it's a honeymoon for eight!"

"For nine," says Cindy, pointing to her doll.

"Ten," says Jan, indicating Fluffy.

"Twelve," says Alice, who shows up with Tiger.

The kids then argue about who should go up the staircase first—boys or girls? Oldest or youngest? How? Mike seizes command: "There's only one way to handle it: by size, and the biggest one goes first. Left foot first. . . ."

And all the Bradys begin marching up the stairs in military fashion as a martiallike version of *The Brady Bunch* theme is played. Fade out. One can only speculate where everybody found room to sleep.

GUEST STARS:
J. Pat O'Malley (*Mr. Tyler, Carol's father*)
Joan Tompkins (*Mrs. Tyler, Carol's mother*)
Dabbs Greer (*minister*)
James Millhollin (*Pringle, the hotel clerk*)

The beloved British character actor J(ames) Pat (trick) O'Malley (1901–85) is remembered in TV's annals not only as the father of Carol Brady, but also of Rob Petrie. Some of his most notable recurring roles were as Bert Beasley, who married housekeeper Mrs. Naugatuck on *Maude,* and as Tim O'Hara's boss on *My Favorite Martian.* Not long after this episode, he co-starred in the ABC sitcom *A Touch of Grace* (1973). Outside of television, his Irish and British brogues grace the animated Disney features *101 Dalmatians, Alice in Wonderland,* and *The Jungle Book.*

Joan Tompkins, who played Carol's mother, had played a notable TV mom before: that of Kate Miller (Tina Cole), who married Robbie Douglas (Don Grady) on *My Three Sons.* Dabbs Greer is familiar as storekeeper Mr. Jones on *Gunsmoke* from 1955–60, and later as track coach Ossie Weiss on *Hank* and Reverend Robert Alden on *Little House on the Prairie* and its sequels. Sitcom fans will also recognize him as Walt Gilroy, the father of Dobie-crazy Zelda on *The Many Loves of Dobie Gillis.* And James Millhollin had been a regular on the 1963–64 Imogene Coca series *Grindl.*

#1: *"Dear Libby"*
Written by Lois Hire. Directed by John Rich.
Original Airdate: October 3, 1969

Marcia reads an item in the "Dear Libby" advice column that describes a family exactly like theirs, in which one of the parents is extremely unhappy. Of course, she and the kids are sure that either Mike or Carol wrote the letter. And of course, we know that Mike or Carol would never do such a thing.

GUEST STAR:
Jo de Winter *(Libby)*

Like *Brady* theme composer Frank De Vol, scriptwriter Lois Hire was a veteran of *My Three Sons.* Jo de Winter went on to play Dr. Maggie Lawrence in the *All in the Family* spinoff *Gloria.*

#2: *"A Clubhouse Is Not a Home"*
Written by Skip Webster. Directed by John Rich.
Original Airdate: October 31, 1969

The boys are having a hard time adjusting to living with girls in their house. The difficulties reach a boiling point when the girls want to move into the

With guest Jo de Winter in "Dear Libby."

boys' backyard clubhouse. Mike agrees that the boys should have their own space, but eventually he changes his mind, in the spirit of sharing and family unity.

Fledgling TV scriptwriter Skip Webster would go on to write for *The Partridge Family, The Love Boat, Fantasy Island, Charlie's Angels,* and other lite shows, as well as the dramas *Matt Houston* and *The Rookies.*

#3: *"Kitty Karry-All Is Missing"*
Written by Al Schwartz and Bill Freedman. Directed by John Rich.
Original Airdate: November 7, 1969

Some heartless felon has stolen Kitty Karry-All, Cindy's favorite doll. Cindy suspects Bobby, who had angrily told her that he hoped her doll got lost.

Bobby didn't steal the doll, but he has his own problems, too: someone has stolen his kazoo. Even with that, Bobby does try to make amends by buying a new Kitty Karry-All for Cindy—but Cindy refuses to accept the present because it's not the real Kitty. Eventually, both items turn up—in Tiger's doghouse (which will prove to be the repository of many lost items in episodes to come). "You should be ashamed of yourself," Mike chastises Tiger.

GUEST STAR:
Pitt Herbert *(Mr. Driscoll)*

Al Schwartz is the older brother of *Brady* creator Sherwood Schwartz and, in fact, the guy who brought Sherwood into the business. Bill Freedman had written for *Run, Buddy, Run* and other shows. Pitt Herbert was a minor player in TV shows and such TV movies as *Victory at Entebbe* and *Cry Panic*.

#4: *"Katchoo"*
Written by William Cowley. Directed by John Rich.
Original Airdate: October 24, 1969

Oh no! Jan is sniffling and sneezing, so Carol keeps her home from school, thinking she has a cold. But when the sneezing continues, it becomes obvious that she's allergic to something. Is it Mike? Is it Tiger? And if it is Tiger, can the family deal with his being taken away? After each family member independently bathes Tiger, it's discovered that what Jan is allergic to is not Tiger, but Tiger's flea powder!

#5: *"Eenie, Meenie, Mommy, Daddy"*
Written by Joanna Lee. Directed by John Rich.
Original Airdate: October 10, 1969

Cindy is excited when she comes home with the announcement that she has been chosen to play the fairy princess in the school play. But her mocd sinks when she learns that she can only get one ticket. This begins an elaborate round of charades and soul-searching: Should she invite her mommy or her daddy. Finally, the teachers come to Cindy's rescue (as if the other kids didn't have the same dilemma!) and allow the entire Brady clan (including Alice) to attend a "special performance" of the play put on just for them.

GUEST STARS:
Marjorie Stapp (Mrs. Engstrom)
Tracy Reed (Miss Marlowe)
Brian Forster (elf)

Tracy Reed went on to co-star in the sitcom based on Neil Simon's *Barefoot in the Park* (ABC, 1970–71); she was also a repertory player on *Love American Style* and has been in numerous TV movies, including *Death of a Centerfold: The Dorothy Stratten Story* (along with unrelated *Brady* co-star Robert Reed). Brian Forster went on to succeed Jeremy Gelbwaks as Chris Partridge on *The Partridge Family*. Scripter Joanna Lee was one of Sherwood Schwartz's *Gilligan* veterans; her other credits are as diverse as *Gidget* and *The Waltons*.

#6: "Alice Doesn't Live Here Anymore"
Written by Paul West. Directed by John Rich.
Original Airdate: October 17, 1969

Despite the similarity in title to the 1975 Ellyn Burstyn–Kris Kristofferson movie, this episode is not about a divorcée finding herself. It's about what happens when Alice believes the Bradys no longer need her. She makes up an excuse about visiting a sick aunt in Seattle and announces she's leaving. The heartbroken Bradys concoct "Operation Alice," a scheme to keep her. After it works and Alice agrees to stay, she admits she knew about the scheme all along. That Alice, what a card!

GUEST STAR:
Fred Pinkard (Mr. Stokey)

Bringing the family sitcom up to the minute was Paul West, one of the main writers on *Father Knows Best*. He went on to script that series' two 1977 reunion specials.

#7: "Father of the Year"
Written by Skip Webster. Directed by George Cahan.
Original Airdate: January 2, 1970

After Mike shows Marcia how important she is to him, Marcia writes an essay for a newspaper's "Father of the Year" contest. But when she tries to hide what she's doing, Mike gets the wrong idea and grounds her from a family ski trip. All is forgiven when the newspaper photographers come to the Brady residence to present the award and Mike realizes why Marcia has been so secretive.

GUEST STARS:
Oliver McGowan *(Hamilton Samuels)*
Bill Mullikin *(Lance Pierce)*
Lee Corrigan *(photographer)*
Bob Golden *(Mr. Fields)*

George Cahan had directed for *Gilligan* and had served as producer on the 1966–67 sitcom *It's About Time,* for which Sherwood Schwartz was executive producer. Cahan's TV credits stretch all the way back to 1949, when he directed one of ABC's first shows, *The Ruggles*: a family sitcom with situations—like first-date adventures and getting in line for the bathroom in the morning—that eerily resemble the Bradys's.

#8: *"The Grass Is Always Greener"*
Written by David P. Harmon. Directed by George Cahan.
Original Airdate: March 13, 1970

Who has the harder job? Mike or Carol? The Bradys decide to settle this world-shaking argument by switching roles for one day. Mike tries to help the girls with cooking while Carol attempts to teach the boys how to play baseball. At episode's end, tired and sore, Mike and Carol realize that strictly defined sex roles are the only way to go.

Prolific scriptwriter David P. Harmon's early days in the business included *Gilligan's Island, Star Trek* ("A Piece of the Action," with Gene L. Coon; "The Deadly Years"), *Mr. Terrific, The Rifleman,* and other '60s shows. Later, in addition to writing for *All in the Family, Mannix, McCloud,* and other series, he had the distinction of scripting two of the three *Gilligan's Island* reunions.

Gender-bending in "The Grass Is Always Greener."

#9: "Sorry, Right Number"
Written by Ruth Brooks Flippen. Directed by George Cahan.
Original Airdate: November 21, 1969

Mounting phone bills and arguments over the use of the phone are driving Mike nuts. But after Alice sees a pay phone at Sam's butcher shop, she suggests that Mike install one at home. The first phone call is for a wrong number ("This is not O'Brien's Taco and Tamale Shop," Mike angrily tells the errant caller), but eventually things look like they might work out—*until* Mike loses an important business deal with a potential client, Mr. Crawford, because he doesn't have change for the pay phone! But the next day Mr. Crawford changes his mind and gives Mike the deal when he realizes how ingenious Mike is to have a pay phone at home. In fact, that old Mr. Crawford decides to install one in his own home!

GUEST STARS:
Allan Melvin *(Sam Franklin)*
Howard Culver *(Mr. Crawford)*

Allan Melvin makes the first of eight appearances as Sam the butcher, Alice's occasionally seen beau. One of the great everyman character actors, he was a regular on *The Phil Silvers Show* (as the immortal Corporal Henshaw) and a recurring player both on *Gomer Pyle, USMC* (as Sergeant Hacker) and *All in the Family/Archie Bunker's Place* (as Barney Hefner). He was also one of two actors to play Rob Petrie's army buddy Sol Pomeroy on *The Dick Van Dyke Show,* and has done countless cartoon voice-overs—most famously as Magilla Gorilla. Initial *Brady* director John Rich had suggested him for the role.

Howard Culver (1918–75) played hotel clerk Howie throughout *Gunsmoke*'s entire twenty-year run. Scriptwriter Ruth Brooks Flippen had written for *Bewitched, The Ghost and Mrs. Muir, Gidget,* and *My World ... And Welcome to It.*

#10: "Is There a Doctor in the House?"
Written by Ruth Brooks Flippen. Directed by Oscar Rudolph.
Original Airdate: December 26, 1969

Another battle of the sexes occurs when the kids come down with the measles. Peter is the first to break out, and Mike calls his family doctor—a man. When Jan succumbs, Carol calls her family doctor—a woman. But when the others also become sick, which doctor should the family call? The boys don't want to be treated by a woman, and the girls don't want to be treated by a man. The typically Solomonic (or Bradyic) answer: The girls will stick with the woman MD, the boys with the male. But no feelings are bruised since both doctors have suddenly decided to combine their practices!

GUEST STARS:
Marion Ross *(Dr. Porter)*
Herbert Anderson *(Dr. Cameron)*

This episode is full of famous TV parents: Herbert Anderson was Dennis's father on *Dennis the Menace,* while Marion Ross would go on to play Richie Cunningham's mom on *Happy Days.* This episode is the also the first of twenty-nine directed by that most prolific of *Brady* helmers, Oscar Rudolph—the father of movie director Alan Rudolph and a veteran TV director of everything from *Batman* to *All in the Family.*

#11:   "54–40 and Fight"
Written by Burt Styler. Directed by Oscar Rudolph.
Original Airdate: January 9, 1970

When they learn that the trading-stamp company is going out of business, the Bradys battle over what to do with their stamps. The problem is that the boys have forty books and the girls have fifty-four. Only by combining books can they get one really great premium. The boys want a rowboat, the girls want a sewing machine. To settle the dispute, Mike and Carol make the kids play a game in which each kid builds a house of playing cards; the one whose card causes the house to collapse loses. As Greg is gingerly placing his card, Tiger bumps into him and the cards topple. So the girls win by default. But when they go to the store, they change their mind about getting a girlish present and they buy something the entire family can use: a color TV set.

GUEST STAR:
Herb Vigran *(Harry)*

Lovable Herb Vigran (1910–86) was one of TV's best and most ubiquitous character actors. Anybody who didn't grow up watching him play natty comic crooks on *The Adventures of Superman* and elsewhere just didn't grow up right. This was the first of his two *Brady* appearances.

An eerie promotional still from "54-40 and Fight."

#12: "A-Camping We Will Go"
Written by Herbert Finn and Alan Dinehart. Directed by Oscar Rudolph.
Original Airdate: November 14, 1969

In a ploy to bring the boys and girls closer together, Mike and Carol plan a family camping trip. The girls have never been on one, and naturally, the boys don't want them along. But off they go, with Alice in ranger garb. Of course, the usual series of Bradys mishaps occur: no one can catch any fish, the girls get scared of strange noises, Alice's hair curlers puncture her air mattress. When Jan and Cindy scare Bobby by making hand shadows that look like a bear, all the men rush out of their tent into the women's, causing it to collapse. But the trip turns out to be a success, even though Carol admits that "togetherness can be exhausting."

Herbert Finn and Alan Dinehart had written for Sherwood Schwartz's *Gilligan's Island* and *It's About Time*. More significantly, Finn was one of the staff writers of no less than that 1950s TV classic *The Honeymooners*.

#13: *"Vote for Brady"*
Written by Elroy Schwartz. Directed by David Alexander.
Original Airdate: December 12, 1969

Greg and Marcia run against each other for student-body president. Mike and Carol profess their neutrality, but the kids take sides, leading the parents to lecture them on the value of family unity. In the end, Marcia graciously withdraws, deferring to the older Greg's experience.

GUEST STARS:
Martin Ashe *(Mr. Dickens)*
Stephen Liss *(Rusty)*
Casey Morgan *(Scott)*

Elroy Schwartz is, not surprisingly, Sherwood Schwartz's brother; Elroy's son Douglas would produce NBC's 1989 series *Baywatch*. David Alexander has directed for *Star Trek* ("The Way to Eden") and a myriad of '60s sitcoms such as *F Troop* and *My Favorite Martian*. Guest Martin Ashe went on to appear in *Rescue from Gilligan's Island*.

#14: *"Every Boy Does It Once"*
Written by Lois and Arnold Peyser. Directed by Oscar Rudolph.
Original Airdate: December 5, 1969

The overly sensitive Bobby thinks the world is out to get him. He has to wear hand-me-downs; he thinks he has an evil stepmother (after having watched *Cinderella* on TV), and he gets paranoid when his stepsiblings don't include him in their plans and leave him home. His solution is to run away. As Bobby is lugging his suitcase down the stairs, Mike tries some reverse psychology. He encourages him to run away, but makes him wonder about how he will support himself. That gives Bobby some food for thought and he decides to stay home. Sigmund Freud's got nothing on Mike Brady!

GUEST STARS:
Larry McCormick *(TV announcer)*
Michael Lerner *(Johnny)*

Larry McCormick later played Marla Gibbs's boyfriend, Buzz Thatcher, on *The Jeffersons*. Co-writers Lois and Arnold Peyser had written for *Gilligan's Island,* among other shows.

Shopping for Bobby's bike in "Every Boy Does It Once."

#15: *"The Voice of Christmas"*
Written by John Fenton Murray. Directed by Oscar Rudolph.
Original Airdate: December 19, 1969 (rerun December 25, 1970)

The classic *Brady Bunch* holiday episode. It's the day before Christmas and the Bradys are wrapping their presents. But the good vibes are shattered when Carol comes home and announces in a whisper that she can't talk—which means she won't be able to sing with the church choir on Christmas unless a miracle occurs. She and Mike hug each other, sadly.

Mike phones the doctor, who informs him that Carol has laryngitis and that the only thing that may cure her is complete rest and quiet. Carol panics since there's so much to do to prepare for Christmas, but Mike tries to ease her worries. The boys come home with the tree, but they're saddened when they learn about their mom. Not to worry, Alice tells them, she'll cure Carol's laryngitis by having her wear a towel that has been soaked in an old family recipe (mustard, oil of camphor, vinegar, and pepper). Carol reluctantly agrees to wear this concoction, and when Mike kisses her good-bye, he holds his nose.

Mike takes Cindy to the department store to see Santa. Instead of asking for a present, Cindy asks Santa to "give my mommy her voice back." Santa realizes he might not be able to, but taken in by Cindy's selflessness and charm, he says he will cure Carol.

When Cindy tells Mike, he's less than pleased. "He's not a doctor," Mike admonishes Cindy. "He's better than a doctor!" Cindy cheerfully replies. "He's Santa Claus!"

Trying to make Cindy realize the cruel hard facts of the world, Mike tells her that she shouldn't expect a miracle. And Cindy—ever the logician—responds that she wasn't looking for a miracle, she just wants Mommy to get her voice back.

It's now Christmas Eve at the Brady residence, and Greg sneaks downstairs to look at his present. Soon, the other kids join him. They're all bummed ("Some Christmas! It's no fun this year") and think maybe they should cancel Christmas until Carol gets better. Awakened by the racket, Alice comes out of her room and tells the kids that their mother would be disappointed if they canceled Christmas. The kids realize that Alice is right and she shoos them back to bed.

Meanwhile, in Mike and Carol's bedroom, Carol is humming "O Come, All Ye Faithful" in her sleep, which wakes up Mike, who realizes she's gotten her voice back. Cut to the next morning at church, where Carol sings a lovely solo of the same song.

The next day, Cindy writes a thank-you letter to Santa. Mike now appreciates Santa and tells Cindy: "You were right, sweetie. Christmas is the season for miracles!"

GUEST STARS:
Hal Smith *(Santa)*
Carl Albert *(little boy)*

Hal Smith is best known for playing Otis the drunk on *The Andy Griffith Show*. Which would explain the red nose.

#16: *"Mike's Horror-Scope"*
Written by Ruth Brooks Flippen. Directed by Oscar Rudolph.
Original Airdate: January 16, 1970

Carol reads Mike's horoscope, which claims a strange woman will come into his life. Mike pooh-poohs the notion, until glamorous cosmetics heir Beebe Gallini shows up to hire him to design a new factory.

GUEST STARS:
Abbe Lane *(Beebe Gallini)*
Joe Ross *(Duane Cartwright)*

Old-timers will remember Abbe Lane as the songstress first wife of Latin bandleader Xavier Cugat. And in case there's any doubt, guest Joe Ross is definitely not *Car 54*'s Joe E. Ross.

#17: *"The Undergraduate"*
Written by David P. Harmon. Directed by Oscar Rudolph.
Original Airdate: January 23, 1970

Greg appears to be sick, but he's actually lovesick, as Alice discovers when she finds a love note to a mysterious "Linda." Mike and Carol are surprised to find out that Linda is not a teenager by that name, but Greg's teacher, Linda O'Hara. Greg gets set straight when he meets Linda's boyfriend—played by Los Angeles Dodgers first baseman Wes Parker as himself.

OTHER GUEST STARS:
Gigi Perreau *(Miss O'Hara)*
Teresa Warder *(Linda)*

Ironically, guest Gigi Perreau was sort of a grown-up *Brady* girl—a popular child actress of the 1940s and '50s whose adult career was much less distinguished. Born Ghislaine Elizabeth Mariet Thérèse Perreau-Saussine in 1941, her films include *Madame Curie* (1943), *Mr. Skeffington* (1944), and *Bonzo Goes to College* (1952).

#18: *"To Move or Not to Move"*
Written by Paul West. Directed by Oscar Rudolph.
Original Airdate: March 6, 1970

The children have been moaning to Mike and Carol that the house is too small, so Mike decides to sell. But then the kids realize their attachment is too strong, and so to scare off prospective buyers and change Mike's mind, they make it seem as if the house is haunted. When a house hunter shows up, so do two ghosts—actually Bobby and Cindy in sheets. When Mike sees the extreme measures the kids have been taking, he realizes he can never sell.

GUEST STARS:
Fran Ryan *(Mrs. Hunsaker)*
Lindsay Workman *(Bertram Grossmann)*

Fran Ryan is one of the most familiar faces on television, having played everything from the original Doris Ziffel on *Green Acres* to Miss Kitty's successor, Miss Hannah, on the last season of *Gunsmoke*. Her most recent regular cast role was as Tillie Russell in the adventure series *The Wizard* (CBS, 1986–87).

#19: *"Tiger! Tiger!"*
Written by Elroy Schwartz. Directed by Herb Wallerstein.
Original Airdate: January 30, 1970

Where is Tiger? When Bobby goes out to feed the family dog, he can't find him. The family chips in $42.76 for a reward and they even buy a lost-dog ad in the newspaper. Mike and Carol suspect that perhaps a gang of robbers lured Tiger away in order to burglarize the Brady residence. So Greg sets up an antiburglar booby trap, but the only person it catches is Alice. After several false leads, Greg gets a call from a friend that Tiger has been spotted in the neighborhood. This sets the Bradys off on a search-and-find mission that would do a SWAT team proud: by car and bicycle, they fan out on neighborhood streets, keeping each other abreast of Tiger's whereabouts by telephone. (A little snatch of the *Dragnet* theme is heard here on the soundtrack.) Each time, Tiger manages to elude the manhunt—er, doghunt. Finally, Peter calls, announcing he has found him—safe and sound.

GUEST STARS:
Maggie Malooly *(Mrs. Simpson)*
Gary Grimes *(teenage boy)*

Maggie Malooly played Robert Young's housekeeper on the short-lived series *Little Women* (NBC, 1979), which co-starred Eve Plumb. Gary Grimes later appeared as Jack Devlin in the military mini-series *Once an Eagle* (NBC, 1976–77). Herb Wallerstein, turning in his only *Brady* assignment, has directed everything from *Happy Days* to *Star Trek* ("That Which Survives," "Whom Gods Destroy," and the final episode, "Turnabout Intruder").

#20: "Brace Yourself"
Written by Brad Radnitz. Directed by Oscar Rudolph.
Original Airdate: February 13, 1970

Marcia is devastated when she learns she has to wear braces. Even though her family assures her she still looks pretty, she becomes even more upset when Alan, a boy who was going to ask her to the school dance, cancels on her. She assumes it was because of the braces. To make her feel better, Greg, Alice, and her parents try to con three other boys to take her to the dance. All three show up at the Brady residence at the same time—as does Alan!

GUEST STARS:
Molly Dodd *(saleslady)*
John Daniels *(Eddie)*
Jerry Levreau *(Harold)*
Mike Robertson *(Craig)*
Brian Nash *(Joey)*

The late Molly Dodd—no relation to the Blair Brown TV series—had previously appeared as George Baxter's secretary, Miss Scott, on *Hazel*. Later in the *Brady* canon, she played the bitchy neighbor on the episode/pilot "Kelly's Kids." And in another one of those darn weird-name coincidences, Brian Nash had played Joel Nash, one of the kids on the NBC sitcom *Please Don't Eat the Daisies*.

#21: *"The Big Sprain"*
Written by Tam Spiva. Directed by Russ Mayberry.
Original Airdate: February 6, 1970

A really intense crisis hits the Brady household when Carol goes out of town to care for her ailing aunt Mary, and Alice sprains her ankle when she trips over the kids' Chinese checkers. (An angry Mike informs them, "Leaving them on the floor is a strict violation of family policy!") Mike tries to salvage the situation by dividing the household chores among the kids—even though the girls can't cook and the boys can't clean. Meanwhile, the injured Alice is upset that she won't be able to go with her boyfriend Sam the butcher to the Meatcutters' Ball on Saturday night. The kids feel they're responsible. But everything turns out okay, of course.

GUEST STAR:
Allan Melvin *(Sam Franklin)*

Allan Melvin makes his second appearance as Sam the butcher. Making their *Brady* debuts are series story editor Tam Spiva on the script, and director Russ Mayberry, who would go on to to become a prolific helmer of TV movies (*The $5.20 an Hour Dream, The Fall Guy,* etc.) and mini-series (*Seventh Avenue, The Rebels*).

#22: *"The Hero"*
Written by Elroy Schwartz. Directed by Oscar Rudolph.
Original Airdate: February 20, 1970

While shopping in a toy store, Peter sees a wall about to fall on a young girl. He rushes over, pushes her out of the way as the wall tumbles down. The girl's mother calls the local newspaper, which prints a story about Peter's heroic act. As a result, Peter's head swells, which turns off his brothers and sisters. When Peter decides to throw a party with the fifty dollars he won for receiving the newspaper's "Outstanding Citizen" award, his friends and siblings refuse to attend.

GUEST STARS:
Pitt Herbert *(Mr. Driscoll)*
Dani Nolan *(Mrs. Spencer)*
Dave Morick *(Earl Hopkins)*
Joe Conley *(deliveryman)*
Randy Lane *(Steve)*

Iler Rasmussen *(Jason)*
Susan Joyce *(Jennifer)*
Melanie Baker *(Tina Spencer)*

Guest Joe Conley played general-store owner Ike Godsey in *The Waltons* for nine years plus three TV-movie reunions. Pitt Herbert had also appeared as Mr. Driscoll in episode #3, "Kitty Karry-All Is Missing." The rest, sad to say, don't even qualify for "Where are they now?"

#23: "Lost Locket, Found Locket"
Written by Charles Hoffman. Directed by Norman Abbott.
Original Airdate: March 20, 1970

Feeling depressed, Jan has her spirits lifted when she receives a locket in the mail with no note attached. The only clue is that the "y" on the typed address is crooked. That sends Mike and Carol hunting for the broken type-writer, which will prove the sender's identity. Later on, Jan loses the locket and gets briefly hysterical, but she calms down when she realizes it fell out the window when she was gazing at the Little Bear constellation. And when all is said and done, it's revealed that Alice sent the locket.

GUEST STAR:
Jack Griffin *(guard)*

Director Norman Abbott has directed a zillion TV shows, including a host of Bob Hope and Jack Benny specials and the first *Father Knows Best* TV-movie reunion.

#24: "The Possible Dream"
Written by Al Schwartz and Bill Freedman. Directed by Oscar Rudolph.
Original Airdate: February 27, 1970

Cindy accidentally gives away Marcia's diary—the book that contains Marcia's confession of her secret crush on Desi Arnaz, Jr. Marcia responds by ignoring Cindy, while Mike and Carol search used-book stores. Desi Jr. saves the day by showing up at the Brady residence.

OTHER GUEST STARS:
Gordon Jump *(Collins)*

Pat Petterson *(friendly handyman)*
Jonathan Hole *(Thackery)*

It may be hard now to see what all the hubbub was about, but Desi Arnaz, Jr., was quite the teen idol at the time. TV's most celebrated baby, he is the son of Lucille Ball and Desi Arnaz; his newborn photo graced the cover of *TV Guide*'s premier issue. By the time of his *Brady* appearance, he'd just broken up his bubblegum-pop band Dino, Desi & Billy ("I'm a Fool," "Not the Lovin' Kind," both top-25 in 1965). Later on, Desi and Dino—Dean Martin's son—would form part of the (one hopes ironically titled) Beverly Hills Blues Band. Desi Jr. went on to do a few TV movies, and as late as 1983–84 was starring in his own series, *Automan*.

Gordon Jump, making his first of two appearances, would gain fame as radio station manager Arthur Carlson of *WKRP in Cincinnati*. A cuddly character actor who once played against type as a child molester in an episode of *Diff'rent Strokes*, he's since succeeded the venerable Jesse White in the Whirlpool appliance commercials—going from *WKRP*'s "big guy" to Whirlpool's "lonely guy." And Jonathan Hole had been a TV performer at least as far back as 1950, when he was a regular on author Studs Terkel's anecdotal show *Studs' Place*.

#25: "Going, Going . . . Steady"
Written by David P. Harmon. Directed by Oscar Rudolph.
Original Airdate: October 23, 1970

Marcia goes steady for the first time with Harvey Klinger, a boy whose hobby is collecting bugs. Marcia is so buggy about landing Harvey that she spends most of her spare time reading up on insects. Mike and Carol don't approve of thirteen-year-old Marcia going steady, even though Marcia claims that today's thirteen-year-old girl is more like a twenty-year-old, and a thirteen-year-old boy is more like twenty-two. Hearing this, Mike asks Harvey over for a man-to-man talk about his future plans. That scares the young couple and they stop going steady. But that doesn't stop boy-hungry Marcia: at episode's end, she has a new steady—Lester.

GUEST STARS:
Billy Corcoran *(Harvey)*
Rory Stevens *(Lester)*

Whatever became of Harvey the bug boy? Billy Corcoran's acting career seems to have faded after that. Rory Stevens at least went on to the 1977 NBC sitcom pilot *Hollywood High*, starring *Designing Women*'s Annie Potts.

#26: "The Dropout"
Written by Bill Freedman and Ben Gershman. Directed by Peter Baldwin.
Original Airdate: September 25, 1970

Don Drysdale, the Los Angeles Dodgers pitcher, then in the twilight of his career, guest-starred in this second-season debut episode. Mike is designing Drysdale's new home ("Baseball's been real good to me," the pitcher notes, anticipating Chico Escuela of *Saturday Night Live*), and Mike mentions that Greg would love to meet him. Drysdale encourages Greg's pitching and makes a chance remark that someday Greg might be a bonus baby for the Dodgers. Buoyed by these compliments, Greg becomes obsessed with baseball (memorizing important dates in baseball history) and his grades slip. He then shocks his parents by telling them that he's planning to quit school and pursue a big-league career. When Mike and Carol can't convince him to change his mind, Mike persuades Drysdale to paint a bleak picture of what a baseball player's life is really like. That revelation, plus the shelling Greg gets when he pitches in his Pony League game, is enough to get him to reconsider.

Acclaimed sitcom director Peter Baldwin wasn't the most regular *Brady* helmer—that would be Oscar Rudolph, hands down—but he has certainly been the most enduring: so far, Baldwin has directed both *Brady* TV movies, and episodes of 1990s *The Bradys*. He was Emmy-nominated for directing an episode of *The Mary Tyler Moore Show* and won a 1988–89 Emmy for comedy directing, for the "Our Miss White" episode of *The Wonder Years*.

#27: "The Babysitters"
Written by Bruce Howard. Directed by Oscar Rudolph.
Original Airdate: October 2, 1970

Mike surprises Carol with tickets to a hit play, but they might be forced to cancel their plans when they can't find a baby-sitter. Marcia and Greg argue that they're old enough to sit for their younger siblings. Mike and Carol reluctantly agree, after explaining to the kids how to look out for danger. The younger Bradys, however, are less than pleased; Mike and Carol can't enjoy the evening because they're consumed by worry.

GUEST STARS:
Gil Stuart *(restaurant captain)*
Jerry Jones *(officer number one)*

Writer Bruce Howard was yet another veteran of *Gilligan's Island*. He wrote the episode where they almost get rescued but Gilligan fouls it up.

#28: *"The Treasure of Sierra Avenue"*
Written by Gwen Bagni and Paul Dubov. Directed by Oscar Rudolph.
Original Airdate: November 6, 1970

Bobby finds $1,100 while playing football. But the instant tycoon, gender-loyal as always, decides to share the loot with just his brothers. The girls want their share, too, but the boys refuse and the girls respond by giving the boys the silent treatment. After Mike lectures them, they agree to split the money six ways. Just as the kids start acting as if the money was theirs to keep, the rightful owner, an old man named Mr. Stoner, responds to Mike's ad.

GUEST STARS:
Victor Kilian *(Mr. Stoner)*

Guest star Victor Kilian would best be known for playing Raymond Larkin, Mary Hartman's grandfather, and the so-called Fernwood Flasher on the syndicated '70s soap-opera parody, *Mary Hartman, Mary Hartman*. Co-writers Gwen Bagni and Paul Dubov would be Emmy-nominated several years later, for, of all things, the NBC dramatic mini-series *Backstairs at the White House*.

#29: *"The Un-Underground Movie"*
Written by Albert E. Lewin. Directed by Jack Arnold.
Original Airdate: October 16, 1970

As a history project, Greg decides to make a home movie about the Pilgrims, entitled *Our Pilgrim Fathers*. He wants to cast the whole Brady family, but the kids quibble about the roles they want to play. Greg, an "auteur," demands total control of the project, including casting. And he gets it. The film is a success, getting two thumbs-up from Mike and Carol. Coolest casting: Alice with a fake beard and mustache as Massachusetts Governor John Carver.

Jack Arnold, who would direct fifteen episodes of *The Brady Bunch,* was one of the 1950s' B-movie greats. Among his cult-classic, mostly horror and sci-fi films: *It Came from Outer Space* (1953), *The Creature from the Black*

Lagoon (1954), *Revenge of the Creature* (1955), *The Incredible Shrinking Man* (1957), and *High School Confidential* (1958). He also wowed critics as director of, believe it or not, the *British* comedy classic *The Mouse That Roared* (1959).

#30: *"The Slumber Caper"*
Written by Tam Spiva. Directed by Oscar Rudolph.
Original Airdate: October 9, 1970

You might call this the ultimate family episode on the ultimate family program. Three of Marcia's friends are played by the children of key Brady personnel: Karen is Carolyn Reed (daughter of Robert), Ruthie is Barbara Henderson (daughter of Florence; she'd be billed in later episodes as Barbara Bernstein, using Florence's married name), and Jenny is Hope Sherwood (daughter of Sherwood Schwartz). And there was a TV reunion as well: Marcia's principal, Mr. Randolph, was played by E. G. Marshall, who played Reed's lawyer-dad for so many years on *The Defenders*.

Mike and Carol are weighing whether Marcia should have a slumber party at the Brady residence. Mike finally agrees, noting with sagacity that "if Rome can outlast an invasion by the barbarians, what can a few little girls do to the Brady house?" Greg is not amused ("We're gonna be invaded by girls!"), so he and his brothers plan to counterattack by putting itching powder in the sleeping bags and dressing up like ghosts. Oh, those guys!

But there's trouble in Bradyland. Marcia has been summoned to the principal's office, where he confronts her with a scrawled cartoon of Mrs. Denton, Marcia's teacher, under which someone has written "Mrs. Denton: a hippopotamus." Marcia protests her innocence—even though her name is on the drawing, she says she was doodling a picture of George Washington and someone else had written the nasty remark. Old Mr. Randolph is unyielding and unbelieving: he says Marcia must stay after school for a week.

And he calls her parents. The Bradys don't cotton to budding juvenile delinquents, so Carol cancels the slumber party. But Mike, after talking with the principal, decides that Marcia might be telling the truth and he allows the party. Marcia deduces that her friend Jenny did the nasty deed and she promptly disinvites her.

At the slumber party, the girls are screaming, giggling, playing truth-or-dare. But things turn chaotic when the boys launch their attack: The girls scream when they see the ghosts and start scratching like mad because of the itching powder. During the confusion, Marcia's friend Paula innocently lets on that she wrote the insult and says she meant no harm.

When Mike and Carol arrive home, Marcia tells them the news, and the terrible thing she did to Jenny. Carol chastises her: "You were blamed for something because it seems somebody didn't have all the facts, and you turned around and did the same thing to Jenny." Marcia reinvites Jenny, and at episode's end, when she and Paula tell the principal, he forgives her. Marcia's permanent record is clear once more.

OTHER GUEST STAR:
Chris Charney *(Paula)*

One of the series' classics. As Lloyd Schwartz recalls, "I never realized the impact of our show until the night after the slumber-party episode. I was living alone in Hollywood, and I went to a coffee shop for breakfast. It's Saturday morning, and at the next table was a family with a bunch of kids. And one of them said somebody was going to have a slumber party the next day, and the boys sitting at the table said, 'Let's really screw it up like they did on *The Brady Bunch* last night!' I said to myself, 'Ohmigod! This probably isn't an isolated incident.' You think, Oh no!" he says, laughing. "What've we done?" Indeed.

Lloyd's sister, Hope, wound up on the show, recalls dad Sherwood, because "it just so happened that Bob Reed and Florence Henderson and I all had daughters the same age as Marcia. So I said, this might be a good publicity gimmick, to get them all into that show. And it turned out to be. [Hope] liked it and she wanted to be an actress, and so she became Rachel, an on-and-off girlfriend of Greg's." She remained in show business, and today, known under her married name of Hope Juber, she performs with a satiric comedy trio, the Housewives.

#31: *"Confessions, Confessions"*
Written by Brad Radnitz. Directed by Russ Mayberry.
Original Airdate: December 18, 1970

Peter is bummed: he's sure his weekend camping trip will be canceled when he breaks his mother's favorite vase. Greg and the others decide to cover for him, but Mike and Carol hear too many confessions and they suspect something is up.

GUEST STAR:
Snag Werris *(hardware man)*

Snag Werris was an old-time TV comedy writer (*The Jack Carter Show, Show Biz*) who also occasionally acted. He made three *Brady* appearances.

#32: "The Tattletale"
Written by Sam Locke and Milton Pascal. Directed by Russ Mayberry.
Original Airdate: December 4, 1970

Cindy angers her siblings when she rats on them to Mike and Carol. The troubles get deeper when she causes Alice to have a fight with her boyfriend Sam the butcher because of something Cindy said.

This was the first of five episodes by the Locke-Pascal writing team. Sam Locke was a *Gilligan* veteran; Milton Pascal had written for *Please Don't Eat the Daisies* and other shows.

#33: "Call Me Irresponsible"
Written by Bruce Howard. Directed by Bill Cooper.
Original Airdate: October 30, 1970

Greg knows how to plan for the future and he knows he'll be a red-blooded teenager real soon. And any red-blooded teenager needs a car. So he announces his plans to own a car in two years, but starts asking his brothers and sisters for gas money in advance. To pay for his car, Mike gives Greg a job as a part-time office boy working at his architectural firm—but on the first day on the job, Greg loses the important designs he is supposed to deliver, and is fired. After Mike intercedes, Greg is re-hired, and loses the plans *again*! But this time he has the resourcefulness to track them down and prove to Mike that he's a responsible young man.

GUEST STARS:
Jack Collins *(Mr. Phillips)*
Annette Ferra *(Randy)*
Barbara Morrison *(drama coach)*
Gordon Jump *(mechanic)*
Bob Peoples *(Mr. Peterson)*

Jack Collins, making the first of three appearances as Mike's boss, Harry Phillips, had previously co-starred as the boss on the 1966–67 NBC sitcom *Occasional Wife*. He was an old TV hand, having been a regular on *The Milton Berle Show* from 1953–55. Barbara Morrison went on to the 1976 NBC mini-series *Captains and the Kings*. And the always-welcome Gordon Jump was back. Writer Bruce Howard scripted for *Gilligan, The Flying Nun, It's About Time, The Dukes of Hazzard,* and other distinguished programs.

#34: *"The Impractical Joker"*
Written by Burt Styler. Directed by Oscar Rudolph.
Original Airdate: January 1, 1971

Jan never struck us as a wild and crazy gal but in this episode she emerges as a practical joker, pulling stunts like fake ink stains on Alice's dress and scaring her sisters with rubber spiders. But she goes too far when she takes Greg's pet mouse Myron and hides him in the hamper. The mouse wriggles out, setting the Bradys on a mad chase for him—one step ahead of the exterminator, whom Alice has hired to get rid of the mouse she saw. When they can't find Myron, the kids think he's been done in by the exterminator. But lo and behold, Myron is alive and hiding in that typical Brady inner sanctum, the home of all lost items: Tiger's doghouse.

GUEST STAR:
Lennie Bremen *(the exterminator)*

Lennie Bremen had the distinction of appearing in a 1957 sitcom pilot called *It's a Small World,* a.k.a. *Wally and the Beaver.* Guess what show it launched? The same year, Lennie played a youngster on a pilot called *New Girl in His Life,* a.k.a. *Uncle Bentley,* which sold the John Forsythe series *Bachelor Father.* Scripter Burt Styler has written for everything from *The Flying Nun* to *M*A*S*H,* including the 1979–80 sitcom *Joe's World,* in which Chris Knight co-starred.

#35: *"A Fistful of Reasons"*
Written by Tam Spiva. Directed by Oscar Rudolph.
Original Airdate: November 13, 1970

Peter comes home with a black eye he received after being goaded into a fight by noted bully Buddy Hinton. The fight was caused by Buddy making fun of Cindy's lisp. At first Mike suggests that Peter reason with the bully, but after Peter tries that tactic, he gets belted again. When Mike and Carol try unsuccessfully to persuade Buddy's parents to stop their son, Mike reluctantly concludes that sometimes fighting is the only answer. The family helps Peter learn how to box; and the next time he runs into Buddy, Peter floats like a butterfly and stings like a bee, and knocks out Buddy's front tooth. The result is that because of the gap in his teeth, Buddy now sounds like Cindy!

GUEST STARS:
Russell Schulman *(Buddy Hinton)*
Paul Sorenson *(Mr. Hinton)*
Ceil Cabot *(Mrs. Hinton)*

Ah, the ever-malevolent Buddy Hinton! Russell Schulman, like the actor who played Harvey the bug boy, seems to have vanished into TV history. So did Paul Sorenson, who played Mr. Hinton. (Maybe Mike Brady hired a hit man?) Ceil Cabot fared a little better, continuing to act into the '80s, and playing Mrs. Barish, the baby-sitter, on the unfortunate *Columbo* spinoff, *Kate Loves a Mystery* (NBC, 1979).

#36: *"What Goes Up . . ."*
Written by William Raynor and Myles Wilder. Directed by Leslie H. Martinson.
Original Airdate: December 11, 1970

Bobby is self-conscious about his height, and in this episode at least, he's also scared of heights. Peter gets the other guys to let Bobby join his tree-house club. But then Bobby falls and sprains his ankle (a typical Brady ailment) and is afraid to climb again. But it turns out Bobby's fear is psychosomatic when he climbs a tree to rescue his pet parakeet.

GUEST STARS:
Jimmy Bracken *(Jimmy)*
Sean Kelly *(Tim)*
Brian Tochi *(Tommy)*

Brian Tochi went on to play the Crown Prince Chulolongkorn in the Yul Brynner sitcom (!) *Anna and the King* (CBS, 1972). He also went on to do voice-overs for Saturday-morning cartoons. Writers Raynor and Wilder wrote together on *McHale's Navy, Bachelor Father, The Dukes of Hazzard,* and other shows. And bowing in with the first of his six episodes is Leslie H. Martinson—none other than the director of the movie *Batman* . . . the good old 1966 version. That, much more so than *Hot Rod Girl* (1956), *Hot Rod Rumble* (1957), or even *Lad: A Dog* (1961) and *PT 109* (1963), assures that his name will live forever.

#37: "Coming Out Party"
Written by David P. Harmon. Directed by Oscar Rudolph.
Original Airdate: January 29, 1971

Mike's immediate boss, Mr. Phillips, has invited all the Bradys on a fishing trip on his boat. Wouldn't you know that Cindy gets tonsillitis and has to go to the hospital? And wouldn't you know that when the doctor examines Carol, it turns out she, too, needs her tonsils removed. Fortunately, both recover in time for a rescheduled fishing trip (after a typical Brady mix-up), and the only bad result is a little seasickness.

GUEST STARS:
John Howard *(Dr. Howard)*
Jack Collins *(Harry Phillips)*

Jack Collins makes his second appearance as Mike's boss, Harry Phillips. John Howard later reprised his role as a doctor in the classic Marcia episode "Today I Am a Freshman" (#75).

#38: "The Not-So-Ugly Duckling"
Written by Paul West. Directed by Irving Moore.
Original Airdate: November 20, 1970

Jan has her first crush: a groovy guy named Clark Tyson. But Clark likes older chicks, i.e. Marcia. Jan is crestfallen and doesn't understand why; she thinks it might be her freckles that are turning Clark off. To make him jealous and also prove to her family that she's popular, Jan makes up an imaginary boyfriend named George Glass. But eventually she learns that the problem wasn't her freckles, but the fact she dresses like a tomboy, not a young woman. So Jan dresses up and wows Clark, who barely recognizes her.

GUEST STAR:
Mark Gruner *(Clark Tyson)*

#39: *"Tell It Like It Is"*
Written by Charles Hoffman. Directed by Terry Becker.
Original Airdate: March 26, 1971

Carol has been staying up late alone at night, and the family members wonder what she's been doing. It turns out she's embarking on a career as a free-lance writer and is secretly writing a story about her extended family for *Tomorrow's Woman* magazine. Her realistic first effort is rejected as un-believable, but her Pollyanna-ish rewrite scores a hit. But when the editors and a photographer come to the Brady residence to shoot pictures, they find a household totally in disarray. One of the editors sniffs that this is nothing like the story and urges that the article be rejected again. But the editor, now a little wiser, realizes that the first version was the truth after all.

GUEST STARS:
Richard Simmons *(Mr. Delafield, the chief editor)*
Jonathan Hole *(Willie Witherspoon, the photographer)*
Nora Maynard *(Elaine Swann, the haughty editor)*

No, old adventure fans, your eyes aren't deceiving you. That *is* Sergeant Preston of the Yukon, Richard Simmons, playing the magazine editor. He had mushed across Canada and into our hearts and living rooms via CBS from 1955–58.

#40: *"The Drummer Boy"*
Written by Tom and Helen August. Directed by Oscar Rudolph.
Original Airdate: January 22, 1971

Peter's football buddies are getting on his case because he also belongs to the glee club, which they say is for sissies. Peter decides to quit the glee club. But his fate changes the next day at football practice when the Los Angeles Rams' massive defensive end David "Deacon" Jones comes to watch (he's a friend of the coach—sure!). When he sees Peter looking de-pressed, he's curious, and when he finds out why, he's furious. "I sing," he tells the other young gridders, "and am I a sissy? . . . If singing were sissy stuff, we'd be missing a lot of good men in sports." And the coach adds: "Rosie Grier sings and I don't know anyone brave enough to call him a sissy." "Not even me," adds Deacon. The point is made: Pete's no sissy; he remains with both the glee club and the football team.

The episode's title actually reflects a subplot: since Bobby, unlike Peter, failed to make the glee club, his parents decide he should learn an instrument.

He chooses the drums and proceeds to drive all the Bradys and the neighbors crazy when he becomes a pint-sized Keith Moon. At the end of the episode, Bobby decides he'd rather learn to play the trumpet; he wakes up the entire household playing reveille at 5:00 A.M.

OTHER GUEST STARS:
Bart La Rue *(Coach)*
Jimmy Bracken *(Larry)*
Dennis McDougall *(Freddy)*
Pierre Williams *(Jimmy)*

Bart La Rue returned as the coach in episode #60, "Click."

#41: *"Where There's Smoke"*
Written by David P. Harmon. Directed by Oscar Rudolph.
Original Airdate: January 8, 1971

Omigod! What's this? Greg smoking? Thank goodness it's only tobacco. But yes, that's Greg puffing away when Jan and Cindy spy him. Turns out Greg didn't really want to light up, but he was trying to impress some cool school chums who want Greg to join their rock band, the Banana Convention. And Greg couldn't even smoke the damned cigarette; he just coughed.

But that doesn't mean anything to the girls, who tell Marcia, who takes it upon herself to tell her parents. When Mike and Carol find out about Greg, they naturally have a fit. "You did the right thing," they tell Marcia, who feels guilty for snitching. Greg admits his misdeed to Mike and Carol, telling them that he did it because he wanted to be one of the guys. Mike isn't buying: "You can't do something you know is wrong just to go along with the guys. . . . It's stupid. . . ." But his folks are forgiving, as always. As Carol explains: "If you know what you did was wrong, that's more important than any punishment we could give you." Mike even lets on that he smoked when he was a boy, but Carol adds, "We didn't have the evidence then."

Meanwhile, Carol has decided to join a local antismoking group headed by Mrs. Johnson, the mother of Tommy, the drummer in Greg's band. Dig this conversation between the two gals about the band:

Carol: "Greg says Tommy's group is really far out and heavy."
Mrs. J: "Tommy says he really knows where their heads are at."
Carol: "Right on, man!"

The next day Greg comes home from school, flings his jacket on the chair, *and a pack of cigarettes falls out!* This is much to the dismay of Carol and Mrs. Johnson, who has come over to deliver some antismoking pamphlets.

Greg protests his innocence and Carol still believes him, even if Mrs. Johnson doesn't. Alice asks Greg to reconstruct the crime, and when he does, he realizes that he took the wrong jacket from the malt shop (he had ripped the lining of his jacket on his bicycle's handlebars and this jacket's lining was intact).

It turns out that the jacket belongs to Tommy, and when he comes by the Brady residence to get it, he admits that the cigarettes were his. "Do you have to tell my mother?" he whines. Sheepishly, he tells her himself.

But that doesn't stop the Banana Convention from having a successful gig. In fact when Greg returns (wearing a fringed jacket), he tells Mike and Carol that the dance was "kind of a kicky blast ... the guys really got it together and wailed ... we bent the gig out of shape!"

GUEST STARS:
Craig Hundley *(Tommy)*
Marie Denn *(Mrs. Johnson)*
Gary Marsh *(Phil)*
Bobby Kramer *(John)*

The classic Greg episode. While not quite reaching the highs of *Reefer Madness,* it retains the same charm.

A fond memory from Lloyd Schwartz: "The little old lady who played Craig Hundley's mother, Marie Denn, always played these little old ladies. But when she finished this episode, she got on this Harley Davidson with her biker boyfriend and zoomed off! She had a '60s, '70s kind of plastic outfit, knee-high boots—I couldn't believe it!"

#42: *"Will the Real Jan Brady Please Stand Up?"*
Written by Al Schwartz and Bill Freedman. Directed by Peter Baldwin.
Original Airdate: January 15, 1971

Jan is feeling self-conscious about her place in the family again. This time she's not jealous of Marcia or worried about her freckles. It's her hair: Jan believes she is lost in the middle as the second of three blond daughters. Her solution: Believing that brunettes have more fun, she gets a brunette wig. But instead of making people notice her, it just makes her brothers laugh at her. Poor Jan! Her troubles are compounded when she goes to a friend's party wearing the wig, and they make fun of her "Halloween outfit." Jan storms out and goes home, but the kids from the party soon arrive to apologize and to explain that they really admire her natural blond hair.

GUEST STARS:
Pamlyn Ferdin *(Lucy)*
Marcia Wallace *(salesclerk)*
Karen Foulkes *(Margie)*

Anyone who watched any TV whatsoever from the late '60s to the mid-'70s recognizes Pamlyn Ferdin. Born in 1959 and in show business since age three, she was probably the busiest juvenile actress in TV at the time. Ferdin was in the casts of no less than four series (*The John Forsythe Show, Blondie, The Paul Lynde Show,* and, from 1973–74, *Lassie*), and among her many guest credits, she played Felix Unger's daughter Edna as a preteen on *The Odd Couple.* Ironically, her character is named Lucy here—she did the voice of Charles Schultz's Lucy in two "Peanuts" specials. Last we heard, she left acting, happily, at age eighteen to become a nurse.

Another highly recognizable face belongs to the salesclerk, Marcia Wallace—later the inimitable secretary, Carol, on the '70s' *Bob Newhart Show.* "That was her first [TV acting] job in California," according to Lloyd Schwartz.

#43: *"Our Son, the Man"*
Written by Albert E. Lewin. Directed by Jack Arnold.
Original Airdate: February 5, 1971

Jan, Cindy, Bobby, and Peter are chasing each other around the backyard, shrieking in delight. They bring their loud antics into the kitchen, where Greg (wearing a Westdale High School T-shirt) is trying to talk on the phone (no doubt to one of his imaginary phone friends). "Hey, you guys! Cool it!" he tells the other kids. Peter replies, "We're not guys. We're Indian braves" (anticipating next season's visit to the Grand Canyon). "Kids!" sighs Greg.

When Mike comes home, he and Greg have a heart-to-heart. First, Greg tells him that he's just too old to go on the family camp-out this weekend. And he says that now that he's in high school "where they separate the men from the boys," he thinks he should have his own room.

That night, Mike and Carol discuss what to do. They discuss several alternatives, including the attic, which Mike dismisses with "[That] would be great if he were two and a half feet tall"—a strange lapse of reason for an architect, since that's precisely where Greg moves two seasons later. (Perhaps the Bradys had some reconstruction done in the interim.)

They decide to let Greg move into and remodel Mike's den; Mike will move his home office into the family room. Greg gets excited when he hears this: "My own pad! My own scene!"

The next day at school, freshman Greg tries to pick up a senior girl, who wanders off with a hippie-type student instead. That gives Greg the idea to start dressing hipper. The next day he comes down the stairs wearing a headband, shades, beads, a fringed vest, a blue polka-dot shirt, and striped bell-bottoms. He goes into the kitchen and tells his parents in overly familiar tones, "Good morning, Mike. Good morning, Carol." Mike responds, "Look, Greg, calling parents by their first names may be the fad these days, but around here we're still Mom and Dad."

Wearing his groovy threads, he tries to pick up the same girl again. But she puts him down, saying he'll be cute when he grows up. In the end, Greg decides he's still got a lot of growing up to do and goes on the family camp-out after all.

GUEST STARS:
Julie Cobb *(girl)*
Chris Beaumont *(hip guy)*

After "The Slumber Caper," some more celebrity-daughter stuff: Julie Cobb's father was the late, great actor Lee J. Cobb, who created the role of Willy Loman in Arthur Miller's play *Death of a Salesman.* She went on to become a cast member of the series *The D.A.* and *A Year at the Top* and, most recently, played the mother, Jill Pembroke, during the 1984–85 CBS run of *Charles in Charge.* (Jennifer Runyon, the future Cindy of *A Very Brady Christmas,* played her daughter there. Small world, huh?) Scripter Albert E. Lewin had written for *The Ghost and Mrs. Muir* and *My Favorite Martian,* among other '60s sitcoms. And Chris Beaumont makes the first of three *Brady* appearances.

#44: *"The Liberation of Marcia Brady"*
Written by Charles Hoffman. Directed by Russ Mayberry.
Original Airdate: February 12, 1971

Outside her junior high school, a TV reporter asks Marcia whether she thinks "Girls are the equal of boys in every respect?" Marcia replies yes, but she has second thoughts about her bravado and unsuccessfully tries to prevent her family from watching the news. The newscast sets off a debate about the merits of women's liberation, and Marcia—to get back at her brothers' sexist taunts—announces that she's planning to join the Frontier Scouts. Mike, who is the scout leader, studies the rule book and realizes there's nothing against girls joining. Greg gets back at her by announcing he's joining the Sunflower Girls, but he's too old, so it's Peter who must don the girlish uniform. Peter tries to sell Sunflower Girl cookies door-to-door, but he finds it humiliating and quickly abandons the experiment. But Marcia sticks it out with the Frontier Scouts, enduring all the travails of a camp-out and even finishing a long-distance hike.

GUEST STAR:
Ken Jones *(the reporter, as himself)*

Ken Jones was a real-life newscaster, on the Los Angeles independent station KHJ/Channel 9 (now KCAL). For more on this episode, see "Relevance and *The Brady Bunch*" in the chapter "Brady Miscellanea," page 119.

#45: *"Lights Out"*
Written by Bruce Howard. Directed by Oscar Rudolph.
Original Airdate: February 19, 1971

After seeing a magician perform a disappearing act, Cindy insists that she can't sleep unless the lights are left on. Mike and Carol hope working with Peter in his magic act will help her overcome her fear.

GUEST STAR:
Snag Werris *(salesman)*

#46: *"The Winner"*
Written by Elroy Schwartz. Directed by Robert Reed.
Original Airdate: February 26, 1971

Sibling rivalry among the youngest Bradys: Bobby becomes a frantic competitor when he discovers he is the only Brady without a trophy. When Cindy comes home as the winner of a jacks competition, Bobby desperately enters yo-yo, ice-cream eating, and magazine-subscription contests to prove that he, too, is a winner.

GUEST STAR:
Hal Smith *(Kartoon King)*

Hal Smith, the immortal Otis of *The Andy Griffith Show,* makes his second, appropriately flamboyant *Brady* appearance. Co-star Robert Reed went behind the camera to direct, as many actors occasionally do. He would eventually direct four *Brady* episodes.

#47: "Double Parked"
Written by Skip Webster. Directed by Jack Arnold.
Original Airdate: March 5, 1971

Bad news in the neighborhood! City Hall wants to build a courthouse in Woodland Park, where the Brady kids love to romp. So Carol heads up a petition campaign to save the park, enlisting Alice's help in canvassing door-to-door. *But,* Mike's firm is designing the courthouse, forcing him into a moral dilemma.

GUEST STARS:
Jackie Coogan *(man who signs the petition for Alice)*
Jack Collins *(Harry Phillips)*

Turning in a neat though oddly brief appearance is former child actor Jackie Coogan (1914–84), perhaps best known to the '60s-sitcom generation as Uncle Fester on *The Addams Family*. To film connoisseurs, however, he'll always be remembered as Charlie Chaplin's six-year-old co-star in his classic comic tearjerker *The Kid*. He once estimated he had made 1,400 TV-show appearances. Two of them were on *The Brady Bunch*.

#48: "Alice's September Song"
Written by Elroy Schwartz. Directed by Oscar Rudolph.
Original Airdate: March 12, 1971

Alice's old boyfriend Mark Millard comes to town to court the housekeeper. The romance appears serious when Alice devotes all her free time to Mark, much to the chagrin of her regular beau Sam the butcher.

GUEST STARS:
Steve Dunne *(Mark Millard)*
Allan Melvin *(Sam Franklin)*

Steve Dunne (1918–77) was an actor and emcee from way back, having starred with Barbara (Mrs. Cleaver) Billingsley in the CBS sitcom *Professional Father* in 1955 and emceeing the game shows *You're on Your Own* and a nighttime version of *Truth or Consequences*.

#49: *"Ghost Town USA"*
Written by Howard Leeds. Directed by Oscar Rudolph.
Original Airdate: September 17, 1971

The Bradys begin their third season with a three-part episode, starting with dramatic voice-over narration by Carol. In flashback, we see the Bradys loading up their station wagon and camper to head out to the Grand Canyon. On the way, they camp out in an old, deserted mining town. There they meet a grizzled prospector named Zacchariah (of course), who thinks they have come to jump his gold claim. He locks all eight Bradys and Alice in the ghost-town jail and makes off with their station wagon (*and* the camper!). Mike reaches through the cell bars and manipulates the old-fashioned, western-movie key ring. Everybody escapes, and Mike and Peter go look for help.

GUEST STARS:
Jim Backus *(Zacchariah)*
Hoke Howell *(gas station attendant)*

In his long and distinguished career, Jim Backus (1913–89) was best known for his role as millionaire Thurston Howell III on *Gilligan's Island*. Sherwood Schwartz had known him from their radio-comedy days, and worked with him when Backus co-starred on the early TV sitcom *I Married Joan*. Hoke Howell had just come from a recurring role as logger Ben Perkins on *Here Come the Brides* and from playing Barry Williams's father in the unsold 1970 sitcom pilot *The Shameful Secrets of Hastings Corners*. He is not, we suppose, a long-lost relative of Thurston Howell.

#50: *"Grand Canyon Or Bust"*
Written by Tam Spiva. Directed by Oscar Rudolph.
Original Airdate: September 24, 1971

In part two, the Bradys are in a very Gilligan-like situation: stranded with no contact with the outside world. Instead of a tropical isle, they're marooned in a ghost town. The old prospector, Zacchariah, has taken their station wagon, and they have no way of getting out of town. Alice tries saddling up a mule, but gets dumped onto the ground, while Greg hooks up an old telephone—only to get Cindy on the other end. Miraculously, Mike and Peter (who at the end of the previous episode had gone to look for help) come back with the car and the prospector, who apologizes for the misunder-

At the Grand Canyon.

standing. He gives the Bradys a share in his gold mine and amid cries of "Good-bye, ghost town, hello, Grand Canyon," the Bradys take off.

On the road to the Canyon, the Bradys amuse themselves by singing "My Darling Clementine" and gawking at the sites. When they look at the canyon, Mike points out that it was caused by "thousands of years of water running," which prompts Bobby to reply, "Wow! No wonder you don't want us to leave the water faucets dripping." The next day the Bradys travel by mule to the bottom of the Canyon, where they pitch camp. Mike warns the kids that the campsite is not a playground and they shouldn't wander off. Naturally, Bobby and Cindy do, and as the episode ends—and night falls—the two youngest Bradys are lost as the rest of the family vainly searches for them.

GUEST STARS:
Jim Backus (Zacchariah)
Michael Campo (Jimmy Pakaya; cameo)

#51: *"The Brady Braves"*
Written by Tam Spiva. Directed by Oscar Rudolph.
Original Airdate: October 10, 1971

Bobby and Cindy are wandering lost when they run into a young Indian boy named Jimmy Pakaya, who is running away from his grandfather. After Jimmy makes them promise to give him food, he leads them back to camp, where Bobby and Cindy have a tearful reunion with their parents. That night around the campfire, as guitar-strumming Greg leads the clan in singing "Down in the Valley," Bobby and Cindy sneak off with food for Jimmy, who is hiding outside of the campsite. Mike discovers this and has a heart-to-heart, very Brady-like talk with the Indian youngster. Jimmy tells him he's running away because his grandfather, Chief Dan Eagle Cloud, can only think of the old days. Jimmy, on the other hand, says, "I'm tired of being an Indian—I want to be an astronaut." (The two things aren't mutually exclusive, of course, but hey, he's just a kid.)

Meanwhile, Alice goes off to fetch water and she runs into Tonto—er, Jimmy's grandfather, played by the Lone Ranger's ex-sidekick, Jay Silverheels. The chief comes back to the Brady camp, where he tells Mike that he does understand his grandson: "The foolishness of this child: just because I speak of buffalo, doesn't mean I can't understand 'blast off.' " Carol says the Bradys have the same problems and the generation gap is universal. The chief is so taken by the Bradys that he invites them to a ceremony making them honorary members of his tribe. "You younger folks will have a groovy time," he tells them. At the ceremony the Bradys are all given new names and are asked to dance. (They do, looking like they're undergoing mass psychosis, or at least have ingested a few too many peyote buttons.) When they finally leave the Grand Canyon to head back to the Brady residence, they tell the park tollbooth attendant that they "used to be the Brady family—but now we're the Brady Braves!"

OTHER GUEST STAR:
Michael Campo *(Jimmy Pakaya)*

Jay Silverheels (1919?–80), born in Ontario, on Canada's Six Nations Indian Reservation, the son of a Mohawk chief, played Tonto to Clayton Moore's Lone Ranger from 1949–57 on TV. An occasional episodic-series guest star afterward, he eventually spoke out against the media's misguided portrayal of Native Americans. Then, after turning to horse breeding and racing, he began a second career as a professional harness racer. His son, Jay Jr., became a TV-cartoon vocal artist.

#52: *"Juliet Is the Sun"*
Written by Brad Radnitz. Directed by Jack Arnold.
Original Airdate: October 29, 1971

Marcia gets a swelled head after she's cast as Juliet in a school production. Her family members aren't too happy—especially since they were responsible for encouraging her to pursue the role during a time she was consumed by self-doubt. After she becomes so burdensome, Carol announces that she is removing Marcia from the play. Marcia cries and cries and finally, after much soul-searching, she agrees to take a lesser role, having learned a typical Brady lesson in humility.

GUEST STARS:
Lois Newman *(Miss Goodwin)*
Randy Case *(Harold)*

#53: "The Wheeler Dealer"
Written by Bill Freeman and Ben Gershman. Directed by Jack Arnold.
Original Airdate: October 8, 1971

As we know from seasons past, Greg has been coveting a car for many years. So naturally he jumps at the opportunity when his friend Eddie convinces him that Eddie's old, beat-up convertible can be turned into a groovy set of wheels. But as Greg drives the car home, he realizes he may have bought a lemon.

GUEST STARS:
Chris Beaumont *(Eddie)*
Charlie Martin Smith *(Ronnie)*

Reverting to his formal first name of Charles, "Charlie" Martin Smith went on to co-star as Terry the Toad in George Lucas's 1973 film *American Graffiti* and, among his other credits, to star in the 1983 movie *Never Cry Wolf.*

#54: "The Personality Kid"
Written by Ben Starr. Directed by Oscar Rudolph.
Original Airdate: October 22, 1971

As Peter got older, he began experiencing the insecurities of adolescence. In this episode, he attends a friend's party and comes home bummed because no one has talked to him. Convinced that he has no personality, Peter begins a total transformation. First he imitates movie stars, including Humphrey Bogart. Finally, he discovers that he has talent as a joke teller and he throws a party to reveal his new personality.

GUEST STARS:
Monica Ramirez *(Kyle)*
Margie DeMeyer *(Judy)*
Karen Peters *(Susie)*
Sheri Cowart *(Kathy)*
Jay Kocen *(first boy)*
Pierre Williams *(second boy)*

Ben Starr—a comedy writer's name if we ever heard one—was, like Sherwood Schwartz, a writer for Bob Hope; he also worked alongside Sherwood on *I Married Joan* and wrote for *Mr. Ed, My Favorite Martian, Mork and Mindy, All in the Family,* and many other shows.

#55: *"Her Sister's Shadow"*
Written by Al Schwartz and Phil Leslie. Directed by Russ Mayberry.
Original Airdate: November 19, 1971

Jan is jealous of all the awards Marcia wins and all the praise her older sister gets from teachers. Carol advises her to try to do what she can do best. She first tries out as a pom-pom girl, but doesn't make the cut. But then something good happens to Jan: An essay she wrote on "What America Means to Me" wins the honor society award with a grade of 98. But when Jan adds up the score again, she realizes it's only a 93 and someone else has won. After much soul-searching, Jan realizes that honesty is the best policy, and to a shocked assembly audience she admits the mistake. Carol is delighted, exclaiming: "Sometimes when we lose, we win!" And her teacher boasts that Jan's "behavior should be an example to all of us!"

GUEST STARS:
Lindsay Workman *(principal)*
Gwen Van Dam *(Mrs. Watson)*
Peggy Doyle *(teacher)*
Julie Reese *(Kathy)*
Nancy Gillette *(pom-pom girl)*

#56: *"The Teeter-Totter Caper"*
Written by Joel Kane and Jack Lloyd. Directed by Russ Mayberry.
Original Airdate: December 31, 1971

Bobby and Cindy are annoyed that they aren't invited to Carol's aunt Gertrude's wedding because they're too young. Looking for something they can do on their own, they turn on the TV set and see two college boys trying to set a new teeter-totter record. They decide that's a record they can try to break themselves. As they make the attempt, the ubiquitous newspaper reporter comes to the Brady residence to write about the kids. And although they don't break the college students' record (124 hours), they do set a record for kids their own ages.

GUEST STAR:
Dick Winslow *(Winters)*

Co-writer Joel Kane had written for Sherwood Schwartz on *It's About Time* and had also scripted episodes of *The Many Loves of Dobie Gillis*, *The Ghost and Mrs. Muir*, *Please Don't Eat the Daisies*, and such adventure dramas as *The Invaders* and *The Wild Wild West*.

#57: *"My Sister Benedict Arnold"*
Written by Elroy Schwartz. Directed by Hal Cooper.
Original Airdate: October 15, 1971

Greg is annoyed that he has been beaten out both for first-string basketball team and for student-body president by Warren Mulaney. He really gets irked, though, when Marcia comes home aglow, announcing she is going to have her first date with a high-school boy: the same Warren Mulaney. After they go out, Marcia is lukewarm about Warren, but because Greg has threatened her about him, she decides to pretend she really likes him. Greg retaliates by asking out Kathy Lawrence, who had beaten Marcia out for cheerleader, even though he really isn't so keen on her. The upshot is that Greg and Marcia learn a lesson in trifling with other people's feelings—while Kathy and Warren decide to date each other.

GUEST STARS:
Sheri Cowart *(Kathy)*
Gary Rist *(Warren)*

#58: *"The Private Ear"*
Written by Michael Morris. Directed by Hal Cooper.
Original Airdate: November 12, 1971

A year before Watergate, Peter proved he would have made a fine White House plumber. When he discovers Mike's tape recorder, he begins eavesdropping on and recording the confidential conversations of family members (Marcia tells Jan about her new crush; Greg confesses he has—gasp!—overdue library books). When Greg and Marcia get wind of Peter's shenanigans, they take revenge by planting a phony message about a surprise party on the tape recorder. When Peter hears the message, he gets all excited, then is shocked when no one shows up. Of course, Mike and Carol accidentally hear the trick message as well and they save the day by actually throwing a surprise party for Peter.

Longtime scripter Michael Morris had written for *The Flying Nun, McHale's Navy, Bewitched,* and other '60s sitcoms, and would later write for *All in the Family.* His career stretched back practically to the dawn of television, when he and Gertrude and Cherney Berg together wrote the classic TV sitcom *The Goldbergs* (various networks and syndicated, 1949–56).

#59: *"And Now a Word from Our Sponsor"*
Written by Albert E. Lewin. Directed by Peter Baldwin.
Original Airdate: November 5, 1971

Paul Winchell, the famous ventriloquist, guest-stars as Skip Farnum, a soap manufacturer. Skip sees the Bradys coming out of the supermarket and decides they are the ideal family to appear in a soap commercial. Mike, skeptical as always, thinks that Skip is a huckster. But when he discovers that the offer is legitimate, the Bradys are ready for commercial stardom— if only they could believe in the product.

OTHER GUEST STARS:
Lennie Bremen *(truck driver)*
Art Lewis *(Felder)*
Bonnie Boland *(Myrna)*

Paul Winchell, the creator of such well-known dummies as Jerry Mahoney and Knucklehead Smith, was a TV perennial from the moment he debuted in 1947 on the seminal variety series *Show Business Inc.* He has since become one of the most prolific cartoon vocal artists in Saturday-morning television. Also, would you believe that in 1975 he invented an artificial heart? Check the headlines for yourself. More recently, he was upheld in a landmark, multimillion-dollar lawsuit against a production company that maliciously erased videotapes of his old shows. Appearing with him in this episode was actress-comedienne Bonnie Boland, who played Mabel the postal worker for a season on *Chico and the Man.*

#60: *"Click"*
Written by Tom and Helen August. Directed by Oscar Rudolph.
Original Airdate: November 26, 1971

Greg wants to go out for the football team, but Mike and Carol have opposing views. Being the protective mom, Carol worries about Greg's safety. After much persuasion, Carol reluctantly agrees. So what happens? Greg cracks a rib during practice. After being down on himself, Greg finds a new calling as the team's photographer. (To compare this with a similar episode of *The Wonder Years:* Kevin Arnold gets bruised and cut playing neighborhood football with his own mom's reluctant permission. But on his arrival home, in a touching interior monologue, he goes through that moment when a kid first realizes that he can't always go run to his parents anymore.)

GUEST STARS:
Bart La Rue (Coach)
Elvera Roussel (Linette Carter)

Bart La Rue makes his second and final appearance as the football coach. Elvera Roussel might be familiar to soap-opera fans as the onetime Hope Bauer Spaulding of *The Guiding Light*.

#61: *"The Not-So-Rose-Colored Glasses"*
Written by Bruce Howard. Directed by Leslie H. Martinson.
Original Airdate: December 24, 1971

Jan has mistakenly taken someone else's bicycle from the playground. "What a dumbhead I am," she wails when she realizes it. This is the first tip-off that Jan will need glasses, a physical change as traumatic to her as getting braces was to Marcia. Meanwhile, Mike tries to sneak the kids out of the house to get a surprise photo portrait taken for his and Carol's anniversary. They get Carol out of the way by having Alice pretend to have a toothache so that Carol will have to drive her to the dentist. Later, more clues surface about Jan's condition when Carol gets a letter from Jan's teacher saying her grades are falling. Told she needs glasses, Jan gets angry ("Glasses! I'll look positively goofy"). The photographer delivers the portrait to Alice, who hides it in the garage, where Jan crashes her bicycle into it, destroying the photo. The kids sneak out to the photographer to re-pose without Mike's knowledge. He finds out when he sees the new portrait because Jan was not wearing glasses in the original, but she is in the new one. Mike grounds Jan for two weeks, but in an O. Henry ending, the joke's on Mike: Jan can't ride her bike anyway because she sold it to pay for the portait.

GUEST STAR:
Robert Nadder (Mr. Gaylord)

#62: *"Little Big Man"*
Written by Skip Webster. Directed by Robert Reed.
Original Airdate: January 7, 1972

Tiny Bobby's hung up on his height again. Tired of everyone making fun of his size, he decides to do exercises that will stretch him. When these fail, he decides to become a mental giant. But he learns the value of being short when he and Greg are accidentally trapped in Sam the butcher's meat locker and only little Bobby can crawl out the window to get help. (Greg has another job here—working as Sam's delivery boy to raise money for a surfboard.)

GUEST STAR:
Allan Melvin *(Sam Franklin)*

#63: *"Getting Davy Jones"*
Written by Phil Leslie and Al Schwartz. Directed by Oscar Rudolph.
Original Airdate: December 10, 1971

One of the show's classic episodes featured a guest appearance by erstwhile Monkee Jones, then trying (not too well) to pump up his post-Monkees solo career.

In a fit of ego, Marcia, the president of the Fillmore Junior High chapter of the Davy Jones fan club, promises her friends that she can get Jones to appear at the school prom—even though she has no idea how to get in touch with him. Marcia remains adamant: "If I say I can get him ... I can get him." Her hopes rise when she sees an article in the paper saying that Jones is in town for personal appearances. This sets up a whole bunch of scheming and scrambling to get in touch. The kids go to the TV studio to ambush Davy, but Marcia is crestfallen when she learns the show is taped in advance. Finally, the kids get a break when Alice notes that her boyfriend Sam the butcher delivers meat to the hotel where Davy is staying and that the hotel chef is his friend. Greg and Marcia disguise themselves as busboys only to discover that Davy isn't in the room—he's at the recording studio! Off to the studio they go, where they are kicked out, but not before Davy overhears Marcia moaning about her predicament. Of course, Davy saves the day when he shows up at the Brady residence and tells Marcia that he'd love to go the prom, but he doesn't have a date. Will Marcia be his date? What do you think?

OTHER GUEST STARS:
Britt Leach *(manager)*
Marcia Wallace *(Mrs. Robbins)*
Kimberly Beck *(Laura)*
Tina Andrews *(Doreen)*
Whitney Rydbeck *(page)*

This is so odd. The Monkees had broken up in 1969 (just like the Beatles!) and so by the time of this episode, Davy Jones was past his initial peak. But, as Ann B. Davis recalls, "All of our kids went bananas! They were all standing around staring at Davy Jones. And he was standing around staring at them!"

Jones had been a juvenile actor who in his teens earned a Tony Award nomination for his role as the Artful Dodger in the Broadway musical *Oliver*. After the Monkees disbanded, he continued to make occasional TV guest shots while still pursuing a marginal career in music. Lately, of course, the Monkees have experienced a well-deserved resurgence. It seems like everything does eventually.

Britt Leach went on to co-star in the 1976 adventure series *Spencer's Pilots* and appeared as Gilbert, the hospital barber, on *AfterM*A*S*H*. Tina Andrews went on to play Fred Sanford's niece, Angie Wheeler, on *Sanford and Son* and *The Sanford Arms,* and from 1983–84 played Valerie on *Falcon Crest.* Marcia Wallace makes her second *Brady* visit. And Kimberly Beck appeared again in episode #104, "Marcia Gets Creamed."

#64: "Dough Re Mi"
Written by Ben Starr. Directed by Allan Barron.
Original Airdate: January 14, 1972

Greg has been writing a groovy song called "We Can Make the World a Whole Lot Better," but he can't afford the $150 fee charged by the recording studio. Peter comes up with the idea of the kids forming a group called the Brady Six to record the song and they can split the costs. Mike advances the kids money from their allowances, but as they practice, Peter's voice starts changing. Since the recording-studio fee has been paid, the kids wonder whether they should kick Peter out of the group. Greg locks himself in his room, and after much soul-searching, he comes up with the solution. He writes a song called "Time to Change," in which Peter's cracked voice becomes an integral part of the song.

GUEST STAR:
John Wheeler *(Mr. Dimsdale)*

Allan Barron directed such series as *Room 222* and *My World ... And Welcome to It* and went on to such hourlong shows as *Charlie's Angels, The Dukes of Hazzard,* and *Scarecrow and Mrs. King.*

#65: "The Big Bet"
Written by Elroy Schwartz. Directed by Earl Bellamy.
Original Airdate: January 28, 1972

Greg claims that he can do twice as many chin-ups as Bobby. Hurt and angry, Bobby forces Greg into a bet to prove his boast. Bobby is determined to win, so he works out vigorously, while a complacent Greg does nothing. Greg is shocked when Bobby beats him and then must agree to the terms of the bet: he must do everything Bobby says for a week. When Greg wants to take Rachel on a date to the drive-in, Bobby insists on coming along because that conforms to the terms of the bet. Bobby makes a nuisance of himself, naturally, and ends up putting a hole in the convertible's top with his umbrella.

GUEST STARS:
Hope Sherwood *(Rachel)*

Hope Sherwood, the daughter of *Brady* creator Sherwood Schwartz, makes her second appearance—her first as Greg's sometime girlfriend Rachel, which she'd play two more times. Among director Earl Bellamy's roughly six trillion TV credits is the second *Gilligan's Island* TV-movie reunion.

#66: "Jan's Aunt Jenny"
Written by Michael Morris. Directed by Hal Cooper.
Original Airdate: January 21, 1972

While cleaning out the attic, Jan discovers a picture of Carol's aunt Jenny as a young girl and is struck by the resemblance. Curious about what she will look like when she grows up, she writes to Aunt Jenny and asks her to send a picture. Jan is shocked to find that the grown-up Aunt Jenny looks very much like Imogene Coca. But she changes her mind about the importance of looks when Aunt Jenny arrives. She's a free-spirited, world-traveling, Auntie Mame type who travels by limousine and drops celebrities' names.

GUEST STAR:
Imogene Coca *(Aunt Jenny)*

The legendary comedienne Imogene Coca helped create, define, and establish TV comedy with her longtime partner Sid Caesar. On the seminal live variety shows *Admiral Broadway Revue* (1949) and *Your Show of Shows*

(1950–54), she was a soulful urban gamine and peerless farceur. She wasted her talents in the broad time-travel sitcom *It's About Time,* and in the temporary-maid sitcom *Grindl,* but continued to make many memorable appearances until going into semiretirement not long after this episode.

#67: *"Cindy Brady, Lady"*
Written by Al Schwartz and Marty Rhine. Directed by Hal Cooper.
Original Airdate: February 18, 1972

Cindy is uptight about being the youngest girl in the family and wonders why she had to be born last. Determined to be treated like a grown-up, she dresses in Carol's heels and reads *A Farewell to Arms* because that's what Marcia is reading. Soon "Cynthia" (as she wants to be called) is receiving daily packages from a "secret admirer." Alas, it turns out that he's Bobby, who gets lectured at by Mike when he learns of the scheme. Bobby tries to wriggle out of it by making a deal with his friend Tommy to say that he's the secret admirer—and Tommy actually *does* fall for Cindy because they both love collecting lizards.

GUEST STAR:
Eric Shea *(Tommy)*

Eric Shea had played Samantha Eggar's son in the sitcom *Anna and the King* (CBS, 1972), co-starring Yul Brynner.

#68: *"The Power of the Press"*
Written by Bill Freedman and Sam Gershman. Directed by Jack Arnold.
Original Airdate: February 4, 1972

Peter becomes a columnist in his school newspaper. Calling himself "Scoop" Brady, he becomes popular as he puts his friends' names in the column. But as he devotes more and more time to the paper, his schoolwork suffers: he gets a *D* on a science test. Peter has the solution: He'll write a flattering column about the dull teacher. But this teacher's no dummy, and Peter soon regrets this cheap attempt at flattery.

GUEST STARS:
Milton Parsons *(Mr. Price)*
Bobby Rhia *(Harvey)*
Angela Satterwhite *(Diane)*

#69: *"Sergeant Emma"*
Written by Harry Winkler. Directed by Jack Arnold.
Original Airdate: February 11, 1972

Ann B. Davis does the Patty Duke trip when she plays her identical-twin cousin in this episode. When Alice goes on vacation, she's replaced by her cousin Emma, a former WAC. Emma immediately turns the Brady residence into a suburban version of Fort Dix, with white-glove bedroom inspections and early-morning calisthenics, which leave the Bradys exhausted. And never did the Bradys value Alice more highly.

Harry Winkler (no relation to Henry) had written for *The Addams Family* and *The Partridge Family* before turning to the Brady family.

Anticipating the jogging craze in "Sergeant Emma."

#70: *"The Fender Benders"*
Written by David P. Harmon. Directed by Allan Barron.
Original Airdate: March 10, 1972

Jackie Coogan makes his second *Brady Bunch* guest shot. In a parking lot, Carol is involved in a minor fender bender with Harry Duggan (Coogan). At first, both agree to pay their own damages. But later that evening Harry visits the Bradys and claims the accident was Carol's fault. He says he will take her to court if she doesn't pay to have his car fixed.

OTHER GUEST STAR:
Robert Emhardt *(the Judge)*

#71: *"My Fair Opponent"*
Written by Bernie Kahn. Directed by Peter Baldwin.
Original Airdate: March 3, 1972

Marcia gets angry when her friend Molly, a shy, unattractive student, is jokingly nominated for hostess of Banquet Night. Marcia decides to make Molly over, and everyone is amazed by the transformation. So what happens? Molly's opponent has to withdraw and Marcia must run against Molly—transformed into an unsufferable snob who refuses to acknowledge Marcia's help. At the final judging contest, Molly wins (presenting the speech that Marcia had written for her). At the end, though, Molly has a change of heart, showing up at the Brady residence with the banquet night's guest of honor, an astronaut, and telling Marcia that for the first time in the history of Fillmore Junior High, Banquet Night is going to have co-hostesses!

GUEST STARS:
Debi Storm *(Molly Webber)*
William Wellman, Jr. *(astronaut)*
Lindsay Workman *(Mr. Watkins)*
Suzanne Roth *(Suzanne)*

Scriptwriter Bernie Kahn had written for the original *The Smothers Brothers Show* (the 1965–66 sitcom) and *My World . . . And Welcome to It,* among other series.

#72: "Hawaii Bound"
Written by Tam Spiva. Directed by Jack Arnold.
Original Airdate: September 22, 1972

A Brady tradition continues when the season opens with the family on vacation yet again—this time to Hawaii. Mike is able to take the whole family with him when his company sends him to Hawaii to check the construction of a building he designed. The Bradys tour the island they're on, and the boys get involved with an ancient "tabu" that seems to bring them bad luck.

GUEST STARS:
Don Ho *(himself)*
David "Lippy" Espinda *(Hanalei)*
Dennis M. Chun *(young workman)*
Elithe Aguiar *(hula instructor)*
Patrick Adiarte *(David)*

"My mom was an extra a couple of times," says Lloyd Schwartz, Sherwood's son. "She was in the Hawaii episode when they got off the plane. Then in the last episode in a beauty salon." Dad Sherwood himself, however, never did a Hitchcock on *Brady*.

#73: "Pass the Tabu"
Written by Tam Spiva. Directed by Jack Arnold.
Original Airdate: September 29, 1972

Greg is saved from drowning while surfing, but despite this good fortune, bad luck supposedly from the "tabu" idol continues to plague the Bradys after Jan runs across it. The boys decide to return the idol to an ancient Hawaiian burial ground.

GUEST STARS:
David "Lippy" Espinada *(Hanalei)*
Cris Callow *(Mandy)*
Patrick Adiarte *(David)*

#74: *"The Tiki Caves"*
Written by Tam Spiva. Directed by Jack Arnold.
Original Airdate: October 6, 1972

Vincent Price guest-stars in the final Hawaii episode. The boys return the "tabu" idol to the burial cave. There they meet Professor Whitehead (Price), who believes they intend to steal his "latest find."

OTHER GUEST STARS:
David "Lippy" Espinada *(Hanalei)*
Leon Lontoc *(mayor's representative)*

Vincent Price, the great master of the macabre, has made more than a hundred movies in a film career stretching to 1938.

#75: *"Today I Am a Freshman"*
Written by William Raynor and Myles Wilder. Directed by Hal Cooper.
Original Airdate: October 13, 1972

It's Marcia's first day at high school, and boy, is she nervous. She wants to stay home, claiming she doesn't feel well. However, the doctor can't find anything wrong. Carol has the ailment diagnosed perfectly: it's "new-school-itis"—especially since all of Marcia's friends are going to Tower High and she has to go to Westdale. (Guess they moved to that high-school district when Mike and Carol got married.) Carol tries to cheer Marcia up by reminding her of just what a popular and active student she was in junior high. "Was" is right, Marcia whines. "All my best years are behind me!"

Mike and Carol tell her to "get involved," but Marcia takes their advice much too seriously. In fact, she becomes manic, joining school club after school club, showing up in scuba outfits one moment, practicing karate chops the next, and standing on her head to practice yoga. (A yoga club? In the early '70s? This *is* southern California!)

She's also provisionally accepted by the one club she *really* wants to join—the Boosters, a snobby bunch of Heathers who "only date boys who are letter men." But when the Boosters come to the Brady residence to interview Marcia, Peter's science project—a mock volcano—finally erupts, covering everyone with muddy guck. Marcia laughs, and the girls in the Boosters get mad and ban her from joining. Marcia doesn't care, she decides that she doesn't need them and will join just one club: ceramics.

GUEST STARS:
John Howard *(doctor)*
Vickie Kos *(Kim)*
Kelly Flynn *(Tom)*

Marcia's doctor, distinguished-looking John Howard, had previously starred as a physician in the mid-'50s syndicated drama series *Dr. Hudson's Secret Journal*. He went on to star in the syndicated series *The Adventures of the Sea Hawk* and played Dave Welch on several episodes of *My Three Sons*.

#76: *"Cyrano De Brady"*
Written by Skip Webster. Directed by Hal Cooper.
Original Airdate: October 20, 1972

Peter has a crush on Jan's girlfriend Kerry, but he can't get to first base with her. So he asks Greg—who else?—for advice on how to score. But when Greg goes to speak to Kerry for his brother, she ends up falling for him and rejecting Peter.

GUEST STAR:
Kym Karath *(Kerry)*

#77: *"Fright Night"*
Written by Brad Radnitz. Directed by Jerry London.
Original Airdate: October 27, 1972

This spooky episode is often repeated annually on Halloween.
    The girls are frightened when they hear some strange sounds and see a "ghost." But they investigate and realize it was merely the prank-pulling Brady boys, who are manufacturing the eeriness with a slide projector and sound effects. Playing dumb, the girls vow to get back, and make a bet that the boys can't spend a night in the "haunted" attic. So when the boys go upstairs, they also see a ghost—this one created by the girls.
    When Alice says she isn't scared of anything, the kids band together and rig up the house to prove her wrong. With Mike and Carol out for the evening, the tricks work and Alice panics, smashing Carol's sculpture of Mike. That ticks off Mike and Carol, who ground the kids for two weeks, noting that "if you carry a joke too far, somebody could get hurt."

•   •   •

This episode is among the earliest work by director Jerry London, who went on to helm such prestigious TV movies and mini-series as *Chiefs, The Scarlet and the Black,* and, wouldja believe, *Shogun.* In addition to his four episodes of *Brady,* his other early credits include *The Flying Nun* and *The Bob Newhart Show.*

#78: *"Career Fever"*
Written by Burt and Adele Styler. Directed by Jerry London.
Original Airdate: November 17, 1972

Mike mistakenly believes that Greg wants to follow in his footsteps because of a paper his son prepares for English class. Greg doesn't have the heart to tell Mike that he was just doing the paper as an assignment and he really doesn't want to be an architect. He does a drawing of a house that features a moat to show his lack of ability, but that only encourages Mike more.

Meanwhile, the other kids decide to pursue careers: Peter wants to be a doctor; Jan, a nurse; Bobby, an astronaut; and Cindy, a model. Greg does another drawing for Mike, which finally convinces Mike that Greg should try another line of work in the future. (Mike calls Greg "Frank Lloyd Wrong," ho, ho.) As the episode ends, Bobby and Cindy are stuffing themselves, certainly not the kind of activity future astronauts and models should indulge in. It seems the youngest kids have also changed their minds: Bobby now wants to be a pro football player, while Cindy plans on becoming a wrestler (little realizing there'd be a call for that on television twenty years hence!).

#79: *"Law and Disorder"*
Written by Elroy Schwartz. Directed by Hal Cooper.
Original Airdate: January 12, 1973

Bobby becomes extremely unpopular when he decides to be the best safety monitor at school. Putting on that "SM" armband turns him into a pint-sized tyrant who reports his friends (and even Cindy) for minor infractions like running in the halls. He becomes obsessed with sticking to the letter of the laws, and his fascistic behavior carries over to the Brady residence, where he begins compiling reports on rule-breaking by his siblings (Jan didn't set the table, Greg came in after curfew). Bobby suffers a moral dilemma when a hysterical friend asks him to enter a condemned house with a KEEP OUT sign, in order to find her lost cat. Even though he soils his good clothing, Bobby learns that sometimes rules can be broken if there's a good reason.

(We do wonder about the validity of this particular case, however, since the sign was up for a reason—like, what if a dilapidated floorboard had given way under him, or loose bricks had fallen and gashed his skull?)

GUEST STARS:
Shawn Schepps *(Jill)*
Harlen Carraher *(Steve)*
Cindy Henderson *(girl)*
Jon Hayes *(Jon)*

Cindy Henderson (who is not one of Florence's daughters) did the voice of Wednesday Addams for *The Addams Family* cartoon series of the mid-'70s—alongside Jodie Foster, who voiced her brother Pugsley! Harlen Carraher, in the first of three *Brady* guest shots, had just spent two years playing Hope Lange's son Jonathan on *The Ghost and Mrs. Muir.*

#80: *"Jan, the Only Child"*
Written by Al Schwartz and Ralph Goodman. Directed by Roger Duchowney.
Original Airdate: November 11, 1972

That young would-be neurotic Jan is at it again. She complains that she has no privacy and no identity because she has so many brothers and sisters. The kids try to be solicitous of her by being extra nice, but when that doesn't work, they decide to exclude her from their activities. So there!

This was the only *Brady* episode directed by Roger Duchowney, a veteran of *The Partridge Family.* He also directed the 1980 TV-movie detective spoof *Murder Can Hurt You!*

#81: *"The Show Must Go On??"*
Written by Harry Winkler. Directed by Jack Donohue.
Original Airdate: November 3, 1972

Marcia talks her mother into appearing with her in the school family frolics. Once Carol agrees, Greg comes home to request that Mike also perform. Carol and Marcia perform a duet.

GUEST STARS:
Allan Melvin *(Sam Franklin)*
Barbara Morrison *(Mrs. Tuttle)*
Brandy Carson *(woman)*
Karen Foulkes *(Muriel)*
Frank De Vol *(father)*
Bonnie Ludeka *(daughter)*

Frank De Vol was the show's music director. As an actor, he'd played the building contractor who had to deal with bumbling Marty Ingels and John Astin on *I'm Dickens, He's Fenster* (ABC, 1962–63).

#82: *"You Can't Win 'Em All"*
Written by Lois Hire. Directed by Jack Donohue.
Original Airdate: March 16, 1973

Bobby and Cindy both become eligible to appear on a kids' TV quiz show. But while Cindy spends all her spare time studying, Bobby doesn't, and, of course, only Cindy makes the team. But the idea of turning into a TV star gives Cindy a huge ego (sound familiar?) and she turns off her siblings. But when the time comes for Cindy to go on TV, she suffers stage fright and is unable to answer any questions.

GUEST STARS:
Edward Knight *(Monty Marshall)*
Vicki Schreck *(Woodside girl)*
Harlen Carraher *(Clinton boy)*
Claudio Martinez *(Woodside boy)*
Miyoshi Williams *(Clinton girl)*
Tracey M. Lee *(Woodside girl)*

Edward Knight, a longtime little-theater actor, is the father of *Brady* boy Chris Knight. Claudio Martinez went on to the 1976 ABC sitcom *Viva Valdez* and the 1981–82 PBS high-school series *The New Voice.* And Harlen Carraher makes his second *Brady* appearance, playing a different character than in "Law and Disorder."

#83: *"Goodbye, Alice, Hello"*
Written by Milt Rosen. Directed by George "Buddy" Tyne.
Original Airdate: November 24, 1972

Alice decides to leave when she feels that she can no longer communicate with the kids. When the young Bradys claim that they can't trust Alice anymore, Alice makes up an excuse and gets her own replacement. She isn't gone too long before the kids change their minds and realize the mistake they've made.

GUEST STARS:
Mary Treen *(Kay)*
Snag Werris *(Mr. Foster)*
Harry G. Crigger *(customer)*

Mary Treen, who plays Alice's brief replacement, had been Andy Taylor's original housekeeper on *The Andy Griffith Show*. She had supporting roles in the mid-'50s law drama *Willy* and in Joey Bishop's 1960s sitcom. Alas, her fans will likely never see her work on the latter; all prints of the series were destroyed in the mid-1980s, reportedly at the behest of Bishop himself. Director George Tyne makes his *Brady* debut here; among his credits are *M*A*S*H*, *The Bob Newhart Show*, *James at 15*, and *The Love Boat*.

#84: *"Love and the Older Man"*
Written by Martin A. Ragaway. Directed by George "Buddy" Tyne.
Original Airdate: January 5, 1973

Though it sounds like a *Love American Style* episode, this is really just a nice story about yet another of Marcia's silly crushes. This time it's Dr. Stanley Vogel, a handsome young dentist. Her fantasies are encouraged when Jan reads her an article in a teen-romance magazine that says that the ideal older man for a girl to date is someone who is twelve years older—and that's precisely the difference between the twenty-eight-year-old toothpuller and the sixteen-year-old Brady. Meanwhile, when Mike goes to Dr. Vogel, the dentist asks Mike if Marcia will baby-sit for him on Friday. When Dr. Vogel calls her to see if she's free Friday, Marcia escapes into a world of ultra-fantasy, imagining herself as Mrs. Marcia Dentist. Her fantasy rapidly crumbles when Jan's friend tells her that Dr. Vogel is married. A heartbroken and angry Marcia thinks that nasty Dr. Vogel is taking advantage of her.

GUEST STARS:
Don Brit Reid *(Dr. Stanley Vogel)*
Allen Joseph *(minister)*

#85: *"Everyone Can't Be George Washington"*
Written by Sam Locke and Milton Pascal. Directed by Richard Michaels.
Original Airdate: December 22, 1972

Peter tries out for the role of George Washington in the school play, but ends up playing Benedict Arnold. You see, Peter is such a good actor that the teacher decides he can handle the role of the traitor better than the Father of Our Country. Instead of appreciating the teacher's faith in him and putting up with the uninformed wrath of his narrow-minded friends, Peter schemes to get himself kicked out of the play.

GUEST STARS:
Sara Seegar *(Miss Bailey)*
Barbara Bernstein *(Peggy)*
Sean Kelly *(Stuart)*
Jimmy Bracken *(Freddie)*
Michael Barbera *(Harvey)*
Cheryl Beth Jacobs *(Edith)*
Angela B. Satterwhite *(Donna)*

Old sitcom fans, your eyes aren't deceiving you: Miss Bailey is indeed the second Mrs. Wilson of *Dennis the Menace*—the one married to Gale Gordon's John Wilson. Barbara Bernstein, Florence Henderson's real-life daughter, makes her second appearance, playing a different character than in "The Slumber Caper."

This was the first of six *Brady*s directed by Richard Michaels, a veteran of *Bewitched, The Flying Nun,* and *Room 222,* among other sitcoms and dramas. His many TV movies and mini-series include *Sadat* and *Once an Eagle.*

#86: *"Greg's Triangle"*
Written by Bill Freedman and Ben Gershman. Directed by Richard Michaels.
Original Airdate: December 8, 1972

Greg has yet another girlfriend: a shapely coed named Jennifer who seems to throw herself all over him. But she has an ulterior motive: Greg is the head judge on the cheerleading committee and Jennifer wants to be head cheerleader. The only problem is, so does Marcia. Both girls think their connection will ensure victory. After the cheerleader tryout, Greg breaks a tie between them by voting for a third contestant, which leaves both Jennifer and Marcia plenty angry.

GUEST STARS:
Tannis G. Montgomery *(Jennifer)*
Rita Wilson *(Pat)*

Tannis G. Montgomery later played Richie Cunningham's first girlfriend, Arlene, on *Happy Days*. Fellow cheerleader Rita Wilson grew up to co-star in the movie comedy *Volunteers*, where she met her future husband—actor Tom Hanks.

#87: *"Bobby's Hero"*
Written by Michael Morris. Directed by Leslie H. Martinson.

Bobby upsets his parents and teachers when he makes a hero of Jesse James. Bobby's principal, Mr. Hillary, asks Mike and Carol to meet with him when Bobby at school starts pretending he's Jesse James. Mike sets out to change his son's opinion of the outlaw by exposing to him the truth about Jesse.

GUEST STARS:
Burt Mustin *(Jethroe Collins)*
Richard Carlyle *(Mr. Hillary)*
Gordon DeVol *(Jesse James)*
Ruth Anson *(Miss Perry)*

Burt Mustin (1884–1977), a former car salesperson who got into acting at age sixty-seven, was a veteran character actor best known for his recurring role as Justin Quigley on *All in the Family*. He also popped up as Jud Crowley from time to time on *The Andy Griffith Show*. Richard Carlyle was the original lead on the early TV drama *Crime Photographer* (CBS, 1951–52). Gordon DeVol is not related, incidentally, to *Brady* theme composer Frank De Vol.

#88: *"The Great Earring Caper"*
Written by Larry Rhine and Al Schwartz. Directed by Leslie H. Martinson.
Original Airdate: March 2, 1973

Cindy loses her mother's earrings and enlists Peter's aid in finding them. Peter uses his new detective kit to search for them. Will he find them in time before Cindy has to take the fall?

#89 *"Greg Gets Grounded"*
Written by Elroy Schwartz. Directed by Jack Arnold.
Original Airdate: January 19, 1973

Bobby lets slip that Greg was nearly involved in an auto accident. Mike and Carol respond by telling Greg he can't use the car for a week. Greg is frantic because he wants to go to a rock concert. When a friend lends Greg his car, Greg gets tickets—he'd interpreted Mike's punishment as meaning that only the family car was off limits, not anyone else's. Mike doesn't like Greg's loophole mongering, but goes along. Later, Greg takes Rachel to the drive-in, where Peter's pet frog has accidentally remained in the car, and the little amphibian wrecks Greg's romantic evening.

GUEST STARS:
Hope Sherwood *(Rachel)*
Gracia Lee *(Jenny)*

Hope Sherwood, daughter of series creator Sherwood Schwartz, makes her third appearance on the show—her second as Greg's girlfriend Rachel.

#90: *"The Subject Was Noses"*
Written by Al Schwartz and Larry Rhine. Directed by Jack Arnold.
Original Airdate: February 9, 1973

Marcia is swooning because she's just landed a date with Doug Simpson, the school football hero. The only problem is that she's already made a date with nice-guy Charley. Greg tells her how to get out of a date graciously and she does, which bums poor Charley out. Marcia, however, is floating, dreaming about her date with Doug—until she gets a swollen nose when she is hit by an errant football thrown by Peter. During the next few days, she tries covering up the injury, but accidentally lets Doug see it. Not surprisingly—jock-brain that he is—Doug cancels the date, ironically using the same excuse Marcia had with Charley. That sets Marcia to thinking about doing the right thing, which means apologizing to Charley. We can only fantasize, of course, about how she made it up to him.

GUEST STARS:
Nicholas Hammond *(Doug Simpson)*
Lisa Eilbacher *(Vicki)*
Stuart Getz *(Charley)*

Lisa Eilbacher would grow up and go on to co-star with Eddie Murphy in *Beverly Hills Cop*. Nicholas Hammond would become the costumed hero of *The Amazing Spider Man* (CBS, 1978–79).

#91: *"How to Succeed in Business?"*
Written by Gene Thompson. Directed by Robert Reed.
Original Airdate: February 23, 1973

Peter gets a job with Mr. Martinelli, repairing bikes. After he tells his family that he's doing great, his boss decides to let him go because he works too slowly. (This foreshadows a fifth-season episode in which Marcia hires and then has to fire Peter from a job in an ice-cream store.)

GUEST STARS:
Jay Novello *(Mr. Martinelli)*
Harlen Carreher *(Leon)*
Claudio Martinez *(Billy)*

Jay Novello (1904–82) is best known to sitcom fans as Mayor Mario Lugatto of Voltafiore, the tiny Italian town where *McHale's Navy* disembarked its final season. Harlen Carreher and Claudio Martinez had appeared together (as two different characters) in episode #82, "You Can't Win 'Em All."

#92: *"Amateur Nite"*
Written by Sam Locke and Milton Pascal. Directed by Jack Arnold.
Original Airdate: January 26, 1973

The Brady kids are all set to buy an engraved platter for their parents' anniversary, but the additional engraving charge of $56.23 prevents them from getting the gift. To raise the money, they devise a song-and-dance act so they can appear on a local amateur show. They have to keep the act a secret from Mike and Carol, of course. When Mike sees them auditioning their dance steps in the backyard, they pretend they're doing calisthenics. When they audition for the show, they perform a wimpy ditty (in that Cowsills–Partridge groove) called "It's a Sunshine Day (Everybody's Smiling)," in which Bobby sings the possibly LSD-influenced words: "Can you dig the sunshine?" They pass the audition, and when pressed by the host to tell him their name, they blurt out "The Silver Platters."

When it's time to appear on the real show, all the kids sneak out, but the scam is discovered when Alice turns on the TV and sees the Bradys performing. (Live TV, huh?) Naturally, she shrieks and calls Mike and Carol to take a peek. Dressed in matching white sweaters and blue pants, they perform an uptempo rocker that's elaborately choreographed. They come in third place, but as their parents hear them telling the host why they formed the group, they are genuinely touched as only a Brady can be.

GUEST STARS:
Harold Peary *(Mr. Goodbody)*
Steve Dunne *(Pete Sterne)*
Robert Nadder *(Alfred Bailey)*

The great Hal Peary (1908–85) created the legendary radio character Throckmorton P. Gildersleeve, the lovable old windbag of *Fibber McGee and Molly,* and later, *The Great Gildersleeve.* His TV-series roles include Herb Woodley, Dagwood's next-door neighbor on *Blondie* (NBC, 1957) and Mayor La Trivia on the 1959–60 TV version of *Fibber McGee.* Peary continued doing commercials and voice-overs into the 1970s. Former real-life emcee Steve Dunne (1918–73) makes his second *Brady* appearance.

#93: "You're Never Too Old"
Written by Ben Gershman and Bill Freedman. Directed by Bruce Bilson.
Original Airdate: March 9, 1973

In one of the more inventive episodes, Florence Henderson and Robert Reed play dual roles. Thanks to a load of makeup, Henderson plays Carol's grandmother, Connie Hutchins, while Reed plays Mike's great-grandfather, Judge Hank Brady. The kids decide to set the two old coots up with each other. The only problem is that Grandma is a youthful swinger who jogs and plays basketball with the kids, while Great-Grandpa (who looks more than a little like the dirty old man on *Laugh-In*) is stodgy and boring. It looks like the setup won't work out, but by episode's end, Grandma and Great-Grandpa are sneaking out of the house, eloping to Las Vegas.

Bruce Bilson has directed for every show that has ever been on television since 1931. Or so it seems. He'd won an Emmy Award in 1968 for directing the "Maxwell Smart, Private Eye" episode of *Get Smart*. This was his first of four *Brady*s.

#94: "A Room at the Top"
Written by William Raynor and Myles Wilder. Directed by Lloyd Schwartz.
Original Airdate: March 23, 1973

Greg, now a mature seventeen-year-old, realizes he can't share a bedroom with two younger brothers anymore. His friend, college freshman Hank Carter, suggests that Greg move out and room with him. Mike turns this down, but he okays Greg's proposal to move into the attic. Meanwhile, Marcia is feeling the need for some space of her own, and when she asks Carol about moving up to the attic, Carol, unaware of Mike and Greg's agreement, says yes.

Greg and Marcia fight over the space, and reluctantly, Greg relents. However, the younger boys aren't pleased that Greg's back, and they start a harassment campaign against Marcia. By making crank calls they force her to come down the stairs constantly. The ploy works. A disgusted Marcia moves out (instead of asking for a phone extension) and lets Greg take over. This prepares us for the next season when Greg turns his attic into a groovy bachelor pad befitting a soon-to-be high-school senior.

GUEST STAR:
Chris Beaumont *(Hank Carter)*

Making his directorial debut was Lloyd Schwartz, Sherwood's son, who had climbed the ranks from dialogue coach to one of the producers. This episode also marks the last of three appearances by Chris Beaumont, who went on to play Larry Hagman's son on the 1973 ABC sitcom *Here We Go Again*.

#95: *"Snow White and the Seven Bradys"*
Written by Ben Starr. Directed by Bruce Bilson.
Original Airdate: September 28, 1973

Cindy wants to raise money for her teacher's retirement. Her plan is to put on a version of *Snow White and the Seven Dwarfs* starring members of her family. She commits to the idea without consulting the rest of her family, and then digs an even bigger hole for herself when she finds out the theater where she wanted the play to be performed is rented. No problem: the Bradys volunteer their backyard. The play is very silly, but a success.

GUEST STARS:
Allan Melvin *(Sam Franklin)*
Elven Havard *(policeman)*
Frances Whitfield *(teacher)*

Frances Whitfield was the Brady kids' real-life tutor and welfare worker on the studio set. In 1988, she played the nurse who interrupts Dr. Greg Brady's smooching with his wife on the TV-movie reunion *A Very Brady Christmas*.

#96: *"Mail Order Hero"*
Written by Martin A. Ragaway. Directed by Bruce Bilson.
Original Airdate: September 21, 1973

This is like the male version of Marcia's Davy Jones odyssey two seasons earlier. Bobby has a dream that he's playing football with Joe Namath and that Joe throws him the winning touchdown pass. The next day he's playing football in his backyard with his buddies when, in a fit of one-upmanship, he remarks that he knows Joe Namath. His friends don't believe him, but Bobby insists. When Mike and Carol learn he bragged to his friends, they are not pleased and they lecture him about the evils of bragging. Yet Cindy is sympathetic to Bobby's plight, and when she overhears Marcia talking about how a TV star took time off to visit a sick child, she gets an idea. She sends a letter to Joe Namath's office explaining that her brother Bobby is seriously ill, and nothing would make him happier than to have Namath visit the Brady residence.

Her letter succeeds and Joe Namath (playing himself) drops by the Bradys'—much to everyone's surprise, since of course Mike doesn't know anything about Bobby being sick. When the scam is confessed, Mike isn't happy, but Joe understands—and he even plays catch with Bobby, fulfilling the young Brady's dreams.

OTHER GUEST STARS:
Tim Herbert *(Herb)*
Larry Michaels *(Burt)*
Eric Woods *(Tom)*
Kerry MacLane *(Eric)*

Ah, Broadway Joe Namath, the superstar quarterback of the miracle New York Jets and the Los Angeles Rams, for whom he was playing when he made this guest shot. Ann B. Davis remembers "being fascinated by the fact that when he walked, he walked so tentatively because of those rotten knees of his. Of course, the minute the camera started turning, he bounced like he was out on the field."

Florence Henderson has an even more intimate memory. "When Joe Namath came on the show, I pulled a trick on him!" she recalls with a laugh. "I was always full of the devil. At the end of the episode, he was standing in our driveway saying good-bye to everybody, and I was last in line. So I worked it out with the director and cameraman that they would leave the camera rolling. And when he said good-bye to Bob and the kids and then got to me, I LEAPED on him, threw my legs around his waist, and yelled, 'Take me with you! Get me out of here! I hate this family!' And I was kissing him, and his face got bright red, and he looked at me and sort of shrugged and said, 'Okay.' And then he carried me to his car!"

Namath retired from football in 1977, and the following year starred in his own short-lived NBC sitcom, *The Waverly Wonders*.

#97: *"The Elopement"*
Written by Harry Winkler. Directed by Jerry London.
Original Airdate: December 7, 1973

The Bradys think Alice is planning to elope with Sam the butcher. When Marcia and Jan overhear her discussing elopement with Sam, they pass the news along to the family. Carol begins searching for a replacement house-keeper to allow Alice a week's honeymoon, and the whole family gets involved in planning a surprise wedding reception. But the whole thing turns out to be a silly misunderstanding, since it was Sam's cousin Clara who was eloping, and the big plans they heard Sam talking about concerned his Saturday-night bowling tournament.

GUEST STARS:
Allan Melvin *(Sam Franklin)*
Byron Webster *(the minister)*
Bella Bruck *(Gladys)*

#98: *"Adios, Johnny Bravo"*
Written by Joanna Lee. Directed by Jerry London.
Original Airdate: September 14, 1973

The Brady kids are singing on another TV show when a slick woman agent named Tami spots Greg. Taking him aside, she talks about making him a star. She and her assistant—a hip-talking dude named Buddy ("Righteous! Dynamite!")—unveil their plan to turn Greg into Johnny Bravo. "You won't be *in* the top-20," says Buddy. "You'll *be* the top-20!" They give Greg a groovy costume and let a group of screaming girls attack him. Greg's head swells, and he tells Carol and Mike that he doesn't plan to attend college since he's going to be a big star. But Greg comes down to earth when he discovers that Buddy and Tami have electronically altered his voice for the Johnny Bravo record. When Greg protests, Buddy explains why they hired him: "You fit the suit." Greg tells Buddy to shove his suit, and he returns to the warmth and love of the Brady clan.

GUEST STARS:
Claudia Jennings *(Tami Cutler)*
Paul Cavonis *(Buddy Berkman)*
Jeff Davis *(Hal Barton)*

It's the last place you'd ever expect to find her, but there she is: the late Claudia Jennings, "Queen of the B's." The 1970 *Playboy* Playmate of the Year, Jennings by this time had already begun her string of now cult-classic drive-in movies, most of which found her in various states of undress (although no less a critic than John Simon praised her fully clothed performance in the off-Broadway play *Dark of the Moon*). Among her films: *Jud* (1970), *The Unholy Rollers* (1972), *Truck Stop Women* (1974), *Group Marriage* (1974), *Gator Bait* (1976), *The Great Texas Dynamite Chase* (1977), *Moonshine Country Express* (1977), and *Deathsport* (1978). Jennings died on October 3, 1979, at age twenty-nine, in a car accident.

The Guns 'n' Roses of their time ("Adios, Johnny Bravo").

Paul Cavonis went on to the cast of the Don Johnson TV movie/pilot *The City* (1977), which still plays in syndication.

#99: "Never Too Young"
Written by Al Schwartz and Larry Rhine. Directed by Richard Michaels.
Original Airdate: October 5, 1973

Girl-hating Bobby gets kissed by Millicent for defending her at school. He discovers that kissing a girl isn't as bad as he thought—which is punctuated by the director's subtly inserting shots of fireworks. But he also discovers—after going to Millicent's house and kissing her again—that Millicent may have the mumps. He worries that his ailment may quarantine the rest of the family from attending a big Roaring '20s party.

This episode is worth checking out just to see the entire Brady clan dressed in '20s costumes dancing the Charleston in the living room, and a ukelele-strumming Mike dueting with Carol on "I Want to Be Loved by You." By the way, Millicent didn't have the mumps and Bobby is happy and so are all the Bradys.

GUEST STAR:
Melissa Anderson *(Millicent)*

You might recognize Millicent as Melissa Sue Anderson of *Little House on the Prarie.* What you might not know is that according to Lloyd Schwartz, "This was her screen test that got her the part" of Mary Ingalls.

#100: "Peter and the Wolf"
Written by Tam Spiva. Directed by Leslie H. Martinson.
Original Airdate: October 12, 1973

Greg wants a date with Sandra, but Sandra will go out with him only if he can get someone to double with her cousin Linda. Greg assumes her cousin must be ugly, so all his friends turn him down. Finally, he schemes to pass Peter off as an "older man" named Phil Packer. Peter, armed with a false mustache, helps Greg out, and of course, when they pick the girls up, Linda turns out to be foxy. At the drive-in, though, Peter's mustache falls off.

After the date, the girls realize they've been duped, so they plan to get back at Greg and Peter by pretending they've fallen heavily for Phil. And when the foursome go out again to the local pizza parlor, the two girls throw themselves all over "Phil," while Greg fumes.

Meanwhile back at the Brady residence, Mike is entertaining the Calderons, a Mexican couple, who instead of wanting Mexican food for dinner prefer to sample good ol' American food—at the local pizza parlor. And when the Bradys and the Calderons arrive there, they see the girls smooching Peter passionately. The Calderons are outraged by such wanton behavior—and it's even more embarrassing when the Bradys realize that the moustachioed stud is none other than Peter! An embarrassed Peter explains the situation, and Carol tells him that the Calderons didn't approve of his behavior—but they admired how he told the truth.

GUEST STARS:
Cindi Crosby *(Sandra)*
Kathie Gibboney *(Linda)*
Paul Fierro *(Mr. Calderon)*
Alma Beltran *(Mrs. Calderon)*
Bill Miller *(Len)*

Cindi Crosby is the sister of actress Cathy Lee Crosby—no relation to Bing.

#101: *"Getting Greg's Goat"*
Written by Milton Pascal and Sam Locke. Directed by Robert Reed.
Original Airdate: October 19, 1973

That irrepressible Greg steals Raquel, the goat mascot of rival Coolidge High, to get back at the lowlifes who kidnapped Westdale High's bear-cub mascot. Carol is shocked but Mike is more sanguine, recalling that as a young man he had done his share of mascot stealing. Greg tries to keep the goat's presence hidden, but people get suspicious when they hear him cooing to "Raquel." While Carol is having a PTA meeting at the house to deal with the crisis of mascot stealing that has broken out in the community, Raquel breaks loose and causes everyone to panic. Mr. Binkley, the vice-principal, makes Greg write a five-thousand-word essay on mascot stealing, but then lets him off easy because he, like Mike, had done the same thing as a boy. Oh, those men!

GUEST STARS:
George D. Wallace *(Mr. Binkley)*
Sandra Gould *(Mrs. Gould)*
Margarita Cordova *(first PTA lady)*
Selma Archerd *(second PTA lady)*

Sandra Gould should be a familiar face—for six seasons, she was Gladys Kravitz on *Bewitched,* forever unable to convince her husband that strange things were going on at the Stephens' house. She also showed up a few times as Mildred Webster on *I Married Joan,* where Sherwood Schwartz had been a staff writer.

#102: *"The Cincinnati Kids"*
Written by Al Schwartz and Larry Rhine. Directed by Leslie H. Martinson.
Original Airdate: November 23, 1973

Mike takes the family to a Cincinnati amusement park where his firm is submitting plans for an addition. Jan buys a poster and accidentally substitutes it for Mike's blueprints. Imagine Mike's surprise when he unveils blueprints at a meeting and it's a poster of Yogi Bear instead. Jan's foul-up sets the Bradys off on a wild chase to recover the missing blueprints. After the architectural drawings are found, the Bradys, relay-style, hand them off to each other until they reach Mike, who gives them to his clients at the last minute. The episode contains lots of space-filling action shots of the Bradys screaming on the roller coaster and other rides, and provides a great plug for King's Island Amusement Park.

GUEST STARS:
Hilary Thompson *(Marge)*
Bob Hoffman *(attendant)*

Hilary Thompson stayed busy after *Brady*. Among other things, she was in the casts of three series: the detective drama *The Manhunter* (CBS, 1974–75), and the sitcoms *The New Operation Petticoat* (ABC, 1978–79) and *Number 96* (NBC, 1980–81). Most interestingly, perhaps, she twice played rich bitch Veronica in two live-action pilots based on the comic strip "Archie."

By the way, that's associate producer Lloyd Schwartz wearing the bear costume, in an unbilled cameo.

#103: *"Quarterback Sneak"*
Written by Ben Gershman and Bill Freedman. Directed by Peter Baldwin.
Original Airdate: November 9, 1973

A rival high school's quarterback, Jerry Rogers, shows a romantic interest in Marcia. But Greg and Peter are convinced the jock wants to steal not Marcia's heart, but Greg's football playbook. The boys consider Marcia a traitor, and Bobby confirms the boys' distrust of Jerry when he sees him attempt to steal the playbook.

GUEST STARS:
Denny Miller *(Tank Gates)*
Chris Beaumont *(Jerry Rogers)*
Don Carter *(Rich)*

Maureen McCormick at home.

#104: *"Marcia Gets Creamed"*
Written by Ben Gershman and Bill Freedman. Directed by Peter Baldwin.
Original Airdate: October 26, 1973

Marcia gets her first job, as an afternoon manager at Haskell's Ice Cream Hut. She's so devoted to her work, she breaks a date with hunky Jeff. Then, when Mr. Haskell needs more help, Marcia persuades him to hire Peter ("If one Brady is good, then two are better," he says). But Peter turns out to be an incompetent worker, and Marcia has no choice but to fire him. Meanwhile, Jeff turns up at the ice-cream parlor with another girl, which makes Marcia extremely jealous and even more committed to her career. But that career comes to an abrupt end when Jan (whom Marcia has hired to replace Peter) turns out to be a super worker—so good that Mr. loyal-to-the-end Haskell fires Marcia and keeps Jan! But there's a happy ending: Jeff calls Marcia and all is forgiven.

Interesting lesson here: Don't hire anybody *too* good, or you're threatening your own job. Hmmm.

GUEST STARS:
Henry Corden *(Mr. Haskell)*
Michael Gray *(Jeff)*
Kimberly Beck *(girl)*

Henry Corden is probably the most prolific cartoon vocal artist this side of Mel Blanc; most famously, he succeeded Alan Reed as the voice of Fred Flintstone. In the flesh, he guested as Barbara Eden's father on *I Dream of Jeannie,* as Alejandro Rey's Uncle Antonio on *The Flying Nun,* and of course, as Mr. Babbitt, the boys' landlord on *The Monkees.* Kimberly Beck, who got her start at age two in the Glenn Ford film *Torpedo Run* (1958), played the deaf-mute child Kim Schuster on *Peyton Place* and went on to the casts of *Lucas Tanner* and *Rich Man, Poor Man—Book II.* In the 1980s, as Kimberly Beck-Hilton, she was a star of the daytime soap *Capitol.*

#105: *"My Brother's Keeper"*
Written by Michael Morris. Directed by Ross Bowman.
Original Airdate: November 2, 1973

Bobby saves Peter from being hit by a falling tree, and the older brother promises to become Bobby's slave for saving his life. Peter becomes over-protective and insists on doing all Bobby's chores, and Bobby, natch, begins to get off on the situation. In true Brady fashion he begins to take advantage of his brother until learning the error of his ways.

#106: *"Try, Try Again"*
Written by Al Schwartz and Larry Rhine. Directed by George "Buddy" Tyne.
Original Airdate: November 16, 1973

Jan is a failure in her ballet class and is passed over for a recital because she is so clumsy. Trying to find something she is good at, she takes up tap dancing, only to find that when she practices at home, the incessant tap-tapping drives her family nuts.

GUEST STARS:
Judy Landon *(Miss Clairette)*
Ruth Anson *(Mrs. Ferguson)*
Darryl Seman *(Billy Naylor)*

#107: *"Kelly's Kids"*
Written by Sherwood Schwartz. Directed by Richard Michaels.
Original Airdate: January 4, 1974

This episode was the pilot for another Sherwood Schwartz series about a sappy upper-middle-class couple with a bunch of kids. Unlike the Bradys, this couple was childless until they adopted a white boy, a Chinese boy, and a black boy. And unlike *The Brady Bunch, Kelly's Kids* never went to series—at least not until 1986, when Schwartz's idea was finally picked up by CBS as *Together We Stand,* which starred Elliott Gould and Dee Wallace Stone as the couple. (See Sherwood Schwartz's biography for more on that show.)

Here, the couple, Ken and Kathy Kelly, was played by Ken Berry and Brooke Bundy. The episode opens with Ken and Kathy schmoozing with Mike and Carol, explaining why they've bought a larger house. Ken flashes a snapshot of Matt, a blond-haired eight-year-old tyke, and tells the overjoyed Bradys that they have adopted him. "He's already housebroken," says Ken, "which is more than you can say for your group when you got them." Ha-ha.

But when Matt arrives at the Kelly house, he seems upset. He says he misses two of his orphanage buddies, Dwayne and Steve, the other two-thirds of "The Three Musketeers." And that's not the only problem to sour this sugary fantasy: the Kellys' mean neighbor, Mrs. Payne, comes to the house and sniffs that she and her husband do not appreciate having a family with a young boy as their neighbors. And "I hear you're in show business," she grouses. "Yes, I do a nightclub act," says Ken. Well, you know those nightclub acts!

Matt keeps on feeling lonesome, so Ken and Kathy go over once again to Mike and Carol's for some Brady therapy. "The reason the Brady kids are never lonesome is because there's always another kid around," Ken surmises. So Carol suggests that they adopt another kid. No problem, says Ken, so off he and Kathy go to the orphanage, where they meet Matt's pals, Dwayne and Steve. They seem taken aback when they see that Dwayne is black and Steve is Asian. That doesn't bother these nice suburban liberals, but they can't decide which one to adopt. Of course, they decide to adopt both of them. That nightclub act must have been very well-paying.

Matt is ecstatic when he's reunited with his orphanage mates, now his brothers. But the mean Mrs. Payne isn't. "I noticed you now have two more children ... and they're of different colors." Now don't get me wrong, she tells Ken, "I'm no bigot ... why Mr. Payne and I even managed to be cordial to the Shapiros on the next block. But three boys are bound to be destructive, especially the minorities."

Ken won't let Mrs. Payne bother him, even though she has threatened to kick Kathy out of the PTA and her husband won't allow Ken into the Optimists Club. "She makes Archie Bunker sound like a liberal," he observes.

The boys overhear this conversation, and thinking that they're causing problems, they decide to run away—to the Brady residence. ("There are so many kids there," one reasons, "nobody would notice.") Greg discovers them and brings them inside, where Mike and Carol give them hot chocolate. Ken and Kathy come over and say they won't let Mrs. Payne stop them. "We are a family," Ken insists. Alas, we never got a chance to find out how they turned out.

GUEST STARS:
Ken Berry *(Ken Kelly)*
Brooke Bundy *(Kathy Kelly)*
Todd Lookinland *(Matt)*
William Attmore II *(Dwayne)*
Carey Wong *(Steve)*
Jackie Joseph *(Mrs. Phillips)*
Molly Dodd *(Mrs. Payne)*

In 1973, with *The Brady Bunch* in its fifth season, Sherwood Schwartz starting looking around to launch a new series—one that was the same, only different. In this pilot, Ken Berry (the immortal Captain Wilton Parmenter of *F Troop* and a TV veteran since the mid-1950s) co-starred with Brooke Bundy, who'd started out as a teen actress on *Mr. Novak* and other shows. Interestingly, the press material for this episode erroneously gives Ken Kelly's first name as "Jim," which perhaps it was in an early draft of the screenplay.

The late Molly Dodd makes her second and final *Brady* guest appearance. And yes, Todd Lookinland is Mike Lookinland's younger brother.

#108: *"The Driver's Seat"*
Written by George Tibbles. Directed by Jack Arnold.
Original Airdate: January 11, 1974

Greg makes fun of Marcia's driving-test score, so the two make a bet that if she gets a higher score on her road test, the loser has to do the household chores for a month. Marcia fails on her first attempt, but after some positive-thinking coaching from Jan (imagine the road-test instructor in his under-wear, she tells her), she passes. Her total score is the same as Greg's, so that nullifies the bet. But to settle things once and for all, the Bradys set up an obstacle course of traffic department cones. Marcia negotiates the ob-stacles, but Greg doesn't. And as we leave our heroes, Greg is seen ironing Marcia's clothes.

GUEST STAR:
Herb Vigran *(examiner)*

The late, great character actor Herb Vigran had previously appeared in ep-isode #11, "54–40 and Fight."

#109: *"Miss Popularity"*
Written by Martin Ragaway. Directed by Jack Donohue.
Original Airdate: December 21, 1973

Jan is running for Most Popular Girl in her class. The whole family gets into the act—Peter becomes her campaign manager, and Alice bakes fortune cookies that read "Be a smart cookie: Vote for Jan Brady." Jan promises the world to her classmates, like doing homework assignments. When she wins, she becomes an insufferable snob. Meanwhile, she can't keep her promises and her former friends shun her. At the awards ceremony (held the same night Mike and Carol were planning to take a brief vacation), Jan modifies her egotistic acceptance speech with a humbler version, having learned her painful lesson.

GUEST STARS:
Darryl Seman *(Herman)*
Jerelyn Fields *(Shirley)*

#110: *"Out of This World"*
Written by Al Schwartz and Larry Rhine. Directed by Peter Baldwin.
Original Airdate: January 18, 1974

After watching former Apollo astronaut James McDivitt on a talk show, the kids ponder the possibility of the existence of extraterrestrials. They see a weird red light and hear a spooky-sounding noise—it's Greg and Peter fooling around, pulling yet another prank. That night Bobby has a dream about meeting some aliens, the Kaplutians, who are so small they actually make pint-sized Bobby seem like Kareem Abdul-Jabbar. The "sightings" continue, and eventually, military officials are summoned to the Brady residence to investigate. When Mike finds out that it's all Greg's doings, he gets angry and grounds him.

GUEST STARS:
Gen. James McDivitt, USAF (Ret.) *(himself)*
Mario Machado *(himself)*
Frank Delfino *(Herlo)*
Sadie Delfino *(Shim)*
James Flavin *(Captain McCartney)*

Astronaut James McDivitt flew on Gemini 4 and Apollo 9, and later served as manager of the Apollo Spacecraft Program. He retired from NASA and from the U.S. Air Force as a brigadier general in June 1972 to become a senior vice-president for strategic management with Rockwell International.

Mario Machado is a real-life Los Angeles news personality, at the time with CBS affiliate KNXT (now KCBS). Little persons Frank and Sadie Delfino were the Brady children's stunt doubles throughout the run of the show; Frank, also an actor, still shows up on TV occasionally, and was in the cast of the 1977 ABC series *The Feather and Father Gang.* James Flavin (1906–76), had among his credits a co-starring role with Charles Bronson on the late-'50s ABC series *Man with a Camera.*

#111: *"Two Pete's in a Pod"*
Written by Sam Locke and Milton Pascal. Directed by Richard Michaels.
Original Airdate: February 8, 1974

Chris Knight gets his chance at a dual role, playing a new classmate named Arthur Owens who looks just like Peter Brady except for black, horn-rim glasses. (Great Krypton! It's Superman and Clark Kent!) The two of them have fun fooling the other members of the Brady family, but a potentially embarrassing situation arrives when the *faux* Peter agrees to go out with Pamela, the niece of Mike's boss, Mr. Phillips. As it happens, this is the same night that the *real* Peter has finally nailed a date with Michelle, a girl he's been after all semester. Peter tries everything he can think of to straighten the situation out, but despite his best efforts, he can't avoid the merry mix-up when Peter's date comes to the Brady house and sees Arthur dancing with Pamela. But there's a happy ending: Michelle decides she really likes Peter because of all the trouble he has obviously gone through for her.

GUEST STARS:
Denise Nickerson *(Pamela)*
Kathy O'Dare *(Michelle)*
Robbie Rist *(Oliver)*

The second episode featuring Oliver was actually shot before his storyline debut in the following episode, "Welcome Aboard." Of course, it aired in proper order. See the chapter "A Brady Bunch of Background" for more on Oliver's arrival. Robbie Rist went on to play Glendon Farrell on *Lucas Tanner*, Ted and Georgette's adopted son David on *The Mary Tyler Moore Show*, and Dr. Zee on *Battlestar Galactica*.

#112: *"Welcome Aboard"*
Written by Al Schwartz and Larry Rhine. Directed by Richard Michaels.
Original Airdate: January 25, 1974

Carol's nephew Oliver joins the family. Although he is initially welcomed at the Brady residence, a series of accidents make him and some of the Brady kids think that he's a jinx. But Oliver's luck changes when he goes with the family to tour a movie studio and turns out to be the one-millionth visitor. As a result, all the Bradys get to act in a Keystone Kops–like movie, wear turn-of-the-century outfits, and engage in a huge pie fight.

GUEST STARS:
Robbie Rist *(Oliver)*
John Nolan *(Mr. Douglas)*
Judd Laurance *(director)*
Snag Werris *(Keystone Kop)*
Dick Winslow *(truck driver no. 1)*
Ralph Montgomery *(truck driver no. 2)*

Once again, Lloyd Schwartz does a cameo. "I did the slate in the 1920s-movie scene," he says, referring to the handheld chalkboard that gets clapped at the start of filming a shot to help synchronize sound and image. It seems an easy enough chore, and yet, says Lloyd, "We had an extra who didn't quite know how to do it. So I said, 'Pay the extra, *I'll* do the slate!' "

#113: *"The Snooperstar"*
Written by Harry Winkler. Directed by Bruce Bilson.
Original Airdate: February 22, 1974

Cindy (the reformed tattletale) is snooping around reading Marcia's diary. When Marcia finds out, she writes a trick entry about how a Hollywood agent is going to discover Cindy and make her into the next Shirley Temple. Meanwhile, Mike has been trying to win over Mrs. Penelope Fletcher, a snooty millionaire, with his plans for the Penelope Fletcher Cultural Center. She turns them down, and in a last-ditch effort to save the project, Mike invites Mrs. Fletcher to the Brady residence to look at the plans. When she arrives early, Cindy thinks she's the agent, and—in Shirley Temple curls—starts singing "On the Good Ship Lollipop." Instead of being outraged, Mrs. Fletcher is amused and joins Cindy in a duet.

GUEST STARS:
Natalie Schafer *(Penelope Fletcher)*
Robbie Rist *(Oliver)*

It's the *Gilligan–Brady* connection once again, with Lovey Howell herself, Natalie Schafer, doing a turn as Leona with a heart (or is that an oxymoron?). Born in 1912, Natalie went from being a stage comedienne to a movie character actress in the 1940s and '50s—usually portraying, ironically enough, a matron of means. After *Gilligan's Island,* she played Eleanor Carlyle on the early attempt at a prime-time soap, *The Survivors* (ABC, 1969).

#114: *"The Hustler"*
Written by Bill Freedman and Ben Gershman. Directed by Michael Kane.
Original Airdate: March 1, 1974

A truck delivers a large, mysterious package for Mike. It's a pool table, which is strange since Mike doesn't play. It turns out to be from his big boss, Mr. Matthews, a pool-playing nut. (There's no explanation about the previously seen boss, Mr. Phillips, but Lloyd Schwartz says they considered Phillips as Mike's immediate superior and Matthews as chairman of the board. Must have been an *awfully* big company.) Bobby finds he has a real knack for pool and goes off into another of his famous dreams, fantasizing about becoming a world-champion pool player. When Mr. Matthews comes to the Brady residence, he bets Bobby a pack of gum he can beat him. Bobby keeps winning, and several days later another package arrives—dozens of packs of chewing gum, payback from Mr. Matthews.

GUEST STARS:
Jim Backus *(Harry Matthews)*
Robbie Rist *(Oliver)*
Dorothy Shay *(Frances Matthews)*
Charles Stewart *(Joe Sinclair)*
Leonard Bremen *(truck driver)*
Grayce Spence *(Muriel Sinclair)*
Jason Dunn *(Hank Thompson)*
Susan Quick *(Gloria Thompson)*

Backus is back. After his wonderfully curmudgeonly Zacchariah in the Grand Canyon episodes, he returns as Mike Brady's boss Harry Matthews, the man above Mike's immediate superior Mr. Phillips (played by Jack Collins). It's a sweet comic turn, full of the patented bluster and goodhearted pomposity that Backus did so well.

#115: *"Top Secret"*
Written by Howard Ostroff. Directed by Bernard Wiesen.
Original Airdate: February 15, 1974

When an FBI agent visits the Brady residence to give Mike clearance about a top-security project, Bobby and Oliver suspect something is up. When Sam the butcher later asks for Mike's help with plans on a "secret project" (expanding his store), Alice thinks he's going to marry her, while Bobby and Oliver think he's a spy who's going to take away Mike's valuable blueprints. Trailing Sam to the store, the boys lock up him and his landlord, Mr. Gronsky, in the meat freezer and call the cops.

GUEST STARS:
Robbie Rist *(Oliver)*
Allan Melvin *(Sam Franklin)*
Lew Palter *(Mr. Gronsky)*
Don Fenwick *(Fred Sanders)*

This is Allan Melvin's last of eight appearances as Sam the butcher.

#116: *"The Hair-Brained Scheme"*
Written by Chuck Stewart, Jr. Directed by Jack Arnold.
Original Airdate: March 8, 1974

In the final episode, Bobby has turned into a budding entrepreneur, trying to sell Neat and Natural Hair Tonic door-to-door—but without much luck. Feeling sympathetic, Greg buys some from Bobby, only to discover to his horror that his hair has turned orange! (How punk!) Trying to cover it up, Carol takes Greg to her beauty parlor, where he is embarrassed when he runs into two girls he knows. Eventually his hair reverts to its real color, and the Bradys sail off into syndication and spinoff eternity.

GUEST STARS:
Robbie Rist *(Oliver)*
Barbara Bernstein *(Suzanne)*
Hope Sherwood *(Gretchen)*
Bern Hoffman *(first man)*
John Wheeler *(second man)*
Brandy Carson *(woman)*

EPISODE MINI-GUIDE:
THE BRADY BUNCH HOUR

Sunday, Jan. 23, 1977, 7 pm

Guests Farrah Fawcett-Majors and Lee Majors, Rip Taylor, Kaptain Kool and the Kongs. Songs: "Yankee Doodle Dandy," medley (both by the Bradys), "Razzle Dazzle" (Kaptain Kool), "Send in the Clowns" (Florence)

Sunday, Feb. 27, 1977, 7 pm

Guests Milton Berle, Tina Turner, and Collette the Puppette. Songs: "Rubber Band Man" (Tina), "Evergreen" (Florence), "Sing" (Chris and Collette)

Friday, March 4, 1977, 9 pm

Guests Vincent Price, puppets H. R. Pufnstuf and Kiki Bird. Songs: "Traces," "All by Myself" (Florence and Barry), "Time in a Bottle" (Maureen). In a running sketch, Greg leaves the Bradys' new beachfront home to move into his own apartment. Feels like old times, doesn't it?

Monday, April 4, 1977, 8 pm

Guests Redd Foxx, Robert Hegyes, the Ohio Players. Songs: "Fire" (Ohio Players), "How Lucky Can You Get" (Florence)

Monday, April 25, 1977, 8 pm

Guests Rick Dees and the *What's Happening!!* kids (Ernest Thomas, Haywood Nelson, Fred Barry, and Danielle Spencer). Songs: "Dis-Gorilla" (Dees), "This Masquerade" (Florence), "Thank God I'm a Country Girl" (Ann)

Wednesday, May 25, 1977, 8 pm

Guests Paul Williams, Lynn Anderson, and Rip Taylor. Songs: "The Right Time of the Night" (Anderson), "Born to Say Goodbye" (Florence). The latter was appropriate—this was the last show.

EPISODE MINI-GUIDE:
THE BRADY GIRLS GET MARRIED/
THE BRADY BRIDES

THE BRADY GIRLS GET MARRIED

Fridays, 8:30 p.m.

See "The Brady Legacy" (page 23) for more details and the cast list of the re-edited TV movies broadcast as these three episodes on the following dates:

Feb. 6, 1981

Just as Carol and Mike send Cindy off to college, Jan pops up to announce she's getting married—as does an envious Marcia after a whirlwind romance.

Feb. 13, 1981

Hitches develop in Marcia's and Jan's plans for a double wedding ceremony.

Feb. 20, 1981

Grooms Phillip and Wally disagree over whether to have a modern or a traditional wedding. But the wedding does, finally, take place.

THE BRADY BRIDES

March 6, 1981

The two newlywed couples, now housemates, begin to rub each other the wrong way—especially since Wally likes to get up naked in the middle of the night to raid the refrigerator.

March 13, 1981

Wally brings home a giant stuffed gorilla that roars when its nose is pressed—eventually scaring one of Phillip's colleagues and startling a burglar. Professor Thompson: Byron Morrow.

A double wedding in *The Brady Girls Get Married*, as Greg (nice shoes!) and Peter look on.

March 20, 1981

PRE-EMPTED

March 27, 1981

Carol pays an overnight visit.

April 3, 1981

Wally, worried about his delinquent parking tickets, panics and pretends he's Phillip when an FBI agent comes to the door. FBI agent Mann: Patrick Cronin.

April 10, 1981

Phillip decides to try to be "hip." Mrs. Richardson: Gloria Henry (best known as Dennis the Menace's mom).

April 17, 1981

Marcia's jeans-models walk out on her, on the eve of a fashion show for Mr. Blackwell. Brandon: Tom Gagen. Lance: Tom Jordan.

EPISODE MINI-GUIDE:
THE BRADYS

Fridays, 8 p.m

Feb. 9, 1990

"Start Your Engines/Here We Grow Again"
*Written by Sherwood Schwartz and Lloyd Schwartz. Directed by Bruce
   Bilson.*

Two-hour series debut, comprising what would have been the TV-movie *The
Brady 500*. At the Nashville 500, Bobby, a race-car driver, becomes paralyzed
from the waist down after a crash. The family gathers at Mike and Carol's
house to welcome Bobby home from the hospital. Marcia and husband Wally
arrive to stay, Wally having lost the latest in a string of jobs. Jan and husband
Phillip are trying to get pregnant, and they adopt a young Asian girl. Peter
breaks up with his fiancée. Cindy has become a popular radio DJ. Greg
considers going back to med school to switch from gynecology to orthoped-
ics. Bobby eventually marries his college sweetheart, Tracy Wagner.

GUESTS:
Mary Candorette *(Valerie)*
Lenny Garner *(Howie)*
Richard Herkert *(Dr. Stevens)*
Sheila Shaw *(Maxine)*
Hope Juber *(Erica Hopkins)*
Jack Stauffer *(track paramedic)*
Greg Collins *(track security guard)*
John Wheeler *(Joe Fletcher)*
Kim Maxwell *(Lisa)*
Darcy De Moss *(Donna)*
Dinah Lenney *(Laura)*
Jeffrey J. Nowinski *(Steve)*
Barbara Mallory *(Mrs. Powell)*
Nick Toch *(Mr. Powell)*
Leonard Ross *(man)*
Stu Nahan *(track announcer)*
Dabbs Greer *(the minister)*

Feb. 16, 1990

"A Moving Experience"
Written by Sherwood Schwartz and Lloyd Schwartz. Directed by Bob Sweeney.

Mike decides to physically move the house to a new location after the neighborhood is scheduled to be razed for a freeway ramp. Cindy gets involved with her widowed boss, Gary Greenberg, an older, Jewish man. Mike decides to run for councilman.

GUESTS:
Jerry Hauck *(Borden)*
Herbert Edelman *(Gene Dickinson)*
Pat Crawford Brown *(Mabel)*
Aaron Lustig *(Meadows)*
Dyana Ortelli *(Wallach)*
Philip Glasser *(Jake)*
Jennifer Kolcher *(Carly)*

Feb. 23, 1990

"Hat in the Ring"
Written by Sherwood Schwartz and Lloyd Schwartz. Directed by Nancy Malone.

As the "Mike Brady for City Council" campaign kicks into overdrive, Mike's political future is nearly squelched due to a blackmail attempt by an overzealous campaign manager for the competition, Gene Dickinson.

GUESTS:
Charlie Spradling *(Teri Dickinson)*
Herb Edelman *(Gene Dickinson)*
Dyana Ortelli *(Wallach)*
Aaron Lustig *(Meadows)*
Jerry Hauck *(Borden)*
Fran Ryan *(housewife)*
Joe Lucas *(delivery man)*
Frank De Vol *(man #2)*
Jay Arlen Jones *(foreman)*
Lauren Sinclair *(Ginger)*
David Sage *(Glen Martinson)*
Fred Holliday *(Leo)*

March 2, 1990

"Bottom's Up"
Written by Sandra Kay Siegel. Directed by Bruce Bilson.

With Carol eagerly taking on the responsibility of her two grandchildren, Wally obsessed with his council job, Cindy contemplating a new job and promotion, Jan busy running Mike's architectural firm, and Peter and Greg involved with the development of the city's new trauma centers, Marcia is left to wallow in her own misery, and she turns to alcohol for solace.

GUESTS:
Gloria Gifford *(Dr. Stone)*
John Terrence *(Jordan Armstrong)*
Bill Cort *(Morty St. James)*

March 9, 1990

"The Party Girls"
Written by Ed Scharlach. Directed by Dick Martin.

Marcia, Nora, and Tracy get together and start their own catering business —"The Party Girls"—but Greg and Peter find themselves at odds when they realize their lives are moving in separate directions.

GUESTS:
Gerard Maguire *(Austrian Envoy)*
Alison Rockwell *(party guest)*
Bob Garon *(party guest)*

The Bradys' Lost Episodes

It is not generally known, but there was a *sixth* season of *The Brady Bunch*. However, these episodes encountered a rare electromagnetic alignment of the earth and sun that diverted the broadcasts into space.

In mid-1990, the Voyager 2 unmanned spacecraft accidentally intercepted the errant *Brady* signals somewhere on the far side of Neptune and retransmitted them back to Earth. The authors of this book, by special arrangement with NASA, attended a private screening of these episodes at the Johnson Space Center. And so, for the first time anywhere, we present our findings: **the lost season of *The Brady Bunch*.**

EPISODE 1: *"The Old College Try"*
Greg has to decide where to apply for college—a "party" school or his dad's alma mater. Bill Cosby guest-stars as himself.

EPISODE 2: *"Be Cool to Your School"*
Stung by the kids' characterization of them as "uncool" parents, Mike and Carol attend their high-school reunion and discover they may be "hipper" than they thought.

EPISODE 3: *"Tippacanoe and Tiger II"*
The Bradys adopt a stray puppy, and Cindy and Bobby become jealous of the attention being given it.

EPISODE **4:** *"A Moving Experience"*
When Greg moves into his campus bachelor pad, Marcia redecorates the Bradys' attic apartment.

EPISODE **5:** *"Katchoo Katchoo"*
Jan, who only thought she was allergic to the original Tiger, finds she may *really* be allergic to Tiger II.

EPISODE **6:** *"Alice, We Hardly Knew Ye"*
Alice gets a second job, moonlighting for Sam the butcher.

EPISODE **7:** *"Cindyrella"*
Cindy goes on her first date, and gets locked up in the pizza parlor after closing. Written by Joyce Carol Oates.

EPISODE **8:** *"Bobby Pumps Up"*
In order to impress a girl on the cheerleading squad, Bobby starts lifting weights—with advice from Mr. Universe, Arnold Schwarzenegger!

EPISODE **9:** *"Semper Fido"*
The Brady kids see a huge career for Tiger II when he's cast as a "top dog" in a marine recruiting poster.

EPISODE **10:** *"Big Kids"*
Cindy and Bobby fantasize what it would be like to be the oldest siblings and discover it isn't as much fun as they thought. Directed by a young John Hughes—and is that a six-year-old Molly Ringwald in a bit part?

EPISODE **11:** *"Marcia Meets Donny Osmond"*
Marcia meets Donny Osmond. Donny Osmond guest-stars as himself.

EPISODE **12:** *"The French Connection"*
Mike wins a trip to Paris and has to decide whether to take along the kids, or just Carol.

Around midseason, with the ratings dropping precipitously, the producers decided to try being "relevant" like *All in the Family* and *M*A*S*H**. (Unbeknownst to them, the disappointing ratings were actually those of *Kodiak*, a half-hour, English-language Alaskan series whose satellite signals were floating throughout the northern hemisphere and got sucked into the *Brady* time slot.) Still lighthearted and loving, *The Brady Bunch* nonetheless began to tackle the Important Issues head-on.

EPISODE **13:** *"I Am Curious, Marcia"*
When Marcia announces that she wants to leave home and move into a commune, Mike and Carol take a hard look at their lives and values.

EPISODE **14:** *"Why Do You Think They Call It Dope?"*
When young Cindy is offered a marijuana joint in the school yard, Mike and Carol take a hard look at their lives and values.

EPISODE **15:** *"The People Next Door"*
When Mike and Carol decide to "swing" with the neighbors next door, the kids take a hard look at their lives and values. The script, by a young David Mamet, was rewritten over his objections to take out all the "damns" and "fucks."

EPISODE **16:** *"Alice Doesn't Work Here Anymore"*
When Alice takes part in a march against nuclear energy, against the wishes of pro-nuke Mike, the Bradys are forced to confront their feelings about their housekeeper.

EPISODE **17:** *"Button, Button"*
Cindy loses the "WIN" button that Marcia's new Young Republican boyfriend lightheartedly had engraved for her.

EPISODE **18:** *"Carol the Breadwinner"*
When Mike gets laid off from his architecture firm, Carol gets a job as director of a ghetto lunch program. ("For five years I've run a household of six brothers and sisters," she tells the agency head, and then adds hiply, "I can certainly arrange lunch for these 'brothers' and 'sisters'!")

EPISODE **19:** *"Brother Sun, Sister Moonie"*
Mike and Carol grow concerned about Jan's new friends when they find out the friends are disciples of the Reverend Sun Yung Moon.

EPISODE **20:** *"Guess Who's Coming to Dinner?"*
Marcia brings home her new boyfriend: a black pre-med student.

EPISODE **21:** *"Split Decision"*
Mike and Carol agree to a trial separation.

EPISODE **22:** *"Ahoy Hanoi"*
Back together, and with their kids starting to go off to college, Mike and Carol adopt four Vietnamese boat children. Script by Hunter S. Thompson!

EPISODE **23:** *"Greg's Secret"*
On the final episode, long-infatuated Greg and Marcia decide to elope, while Mike shocks Carol by announcing he's bisexual. Sensitively directed by Robert Redford.

When ABC programmers belatedly discovered that none of these episodes actually aired, they decided to delete them from the Brady annals and went back to the original character conceptions for *The Brady Bunch Hour*. We'll never know just how much impact these hard-hitting episodes would have had.

What If the Bradys Were Italian?

SELECTED EPISODES FROM *THE BRAVO BUNCH:*

"Bless Who's Coming to Dinner": Alice burns the lasagna, and the monsignor is due for supper any minute.

"Peter's Altar Ego": Peter becomes an altar boy, and gets so swell-headed he alienates the other kids.

"Cry Uncle": Mike's uncle Emilio from the old country comes to visit, and the kids try to fix him up with Alice—much to the consternation of Sam the butcher.

"Santa Marcia": Marcia becomes queen of the Festival of Santa Lucia and discovers the responsibility may be more than she can handle.

What If the Bradys Were Jewish?

SELECTED EPISODES FROM *THE BERNSTEIN BUNCH:*

"Guess Who's Coming to Seder": Alice still has to learn to cook kosher, and the rebbe is due for supper any minute.

"Peter's Bar Mitzvah": Peter celebrates his passage into manhood and gets so swell-headed he alienates the other kids.

"Cry Bubbe": Mike's mother from the Lower East Side comes to visit, and the kids try to fix her up with Mike's boss, Mr. Matthews (guest star Jim Backus).

"Of Marcia and Menorah": Marcia becomes queen of the Hanukkah Festival and discovers the responsibility may be more than she can handle.

About the Authors

ANDREW J. EDELSTEIN is a television editor and writer at *New York Newsday*. He is the author of *The Pop '60s: A Personal and Irreverent Guide* and co-author of *The '70s: From Hot Pants to Hot Tubs*. His work has appeared in *The New York Times*, the New York *Daily News, TV Guide*, and *Parade*. He is single and lives in Manhattan.

FRANK LOVECE is a TV/film columnist for United Feature Syndicate, and the author of *Thirty Years of Television* and *Hailing TAXI: The Official Book of the Show*. His work appears in *American Film, The Los Angeles Times, New York Newsday, TV Guide, Video*, and elsewhere. As a fiction writer, he is the author of the graphic-novel *Atomic Age*. He lives in Manhattan with his wife Toni and his son Vincent.

Index of The Brady Bunch Cast and Crew Members— by Episode

Following are indexes of Performers, Sports Figures and Other Notable Guest Stars, Directors, and Writers, each *by episode number* (not page number). These are followed by a general index of the text.

PERFORMERS

(Sports figures and other notables listed separately)

SPORTS FIGURES AND OTHER NOTABLE GUEST STARS

DIRECTORS

WRITERS

General Index